THE GREAT
WHITE BARD

THE GREAT WHITE BARD

*How to Love Shakespeare
While Talking About Race*

FARAH KARIM-COOPER

VIKING

VIKING
An imprint of Penguin Random House LLC
penguinrandomhouse.com

First published in hardcover in Great Britain, the Republic of Ireland,
and Australia by Oneworld Publications, London, in 2023

First United States edition published by Viking, 2023

Interior images: Pall Mall *Alto Relievo* courtesy
of Beinecke Rare Book and Manuscript Library; Droeshout portrait
courtesy of Wikimedia Commons; Alexander Pope edition of
Shakespeare courtesy of archive.org; Shakespeare Westminster Abbey
Memorial © Prisma/Alamy; Peacham drawing courtesy of Wikimedia
Commons; Pauline Black as Cleopatra © David Corio; *Othello* Act V, Scene II
courtesy of Victoria University Library (Toronto) for providing the image
and housing the original material; Cesare Vecellio's Moor portrait courtesy
of the Metropolitan Museum of Art; Theodore de Bry *Christopher
Columbus Arrives in America* courtesy of Rijksmuseum; *The Enchanted
Island* courtesy of the Metropolitan Museum of Art.

Photo insert: Shakespeare Chandos Portrait
© GL Archive/Alamy; Shakespeare Bust by Sicinius under
CCBYSA 4.0; Globe Heavens © Pete le May/Globe; *Titus Andronicus*
© John Tramper/Globe; Hitomi Manaka as Lavinia © Ellie Kurttz/RSC;
Moorish Ambassador to Elizabeth I © CPA Media/Alamy; *Death of Cleopatra*
© Peter Horree/Alamy; Mark Rylance as Cleopatra © John Tramper/Globe;
Jonathan Cake and Joaquina Klukango as Antony and Cleopatra © Hugh
Glendinning/RSC; *King's Fountain* courtesy of Wikimedia Commons;
Rialto Bridge © Artefact/Alamy; *Portrait of Laura de Dianti* courtesy of
Wikimedia Commons; Joe Dixon as Caliban © Topher McGrillis/RSC;
Much Ado About Nothing performance © Joan Marcus; Adjoa Andoh
© Ingrid Pollard. All rights reserved, DACS/Artimage 2022.

ISBN 9780593489376 (hardcover)
ISBN 9780593489383 (ebook)

Printed in the United States of America
1st Printing

This book is dedicated to Julian Ahmed Karim a.k.a PoeticJules

Tho I show my true color, yet believed by no other,
I hope you love me again soon as I live
And love and loathe in this vicarious mystery
— PoeticJules

CONTENTS

PROLOGUE

Can you remember meeting William Shakespeare for the first time?

My first encounter was in my English class as a fifteen-year-old. We read *Romeo and Juliet*, Shakespeare's most popular tragedy about sex, drugs and the whirligig of adolescence. The language was challenging and yet the story took hold of me because, in many ways, it felt Pakistani: a young girl in a patriarchal society is forced to marry someone she doesn't know though she's desperate to follow her own heart. This is *the* archetypal South Asian teenage experience. I did not grow up in a terribly religious or patriarchal household; my grandmother, born in pre-partition India, did, however, and her memories stirred my imagination and rankled my modern, Westernised sensibilities. She described how her father kept her under lock and key and how scared she was on her wedding day because she was marrying a man she didn't know. But it was my mother's story of courage and rebellion that provided a direct link with Juliet's character. South Asian women, though oppressed in many instances, are not as meek as Western portrayals make out. At the age of twenty-two my mother married my father, a divorced sea captain with four children. This was, of course, against her father's will, at least at first. But, like Juliet, she knew exactly what she wanted: the love of her life. I suspect my own ability and courage to speak truth to power derives far more from my South Asian heritage and from my mother's glorious example of wilfulness than to my being raised in America, the so-called land of the free.

I love Shakespeare with a passion. But I recall the extraordinarily uninspiring way his plays were taught in high school in the 1980s. If my ninth-grade English teacher hadn't played a VHS cassette of Franco Zeffirelli's 1960s film version, starring Olivia Hussey and Leonard Whiting (with whom I instantly fell in love), I probably wouldn't be a Shakespeare scholar nor sitting here writing this book. In that class, we tried to get our heads around the plot with pop quizzes and essays on themes like family relationships or courtship. So far, so staid. But Zeffirelli's film captured the thrill of teenage rebellion, fury and the passion that was entirely absent from the classroom. I would go on to read a Shakespeare play each year of high school, but the truth is, for my fifteen-year-old heart, no other story packed the same emotional punch as that of 'Juliet and her Romeo'.

Such passion for Shakespeare felt fragile since I was not subsequently encouraged to pursue any further study of him – not then and not even when I was an English graduate student at the University of London in the 1990s. I met with quite a few challenges on my intellectual and professional journey through Shakespeare. While researching my Masters on Shakespeare and Milton, one professor would comment that I didn't have what it took to go on and do a PhD, let alone secure a teaching position. He probably thought he might spare me the effort and heartache of what did in fact ensue – being turned down for roles I was amply, sometimes overly, qualified for. It wasn't obvious to me at the time – thank goodness – but the odds were stacked against me.

Was it my American accent, that most wince-inducing of sounds to English literary scholars in the UK? Or perhaps my ethnicity, recalling the deep-rooted 'truth' of empirical hierarchies? Or was it as simple as my sex and the challenges of breaking into the boys' club of academia at the time? Misogyny in academia would surely make for a colourful read in another book.

Looking back now and noting the colour of the field of Shakespeare studies in the UK, there is no question that my background shaped perceptions of me as I attempted to navigate the exclusionary behaviours and gatekeeping practices of academics and their institutions. Even as I write, Shakespeare scholars employed full-time by British universities are almost exclusively white; there are only three Shakespeare professors of colour in this country, all from South Asian backgrounds, and I am one of them. *There are no Black Shakespeare or Early Modern Studies full professors employed by universities in the UK.* I hope this shocks the reader as much as it did me when I first discovered it. Shakespeare studies aside, Nicola Rollock, a professor of social policy at King's College London suggests the problem is more systemic; for her,

> institutional directives [on the part of universities] to address race inequalities often fail to engage seriously with the fundamental aspects of race and racism. Instead…universities tend to embrace a range of limited short-term strategies and initiatives, which give the appearance of serious engagement, but…make little substantial, long-term difference to the experiences, outcomes and success of students and faculty of colour.[1]

But the problem is even worse when it comes to English literature. Although Shakespeare is taught in schools and is embedded in popular culture through a variety of means, for many he remains unappealing, alien and unrelatable. Teachers are over-worked and have curriculum targets which can make it difficult to find innovative ways to make Shakespeare more relevant and accessible. As the quotation above reminds us, by the time a non-white student gets to university, if they can afford it, they will undoubtedly encounter some form of institutional racism. The main barrier to Shakespeare is far removed from the actual reality of his works; it is the way that he was constructed over the eight-eenth and nineteenth centuries which conveys an idea that he is only for a certain class of white English, American or European. Whichever way we look at it, Shakespeare studies has not been open-armed.

Contemporary society's knee-jerk reaction when faced with these troublesome and oh-so-white legends of literature and art is to dismiss them. Clearly, they are no longer relevant. They are dinosaurs – racists, misogynists, classists, ignorant of the 'lived experience' of the majority of people today – therefore they have nothing left to teach us. We have the power to choose, after all, who the Greats will be for the modern age. And as for Shakespeare, after centuries of reverence and acclaim, perhaps it's fine to say: time's up.

I feel this would be a mistake.

I served as President of the Shakespeare Association of America in 2021–2, and I'm currently Professor of Shakespeare Studies at King's College London and Director of Education at Shakespeare's Globe, where I have headed Research for over seventeen years. Cancelling Shakespeare would put me out of work, so my campaign to protect him is profoundly pragmatic. But, more importantly, I love him. I am a foreign, brown woman – and I feel seen and heard in Shakespeare's plays. A lot of us, certainly many students or audience members at the Globe whom I have spoken to over the years, tend to *admire* Shakespeare, even *worship* him. But to love Shakespeare means to *know* him. To love is to get to grips with the qualities in others and crucially in ourselves that need to be challenged. At some point, love demands that we reconcile ourselves with flaws and limitations. Only then can there be a deeper understanding and affinity with another. Ideally, we would also communicate honestly and say what we are willing to put up with and what hurts and offends us. But humans are complex, fragile creatures. Shakespeare, happily, is not so easily offended – thus we have every reason to scrutinise him to our heart's content.

One way to examine Shakespeare is to look him dead in the eye. This is hard to do if we keep him on his pedestal. Shakespeare teaches us this each time he satirises the poets who worshipped their mistresses in florid terms that turned them into nameless, faceless statues or dolls. Shakespeare couldn't abide it. But there are many people who insist passionately that he should remain in an elevated position of godliness. So we must start by asking ourselves what sort of readers and lovers of Shakespeare we want to be.

A teacher's editorial in the *Washington Post* argued for removing Shakespeare from the curriculum:

> because there is a WORLD of really exciting literature out there that better speaks to the needs of my very ethnically diverse and wonderfully curious modern-day students. I do not believe that I am "cheating" my students because we do not read Shakespeare. I do not believe that a long-dead, British guy is the only writer who can teach my students about the human

condition. I do not believe that not viewing "Romeo and Juliet" or any other modern adaptation of a Shakespeare play will make my students less equipped to go out into the world and understand language or human behavior.[2]

Another instinct is to preserve Shakespeare at all costs – as though he were an ancient fossil that might turn to dust should we touch him. One conservative theatre critic wrote in 2020, 'The woke brigade are close to "cancelling" Shakespeare': 'there's now no "safe space" where the canon can reside, sheltered from the culture war'.[3]

In both these examples, we find a lack of engagement. In the first, we dismiss Shakespeare outright. In the second, we protect him by locking him away, so that any new interaction is impossible.

I believe there is a far more exciting prospect than cancelling *or* fossilising the Bard: that is, to read him *bravely*; to shed the centuries-old elitist constructions of him as the 'greatest writer in the world' that only a few are privileged enough to understand. Instead of worshipping his words, we contend with them. Jump inside the plays and dig. I don't wish to sit back and let him wash over me (not always anyway), revering him passively for all his wonder and wisdom. Shakespeare's plays are too immense and powerful; they demand our active participation – they are a conversation, an invitation to imagine and interrogate, not simply to venerate and safeguard. Reading Shakespeare through race allows us to confront crucial questions of our day: What is the history of racism in Britain, in the USA? Governments, schools and even some far-right academics want to conceal this history. Why? What can studying Shakespeare contribute to this debate?

How are our icons or national treasures complicit with white supremacy and how do we come to terms with and still make space for them in modern times? If we want to *know* Shakespeare's plays and know them intimately, we need to ask: Did 'race' exist in his time? How might he have felt about it? Does his work engage with it? What do his plays say about justice and who has access to it? Why are Black and ethnic minority performers asked to erase their identities, while whiteness is rendered invisible in modern performance conventions? Shakespeare, on the page *and* the stage, is a limitless workhorse for such questions and finding ways to answer them is an endlessly thrilling endeavour.

I am frequently asked by students and visitors to the Globe, 'What does race have to do with Shakespeare?' This book is my response to that question. The plays that spring to mind in this endeavour are *Titus Andronicus, Antony and Cleopatra, Othello, The Merchant of Venice* and *The Tempest*. Each of these explicitly sheds light on what it meant to be 'raced' as Shakespeare understood it. They speak of the lives of people who might have been known as 'strangers' in Shakespeare's England: three 'Moors', a 'Tawny Queen', a Jew, and an indigenous islander. In these complex plays with multiple and tragic narratives, Shakespeare reveals something about the experience of being black or racially marked in ancient Rome or in sixteenth-century Venice, or on an island somewhere between Italy and Africa, all the while gesturing to the multi-racial demographic and context of Shakespeare's England, not least amongst the audiences who attend the great and gorgeous Elizabethan amphitheatres.

For decades, scholars studying Shakespeare and race or post-colonialism have been marginalised in the field because if they wrote about race they were accused of being 'anachronistic'. Academic orthodoxy alleged that 'race didn't exist in Shakespeare's time, so racism couldn't possibly exist'. But nothing could be further from the truth. Shakespeare's texts are a reservoir of what is known as *race-making* or *racial formation*, meaning the social process of creation of racial identities; this is an idea that I'll be returning to throughout *The Great White Bard*.[4] By the time Shakespeare arrives on the theatrical scene in London, the concept of racial identities and ways of thinking about human difference had been developing since the Middle Ages, and even before that in the classical age. The stories of Aaron the Moor, Cleopatra, Othello, Shylock, the Prince of Morocco and Caliban point to the explicit awareness of racial difference in Shakespeare's time; these characters are in popular plays of the period.

It doesn't end there, however. An undeniable presence of race and racial formation can be detected in Shakespeare's tragedies and comedies and we will explore where and how this can be felt as *context* rather than theme. The core vehicles through which Shakespeare's plays dramatically engage with concepts of race is through character, language and imagery, the building blocks of Shakespearean drama. To see how, we must enter Shakespeare's own social and political world to discover how race was constructed and what role black/white–dark/light imagery played. It is easy to see how repeated links between a colour name and a set of values can condition our thinking about racial identities. This is known as *colour coding* – where colour symbolism and racial thinking merge. A study conducted in the 1960s plainly reveals how colour coding works:

> If the preschool child is learning that white things are good and black things are bad, it seems reasonable that these meanings could generalize to groups of persons designated by the color coded as "white" and "black".[5]

What we say and how we describe thoughts and feelings really matter. And yet Western culture persistently neglects to consider the destructive legacy of the symbolism of black and white that dates back hundreds of years.

There are two schools of thought on the issue of colour symbolism and its relationship to race. One says that the colour black's negative meanings should be distinguished from attitudes towards black skin colour. The other school is that centuries of colour coding in relation to black and white has instead shaped our views about racial difference, laying the crucial foundation for the dehumanisation and enslavement of Black Africans from the sixteenth to the nineteenth century. While Shakespeare's imagery has been written about extensively, I often wonder why more of us haven't thought deeply enough about the power of black and white imagery in his work and how it relates to ideas about race in his time. The more we think about it, more questions arise when we consider his canon as a whole: How do the rhetoric of difference and the mechanics of poetic trope help to develop the atmosphere of fear and conflict in Shakespearean tragedies like *Macbeth* and *Romeo and Juliet*? Moreover, the continuities between the past and the present reveal themselves in some of the comedies, like *Much Ado About Nothing* and even *As You Like It*. These delightful, festive but rather troubling plays revel in racialising imagery and racist humour as they speak to cultural norms related to courtship, gender, class and difference.

*

In the last few years, we have witnessed the toppling of monuments of white Western history and culture. These are acts of resistance to idealised notions of the past. Students in universities across the United Kingdom and the United States have demanded that we 'decolonise the canon', asking, 'Why Shakespeare? What does this dead white man have to do with me?' When people enquire if Shakespeare will go by the wayside as this new wave of anti-colonial revolution spreads, my answer is, Shakespeare will indeed survive and perhaps emerge stronger than before. The more conservative amongst us worry that the decolonial and antiracist innovations taking place in schools, universities and theatres is 'wokeness' gone wrong and that somehow directors, teachers and academics are too afraid to stand up to the youth who are demanding something other than the old status quo. But this is culture war fantasy.

I have witnessed Black actors want to throw their scripts across the room and refuse to utter some of Shakespeare's most beloved lines. Surely this reaction to poetic tropes that use racial imagery is worth confronting. We can no longer continue to 'love' this writer, as he says himself in *The Merchant of Venice*, with 'fancy bred in the eye', meaning without substance, a notion he derided often in his reflections on love. Are we really more comfortable loving a Shakespeare that is based on myth and centuries-old narratives? Or, if we don't mind a bit of discomfort, can we finally engage with Shakespeare's words in the way I am fairly certain he intended? In a society that remains racially divided, we must take a deeper look at our monuments and rather than idealise the past through them, we must put them to work as we build the future.

I once received a handwritten letter from someone who had been listening to the Globe's Shakespeare and race podcasts. He asked me to appeal to the actors' union, Equity, to disallow Black actors from playing Henry V. He insisted he wasn't being racist. But he felt it was beyond him to navigate the discrepancy between the historic English King, Shakespeare's play and racially diverse casting; it was too much to handle. As troubling as this may be, the letter allowed me to reconsider the challenges of 'colour-blind' casting. Actors from all backgrounds have been performing Shakespeare for at least two hundred years, but even with the changes taking place across the theatre industry, in most mainstream venues, white actors are still very much at an advantage, from the parts they get to play, to their makeup and lighting. The very practice of 'colour-blind' casting often demands that actors of colour censor their race so that audiences might better imagine the white character they're portraying. Yet there are more ethical and inclusive ways to cast Shakespeare productions that might release the multiple meanings of these ever-yielding plays. If Shakespeare is your favourite playwright, reading his plays through race will not threaten that. It may make you uncomfortable at times, but in the end, I believe you'll *know* him better, *love* him more, and all the more *enjoy* the myriad ways he can be presented by actors of all backgrounds on the 21st-century stage.

One

THE MAKING OF THE GREAT WHITE BARD

[T]his country is only white because it says it is.

James Baldwin

Dear Ms Karim-Cooper…I am sure you will agree that your remit is to preserve and present The Bard's work… you are mere custodians – to give the general public access to the greatest cannon [*sic*] of work in the English language. It is not your business to try to force *all and sundry* to attend events by playing around with Shakespeare's genius!

This letter, which I received in May 2021, is evidence of the centuries-long investment in Shakespeare as a uniquely English genius. When 'all and sundry' – or more precisely, ethnically diverse people – are invited to adapt or examine his work *on their own terms*, it is overstepping, a violation of what was intended. My penfriend's obtuse but not uncommon point of view is what motivated me to write this book.

NOSTALGIA

Cultural nostalgia is sometimes conflated with a love of the past. It is this sentiment that fuelled the success of Shakespeare's Globe after its opening in 1997. People gathered in the Yard under the open sky to watch actors dance an *authentic* Elizabethan jig in fantastically elaborate and painstakingly accurate costumes stitched by hand. This kind of staging of Shakespeare was unique and radical because no other theatres were recreating the aesthetics of Renaissance performance in a working theatre in such detail. This performance style fed the reverence and nostalgic curiosity that brought people through the Globe's newly framed English oak doors. Other Tudor attractions such as Hampton Court Palace and the Shakespeare Birthplace Trust sell the grand notion of a golden time when Queen Elizabeth I was on the throne epitomising sumptuous royal fashion and power, with her excessively whitened face and lavish gowns, ruffs and jewels. But these popular ideas of Tudor England express only one side of the story of Shakespeare and his age, a side of the story which is whitewashed and mythical.

Elizabethan England, now deemed for centuries a golden age of literature and art, witnessed the proliferation of poetry and drama. As a political state, the country saw the rise of mercantilism and witnessed the opening of trade links with the East beyond the Mediterranean and with Africa. These developments ushered in an age of exploration for the English that reflected their grand expansionist and proto-colonial ambitions, though very few of us learned in school about the exploits of the great English sea dogs like Sir Francis Drake. While academics have interrogated more opaque aspects of Elizabethan history, we have only begun to openly deconstruct the more troubling features of the sixteenth century. Analysing our history in good faith provides an opportunity to understand how we became the culture and society we are today. It is time for a true understanding of the long-lasting effect of Tudor and Stuart exploration, trade and the accumulation of wealth: the exceptionalism of English national identity. As the English came into more frequent contact with non-Europeans, it became easier to form a sense of self and 'other'; the creation of a unique brand of English white superiority emerged, patently symbolised in the painted face of the Queen herself. Shakespeare's plays register these developments in manifold ways.

The fact that such a popular, well-known, widely taught figure as Shakespeare emerged from the Elizabethan period is a perfect opportunity for historians and teachers to grapple with the realities behind the myths, inviting diverse readerships and students to engage with them, especially those looking to understand the making of modern Western society. That only white people resided in England prior to the twentieth century falsifies the record. England's extraordinarily multilayered, complex and itinerant past deserves better attention. Film and television period drama certainly have a lot to answer for – think of movies like *Elizabeth*, starring Cate Blanchett, or *Shakespeare in Love* with the fabulous Dame Judi Dench playing the cosmetic-faced Queen. Rarely do we see that Black people lived and worked in England too, nor are we given any hint that the concept of racial difference was already developing. Such whitewashing is somewhat dangerous. When films, television programmes and stage productions cast Black and ethnically diverse actors in historical settings or plays, the reaction from many fearing that Shakespeare is being adulterated is hostile and even violent. The lack of awareness of historical diversity and Shakespeare's role in racial formation emboldens racist attacks against progressive theatrical and filmic interventions into casting. Being truthful about the past can't do any more harm than hiding from it has already done.

*

The triangular trade route charted by Plymouth-based merchant William Hawkins in the early 1550s was a perilous journey in which ships would leave British ports, sail to West Africa to exchange English goods for human beings, then travel through the horrific 'middle passage' to the West Indies or Americas to trade or sell them. Subsequently, Elizabethan privateers Sir John Hawkins and the infamous Sir Francis Drake chartered three early slave-trading expeditions (the second in the year of Shakespeare's birth), which, while incredibly dangerous, proved lucrative, and therefore later receiving backing from the Queen and members of her privy council, including Sir Robert Dudley, the Earl of Leicester. The Queen even granted Sir John Hawkins a coat of arms that illustrated and celebrated his slave-trading ventures.

The crest in this coat of arms shows a 'Moor' whose captivity is denoted by cords or ropes.[1] While there were only three slave-trading expeditions in the Tudor period, it is worth remembering that they laid the groundwork for the horrors that would follow at the end of the seventeenth century through to the nineteenth century. That Shakespeare emerges unscathed from this less than rosy context is rarely acknowledged. Perhaps the Bard would feel less out of reach for young people if the Elizabethan era was taught in schools in ways that took stock of these encounters. But this level of transparency is countered by attempts to stifle the shameful histories of racial oppression in America as well as Britain. In Britain in 2021 over 250,000 people signed a petition demanding that the national curriculum address Britain's role in colonialism and the slave trade, but the then Education Secretary, Gavin Williamson, rejected the idea of 'compulsory' lessons, claiming that such a narrative would risk 'lowering standards', a statement which implicitly confers a higher status upon white people.[2]

In 2018, the Royal Historical Society published a report on *Race, Ethnicity & Equality in UK History*, arguing 'if History wishes to improve its recruitment of BME students and to present a broad and inclusive range of perspectives on the past, the privileging of an "island story" of Britain (in both school-teaching and university-teaching) will need to be addressed'. By the time my daughter completed secondary school in England at age fifteen, she had been taught very little about slavery, and what she had learned referred only to abolition. Nor did she learn about colonialism or the British occupation of India. Being half-Pakistani, she would have loved to learn how her own ancestry fits into British history and culture, how her heritage was in fact woven into the fabric of the country of her birth. The mighty Shakespeare, whose theatre company performed at Elizabeth I's court every Christmas, would have been deeply aware of the shifting attitudes towards racial difference as well as the country's colonial aspirations and he would have encountered many an English privateer at court. It is hardly surprising, then, that he made space for different kinds of histories *and* bodies in his work, even if it isn't always clear where he himself stood on the question of English supremacy.

We have to ask ourselves, how is it that Shakespeare, whose plays seem to speak to so many different identities and experiences, still feels inaccessible to so many communities? At what point in the history of the reception of Shakespeare did he become the unassailable beacon of English identity? Was it in his own time? Not really. For much of it, he was a jobbing playwright working with a company of players, his 'band of brothers', with whom he collaborated rather than dictated to. No more than half of his plays were published in his lifetime and there was no collected works of his in print until 1623, seven years after he died, so he was not yet part of a canon of literature. His plays were popular; it's fairly certain that the playhouses were full when they were being staged. But people in sixteenth- and seventeenth-century London crammed into the amphitheatres to see the plays of Christopher Marlowe, Thomas Middleton and John Webster too. Shakespeare didn't really stand out amongst his fellow playwrights as the colossus he is today.

In a veiled attack, the contemporary prose writer Robert Greene (or the dramatist Henry Chettle posing as Robert Greene) accused Shakespeare of copying other people's ideas and being an 'upstart Crow, beautified with our feathers, that with his Tiger's heart wrapped in a Player's hide, supposes he is as well able to bombast out a blank verse as the best of you: and being an absolute *Johannes Factotum* [jack-of-all-trades], is in his own concept the only Shake-scene in a country.'[3]

And so our beloved playwright is accused of plagiarism and overly bombastic verse. The mocking tone about the rising popularity of Shakespeare in his own day is hard to miss in the reference to 'Tiger's heart wrapped in a Player's hide', a parody of a line from *Henry VI part 3* where Margaret of Anjou is addressed as 'O tiger's heart wrapp'd in a woman's hide!' (1.4.137). Being called a jack-of-all-trades is a slight, of course, too. He was a player (an actor) *and* a writer – imagine that. But despite some of the criticism he received, Shakespeare was also much admired amongst his contemporaries as the verse dedications in the published volume of his plays, the *First Folio*, tell us. Here, for example, his eventual canonisation is accurately predicted when his rival and fellow poet, Ben Jonson, declares 'Thou art a Moniment, without a tombe, / And art alive still, while thy Booke doth live'.

During the Restoration, the plays of Shakespeare were revived for the theatres, new styles of performing them emerged and it became quite popular to rework, rewrite and adapt his plays, something that has continued to this day. In 1687, the poet William Winstanley considered Shakespeare an 'eminent Poet, the Glory of the English Stage'.[4] But it was also a time when he was critiqued as a writer and his plays started to be analysed scrupulously. While Restoration playwrights and critics admired and praised Shakespeare, they were able to see the flaws in his work too and did not hesitate to point them out. As the playwright and poet laureate John Dryden argued in 1668, Shakespeare 'wears almost everywhere two faces; and you have scarce begun to admire the one, ere you despise the other'; in other words, he is 'the very Janus of poets'.[5] So while he praises him, he also says that Shakespeare can be 'insipid', and has a tendency to swell 'into bombast'.[6] Some writers felt Shakespeare didn't always pass muster when it came to observing classical conventions for drama; moreover, he was criticised for his implausible plots and an overreliance upon spectacle and the supernatural.

However, in the eighteenth century, a general shift in his reception occurs, though his plots and characters continued to be (and still are) subject to harsh critique. His works were further tinkered with, rewritten and adapted to fit the imaginings and attitudes of the time and apocryphal works were even passed off as Shakespeare's in a desperate attempt to widen his canon – because how could a genius like Shakespeare not have been more prolific? Shakespeare the man or symbol was nevertheless praised more elaborately, widely and unapologetically than ever before. It was in this period that he was finally christened the 'Bard', by famed actor and Theatre Royal manager David Garrick. Scholars and artists too expended great stores of energy fashioning Shakespeare into something beyond the mortal but which also reflected the values of the era. He was thus finally christened an 'original genius', whose *natural* talent was seen as specifically English. In the preface to his 1725 collected works of Shakespeare, Alexander Pope argued that the famous playwright was an 'instrument of Nature'; ''tis not just to say that he speaks from her, as that she speaks thro' him'.[7] By the end of the eighteenth century, the beauty of his work and the naturalness of his genius were seen to be derived from divine inspiration as well as English essentialness.

A BARD IS BORN

In 1767, the Scottish minister William Duff published 'An Essay on Original Genius', which argued that genius was observable in imagination, reasonable judgment or rationality, and taste. Shakespeare provided an excellent example for him of a genius quite different 'from that of every other Mortal', which already set him apart as a demigod.[8] Many other writers of the time attempted to define what it was about Shakespeare that marked him out above all others. Literary historian Jonathan Bate has even suggested that the idea of genius we have today was 'invented' in the eighteenth century 'in order to account for what was atypical of Shakespeare'.[9]

Over the centuries many have tried to decode the magic of Shakespeare; unearthing what makes him unique. Is it his originality? No – well, not when it comes to his plots; most of his plays come from well-known sources and histories. Characterisation? Very likely. Language? Definitely. Morality? Hardly. His views on love? Sort of. His views on death? Perhaps. His advocacy of human rights? Feminist critics of *The Taming of the Shrew* would say 'not always!' His ability to capture humanity in all of its ugliness, beauty, complexity and diversity? Indeed. His capacity to demonstrate that freedom is available to us in all sorts of guises? As a person who has been free all her life, I'd agree. But freedom was not available to everyone in Shakespeare's day. The truth is, we may never pin down the *why* behind Shakespeare's resonance. So instead, perhaps it is better to look at *how* he has been fashioned through the lens of English exceptionalism and the effects of this fashioning even now.

The eighteenth century was a period of great contradiction, an age when the ideas of taste and high culture were being cultivated, works of art and literature appreciated according to neoclassical definitions of form and beauty. In his *Essays on the Nature and Principles of Taste* (1790), the Episcopalian priest Archibald Alison defines the emotions of taste as being 'distinguished from the Emotions of Simple Pleasure, by their being dependent upon the exercise of our imagination'.[10] Famously, the eighteenth century was also a time when philosophy and politics were preoccupied with the idea of liberty such as that defined by John Locke (1632– 1704), crowned the 'father of liberalism' because of the principles emerging from his Enlightenment values: autonomy, equality and the basics of human rights.[11] Eighteenth-century English culture also witnessed the heightened appreciation of art, literature, music and aesthetic judgment, all leveraged as the chief symbols of a *civilised* society.

Yet, underpinning the Enlightenment was the escalation of maritime commerce and with it the full realisation of the transatlantic slave trade. Only a few historians, such as Simon Gikandi, have dwelled on the bizarre coupling of the institution of slavery with the aspirations of a nation bent on developing its identity as connoisseurs of culture. In so doing, Gikandi asks one of the most salient questions about the past: 'How could such elevated images of art exist in the same harsh world of enslavement and the slave trade?'[12] How do we reconcile the fact that Shakespeare was being lauded as the 'native genius' while the British Empire was being forged? The enslavement of Black people enabled products like sugar and coffee to add flavour to the civilising activities that celebrated English sophistication, such as going to the theatre or, say, an art gallery.

RE-MAKING THE BARD'S IMAGE

Imagine that it is 1789 and you have been invited to an exciting opening of a new gallery in London's Pall Mall. You have heard that the works of the most celebrated British artists of the century will be on display and you'll have the opportunity to buy engravings of these pieces, specially reproduced for middle-class public consumption.

The Shakespeare Gallery was the brainchild of London publishing magnate and print seller, John Boydell. Building on the 'Bardolatry' ushered in earlier by David Garrick's Jubilee in Stratford-upon-Avon and London in 1769, Boydell commissioned British artists such as Benjamin West, Angelica Kauffmann, Henry Fuseli and even Sir Joshua Reynolds, who was then at the helm of the Royal Academy, to create elaborate illustrations of scenes from Shakespeare's plays.

As you entered the gallery, you would be struck first by an *alto relievo* (high relief, wall-mounted sculpture) of Shakespeare by Thomas Banks, one of the most influential sculptors in the British school.

Appropriately called 'Apotheosis of Shakespeare', the sculpture, later depicted in print on the front of Boydell's Shakespeare volume, included three figures.

Shakespeare perches in the middle on a pedestal while on either side of him are the Dramatic Muse and the Genius of Painting. By combining the inspirational figures of drama and visual art through a neoclassical reimagining of the poet, Banks's relief helps Boydell make the point that the eminence and genius of Shakespeare's dramatic poetry would bring a particular lustre to and showcase the superiority of national creativity, a superiority that would be indisputable in light of British maritime success and increasing power. And such power must be depicted appropriately.

The gallery contained three exhibition rooms housing thirty-four pieces by twenty-one different artists; by the time it closed in 1807 – the year King George III signed into law the Act for the Abolition of the Slave Trade – it had over 160 unique pieces. Eventually, a catalogue was created and countless engravings generated from this cluster of imaginative illustrations of the nation's favourite poet and his works. Boydell certainly had his finger on the pulse of British art and sensibility; the age of Enlightenment witnessed an explosion of fan art centred on Shakespeare. Popular scenes from plays, celebrated characters and sculptures, and illustrations and busts of the Bard himself all emerged. This artistic tradition contributed to the popular construction of Shakespeare we rely on today.

Illustrations or busts of Shakespeare from his own time are extremely rare, something that tends to fuel authorship dissenters contending that the man from Stratford-upon-Avon couldn't have written these plays since there was so much portraiture in the Elizabethan age. The fact is poets rarely had

their portraits painted, let alone playwrights, and when they did, there would likely only be one. There are, in fact, three images of Shakespeare that seem most convincingly to have hailed from the seventeenth century, two of which emerged seven years after his death. The most famous of these was engraved by the Flemish-born artist Martin Droeshout. In this iconic image, the Bard's face peers out from the title page of the *First Folio*.

His domed, bulbous head centralised in the frame has come to symbolise the immensity of Shakespeare's creative intellect. But it is an odd picture for modern eyes: cartoon-like, with unfeasible proportions. When we imagine Shakespeare, we tend to think of the Droeshout engraving, or another somewhat iconic portrait: the Chandos, named after the 3rd Duke of Chandos, who once owned it and whose links to the legacy of the slave trade, being a joint-owner of a Jamaican plantation, underline this co-existence of bardolatry and slavery in eighteenth-century England.[13] Though the artist is not named, some believe it was painted by actor John Taylor, perhaps the one listed on the opening pages of the *First Folio* alongside the other members of Shakespeare's theatre company. Remarkably, the Chandos portrait, then owned by the Earl of Ellesmere, was the very first item given to the National Portrait Gallery when it was established in 1856. As the only likely painting emerging from Shakespeare's lifetime, it is in itself a national treasure, a true symbol of curiosity and wonder.

I love this portrait, not just because it depicts Shakespeare as a rather cool dude with an earring, but also because I like to imagine him sitting impatiently for this portrait somewhere in London where it was likely painted and where he had the urgent business of putting on plays. How close did the artist come to his likeness, and did the sitter approve? There are many instances in Shakespeare's work that indicate his appreciation of the skill of painters who can recreate faces from life as if by some divine magic. In *The Merchant of Venice*, the financially troubled gentleman Bassanio takes part in a 'casket test' devised by the late father of a 'lady richly left', Portia, in order to find her a husband. A gold, silver and lead casket are on display and suitors must guess which one contains her 'miniature', a tiny portrait made popular in the sixteenth century by artist Isaac Oliver, known for his many miniatures of Tudor and Stuart monarchs. Bassanio guesses correctly and finds Portia's likeness within the lead casket:

Fair Portia's counterfeit! What demigod
Hath come so near creation? Move these eyes,
Or whether, riding on the balls of mine,
Seem they in motion? Here are severed lips,
Parted with sugar breath; so sweet a bar
Should sunder such sweet friends. Here in her hairs
The painter plays the spider and hath woven
A golden mesh t'entrap the hearts of men
Faster than gnats in cobwebs.

(3.2.115–23)

Nowhere else is there a more perfect description of the unnerving magic of painting. 'Move these eyes?' – we know this unsettling feeling well from viewing portraits that seem to stare back at us.

A great deal of ink has been spilled about these images though there may be nothing controversial about them. They, in fact, tell us very little about the man himself, who remains unfathomable. What these representations did elicit, however, was a desire for subsequent 'truer' depictions of the Bard's features. The compulsion to paint, sculpt and re-imagine Shakespeare has not died, nor should it. Each generation's depiction of him tells us much more about the artist, the time period, culture and geography than they actually do about Shakespeare. Curiously, however, eighteenth-century portraits and sculptures of him propose a Shakespeare that is more beautiful, symmetrical and whiter in complexion than the three Shakespearean faces that emerged in the seventeenth century. While these three faces are instantly recognisable, the eighteenth-century visual fantasy of Shakespeare endures.

Given Shakespeare's evident admiration for the 'demi-god' wonders of visual art, I am not sure he would have appreciated the funerary bust in Holy Trinity Church in Stratford-upon-Avon, which was mounted on the north wall of the chancel in 1623.

The memorial bust, possibly cut by Dutchman Geerart Janssen, which appeared only seven years after the playwright's death, has been famously reviled as unworthy of the Bard, a view that twentieth-century scholar John Dover Wilson articulates when he declared it may be suitable for 'an affluent and retired butcher, but does gross wrong to the dead poet'.[14] At the persuasion of Shakespeare editor Edmond Malone, it was repainted entirely in white in 1793, the same year editor George Stevens declared the *First Folio* 'the most expensive single book in our language'.[15] It was also copied repeatedly – and with varying degrees of artistic license – as an engraving (pictured here), one of which illustrated Pope's edition of Shakespeare's works in 1725.

This latter image is quite altered, perhaps to justify Pope's conviction and reason for editing a complete works: that Shakespeare 'of all English poets' is 'the *fairest* and fullest subject for [literary] criticism'. Did Shakespeare perhaps need to *look* the part of the 'fair' native genius too?

Throughout the 1700s, depictions of Shakespeare increased, fuelling his status as a kind of national saint. The 'father of art history', Johann Winckelmann (1717–1768) helped launch the neoclassical movement in sculpture and art across Europe. Obsessed with ancient Greek statuary, he saw the white marble copies of ancient figures as paragons of true beauty, even though original classical sculptures had been colourfully painted. He wrote extensively about ancient art and his theories were distributed widely. His shaping views of aesthetics thus intersected with the developing systems of human classification of the day that spuriously attempted to tie racial difference to biology, skin colour, skull shape and environment or climate. British

philosopher David Hume's ideas expressed in his work on 'aesthetics' and art-making reflect the received racial 'wisdom' of the day held by anthropologists as well as art theorists: 'I am apt to suspect the negroes, and in general all other species of men (for there are four or five different kinds) to be naturally inferior to the whites.'[16] Meanwhile Winckelmann's art theory, while recognising that beauty is subjective and not all people will share the same idea of human beauty, identified, quite technically, white as a superior colour. Because white 'reflects the greatest number of rays of light, and consequently is the most easily perceived, a beautiful body will, accordingly, be the more beautiful the whiter it is'.[17] No wonder Shakespeare's eighteenth-century visual reimagining would emerge glowingly white and perfectly chiselled to reflect the Caucasian skull underneath. Recapturing ancient Greek and Roman precedents, Shakespeare busts and statuary emerged as a direct response to the neoclassical ideal of bodily perfection – with symmetry and whiteness as the distinguishing features.

It was so important for England that its national poet should once and for all be beautiful enough to reflect his genius and his native origins, that in 1741, a statue of this kind finally appeared in the ultimate corner of the country.

The artist, Peter Scheemakers, a Belgian classicist, who lived and worked in London creating mostly garden sculptures, was commissioned in 1740 to erect a statue of the Bard in Poet's Corner in Westminster Abbey (pictured here). Actors, theatre managers and a Shakespeare 'Ladies Club' all worked tirelessly raising money to memorialise England's greatest poet appropriately. Historian Fiona Ritchie points out that 'women were the primary financial contributors to the fund to commission the statue'.[18] The commemorative statue was seen as bringing to fruition a century-long wish to see Shakespeare remembered in this national way. The poet and scholar William Basse, in one of the earliest elegies to Shakespeare, written sometime between 1616 and 1623, had been one of the first to point out the absurdity of Shakespeare being buried not in the country's national cathedral but instead in the provincial Trinity Chapel in Stratford-upon-Avon.[19]

The Shakespeare of Westminster Abbey is depicted in seventeenth-century dress, with his elbow resting upon a pile of books, the busts of Queen Elizabeth I, Henry V and Richard III carved into the plinth to demonstrate the playwright's connection to British monarchical power through his stories and patronage.

WILLIAM SHAKESPEARE 1564 – 1616
BURIED AT STRATFORD-ON-AVON

Curiously though, he is not really depicted here as a man of the theatre, which is absolutely what he was. Instead, he is shown to be a learned, meditative philosopher literally raised high and unassailable.

> There up to heav'n a mass of rock was piled
> ...
> And on its topmost height, the regal throne
> Of this romantic realm, stood Avon's bard alone.[20]

An idealised notion of Shakespeare, to say the least. When Alexander Pope was creating his edition, he too was keen to correct any evidence of the coarse practice of theatre-making, and rationalised that any deficiencies in Shakespeare were directly attributable to his writing for the 'populace' and 'from our Author's being a Player'.[21] This was part of an effort in the eighteenth century to purify the Shakespearean text, not just of posthumous interventions but also the inherent properties of original performance.[22] What the Westminster Abbey statue captures, then, is Shakespeare the reader, the classically inspired English poet. We know he read avidly from the many contemporaneous, continental and classical sources that inspired and informed his plays and poems. But the Abbey monument suggests that that was all he was about.

Thinking of him as a dramatist first and foremost forces us to see the practicalities of theatre-making, its messiness, its collaborative nature and Shakespeare's own intimate involvement as the house playwright attached to the Globe Theatre. The Enlightenment's idea of genius was incompatible with the realities of the collaborative nature and fragmentation of early modern playwriting. Such a Shakespeare wouldn't do in the crafting of 'the Bard' as national icon. How can you be a natural and native genius if you have actors, other playwrights, theatre impresarios, prompters, censors, audience judgment and theatre architecture helping to shape your plays?

The celebration and acts of commemoration that took place during the eighteenth century divorced Shakespeare from his works, which enabled him to become well and truly a mythological or quasi-religious figure.[23] To visit the monument, one must go to church, in fact to one of England's most treasured cathedrals where Elizabeth I herself is buried. Although Shakespeare is not buried in Poet's Corner alongside Edmund Spenser and Ben Jonson it is still clear that in the 1700s he was crowned not only the national poet, but also cult figure and secular god: 'It is she [Nature] who was thy book, O Shakespeare', proclaims the cleric Martin Sherlock in his eulogy 'The Immortality of Shakespeare', 'it is she from whom thou hast drawn those beauties which are at once the glory and delight of thy nation'.[24]

'GOD OF ALL OUR IDOLATRY'

A few years later, David Garrick would refer to Shakespeare as 'the Bard' for the first time. And though the term had been in use for a while to refer to poets, it didn't stick to others in quite the same way. Garrick was considered an exceptional actor of his day, celebrated as a true marvel of the stage, leaving audiences enthralled by the sheer emotion of his performances. In Fanny Burney's three-volume sentimental novel *Evelina* (1778), the actor is mentioned by name:

> Well may Mr Garrick be so celebrated, so universally admired – I had not any idea of so great a performer.

> Such ease! such vivacity in his manner! such grace in
> his motions! such fire and meaning in his eyes![25]

The German physicist Georg Christoph Lichtenberg raved about Garrick's performance of Hamlet seeing his father's ghost: 'His whole demeanour is so expressive of terror that it made my flesh creep even before he began to speak'.[26] But he is perhaps best known for his passion-fuelled performance of Richard III, captured compellingly by the great visual chronicler of eighteenth-century society, William Hogarth. Garrick felt divinely appointed to commemorate Shakespeare, to elevate him to the status he deserved. And that's precisely what he did.

In 1769 the actor was approached by the corporation of Stratford-upon-Avon to help celebrate their 'son' with…yes, you guessed it, a new statue. At this time Stratford was a minor municipality and certainly not the tourist magnet it is today. Garrick organised what was to be a three-day festival in September of that year, the infamous Shakespeare Jubilee, to accompany the monument's erection. There would be pageants, parades, a masquerade ball, dinners, breakfasts, even a horse race. Thirty cannons were brought into Stratford for the opening day and a special amphitheatre built to host the aristocracy visiting this provincial town. This was probably the first time that souvenirs dedicated to Shakespeare went on sale in Stratford. Oddly, no Shakespeare plays were performed, but never mind; the plays with their multiple ideas and polyvocality would just get in the way of the one, true image of the Bard that Garrick was trying to construct.

The Jubilee was meant to attract the richest and most elite visitors from London while also taking Shakespeare to the everyday person, to the very streets of Stratford. Some might argue this was an act of inclusivity and egalitarianism.[27] This would be true if inclusivity had meant including *only* the white working classes. But British Enlightenment values like liberty and democracy did not apply to different ethnicities, and certainly did not reach English slave ships or the plantations of the Caribbean and Americas.

Unfortunately for Garrick the English weather got the better of him and much of the festival was a washout. But it did serve a purpose nevertheless: Shakespeare was indeed commemorated as the son from Stratford-upon-Avon and therefore the birthplace of the Bard was put on the map as the ultimate literary pilgrimage site forever after – as Garrick's letter written to the town's mayor two years later encouraging him to keep the town clean suggests: 'to allure *every* body to visit the holy land'.[28] Secondly, the events marked out Shakespeare as England's greatest achievement, the very 'demi-god', as Garrick's 'Ode' to the 'Blest genius of the isle' intones,

> Who Avon's flowery margin trod,
> While sportive Fancy round him flew;
> Where Nature led him by the hand,
> Instructed him in all she knew,
> And gave him absolute command!

In his career, Garrick played many roles to acclaim, but he was reportedly a terrible Othello. Critics were not as forthcoming with their accolades as they had been for his other Shakespearean roles. Donning a turban and blackface, his Othello was seen as rather neurotic and anxious. Othello was a beloved tragic character who presented a fantasy of an African man who had acquired dignity and eloquence in his speech despite his origins. Fellow actors and critics were not impressed with Garrick's exoticisation of the role nor his over-the-top performance. Reportedly, the actor James Quin commented on Garrick's appearance: 'Othello! Psha! No such thing! There was a little black boy, like Pompey attending with a teakettle, fretting and fuming about the stage; but I saw no Othello!'[29] When asked why Shakespeare chose to make Othello black rather than white, Garrick declared that such a raging jealous spirit would not suit a white man's disposition:

> Shakespeare had shown us white men jealous in other pieces, but…their jealousy had limits, and was not so terrible… [In] Othello, he had wished to paint that passion in all its violence, and that is why he chose an African in whose veins circulated fire instead of blood…[30]

Garrick's attempt to portray Othello's 'otherness' ultimately worked against him as *his* perception of black men couldn't quite map on to Shakespeare's Moor.

It goes without saying that there was some denial in this period about the extent of Othello's blackness. The writer William Kenrick said in 1774 that Othello could not be black and was 'at worst only of a tawny colour'; how else can such a 'young lady of Desdemona's delicacy of sentiment' have 'fallen in love with a Negro'?[31] It is no wonder then that by the time the famed actor Edmund Kean (1789–1833) took on the role, he did so with lighter makeup, initiating what is known as the great 'bronze age' of performances of Othello.[32] Othellos were 'tawny' until the late nineteenth and twentieth centuries, when darker-skinned Othellos began to reappear, coupled with an overly emotional and stereotypical portrayal of the Moor. Thus, it was eighteenth-century audiences reconciling their attraction to Othello with the growing science of race that played a key role in the justification for the enslavement of Africans.

Between 1640 and 1807 Britain was the most dominant of the European slave-trading countries. British ships leaving from Bristol, Liverpool and London transported 3.1 million Africans to the British colonies in the Caribbean and Americas. By the end of the seventeenth century, bespoke trading companies were formed – such as the Royal African Company, a chartered mercantile company created by the King and the merchants of London in 1672 to hold a monopoly on English trade to West Africa. This enabled Britain to compete with its Iberian rivals, Spain and Portugal, who had been well established in the trade since the fifteenth century. From around 1660 the British Crown granted charters and passed legislation to mechanise the opportunities for companies to supply enslaved subjects to the American colonies and provide labour for their colonial outposts and plantations in the Caribbean. The East India Company, created in 1600, also ventured into slave-trading, collecting Africans from both the East and West coasts of Africa to support its settlements across Asia and India.[33]

Britain's immense maritime efforts were met with celebration and pride. Historians agree that the slave economy as it stood in the eighteenth century was the basis for the commercial, financial and (I would add) cultural structures of Britain's metropolises.[34] The finery and goods pouring into the country were unprecedented; paradoxical at best, grossly obscene at worst. Sugar was the most lucrative import until the nineteenth century, changing the tastes of Georgian England sensorially as well as intellectually. In the 1790s when the Stratford-upon-Avon restorers were painting Shakespeare's memorial bust entirely white, the planter

Bryan Edwards noted that the contribution of the sugar trade in the West Indies to the nation's economy was 'the principal source of national opulence and maritime power'.[35]

The perception of Shakespeare as universal genius and the 'god of all our idolatry' was born during this period of oppression. As the nation began to view itself as the epitome of civilisation, Shakespeare took on this symbolic burden too. He was and is still considered universal, because humanity, reason, creativity and civilisation were qualities strictly attributed to whiteness in the period's writings on race. Shakespeare spoke for and to these qualities, as did his great characters like Hamlet and Lear. European philosophy intersected with racial science and influenced ways of thinking for the English to judge the world through the prism of their own achievements. In the period's meditations on the sublime and the beautiful, for example, racial science becomes a point of fact, as philosopher Immanuel Kant's *Observations on the Feeling of the Beautiful and the Sublime* tells us: 'The negroes of Africa have by nature no feeling that arises above the trifling. Mr Hume challenges anyone to cite a single example in which a Negro has shown talents, and asserts...not a single one was ever found who presented anything great in art or science or any other praiseworthy quality... So fundamental is the difference between these two races of man.'[36]

According to Kant, white supremacy was the foundation of artistic genius. This notion produced the shaky logic that Shakespeare was a genius because he was white. White bodies and minds were exceptional, and the domination of the world by European powers simply confirmed this and provided the confidence necessary to declare it boldly, violently and repeatedly. Beautiful art, music and poetry, theatres, coffee houses, galleries, gardens and opera houses, statues and celebrations of Shakespeare not only co-existed with race-based slavery, but rather depended on it.

'MASTER-TOUCHES'

According to the parish register of Holy Trinity Church, Stratford-upon-Avon, Shakespeare was baptised on 26 April 1564. This means he could have been born anytime between 21 and 24 April but his birthday is traditionally observed on the 23rd – St George's Day, yet another tether to English nationalism. Conflating Shakespeare with the patron saint of England seems nothing less than strategic in the construction of the Great White Bard. Most of us know very little about St. George. But he was probably, by blood, Cappadocian and Palestinian, and very possibly brown-skinned. In Eastern Europe he was known as 'dragon slayer', but by the eleventh century he had been adopted by Western crusaders to inspire them in their horrific battles with Islamic 'infidels', as they were called, and in 1415 the red cross flew over the Battle of Agincourt as King Henry V famously led his troops to victory, after which St George's Day was officially made a feast day in the English calendar. It's no coincidence then that the 23rd was the chosen date of Shakespeare's birth sometime in the eighteenth century – it created the illusion of a divinely ordained outcome. We overlook that he may not in fact have been born on the 23rd or that his connection to St George is in fact a connection to foreign lands. How much less poetic to say so!

It can feel impossible to extricate Shakespeare from this legacy because of patriotism's powerful hold. Whether it's Brexiteer Boris Johnson's invocations of Shakespeare to assert the primacy of English culture and language: 'this is our language, the language of Shakespeare',[37] or the use of speeches such as *Henry V*'s 'Once more unto the breach' to inspire English victory in war, or on football and rugby pitches:

> And you, good yeomen,
> Whose limbs were made in England, show us here
> The mettle of your pasture; let us swear
> That you are worth your breeding – which I doubt not,
> For there is none of you so mean and base
> That hath not noble lustre in your eyes.
> I see you stand like greyhounds in the slips,
> Straining upon the start. The game's afoot.
> Follow your spirit, and upon this charge
> Cry, 'God for Harry! England, and Saint George!'
>
> (3.1.25–34)

It is one of the most effective pep talks in the English language. If you've seen either Mark Rylance in 1997, Jamie Parker in 2012 or Sarah Amankwah in 2018 perform these lines to an excited crowd of groundlings in the Globe Theatre, you will have witnessed the speech's riveting, nostalgic force. But Shakespeare's works do not advocate for empty rhetoric nor was he entirely unquestioning of nationalism. While *Henry V* tells the story of a brilliantly triumphant moment in English history, it does not lack complexity and criticism of Shakespeare's own political moment. Phrases like 'noble English', 'Englishman' and 'those men of England' appear frequently in the play, which is why some have viewed it as evidence of Shakespeare's patriotism, but scholars have shown how the play instead reveals Shakespeare's sensitivity to the instability in England around 1599 when the play was written and first staged, as questions of succession were looming as the 'virgin' Queen Elizabeth I was ageing without a named heir. The play also interrogates the very premise of English nationhood in the context of the country's assertion of English domination and colonialism when it came to Ireland, Scotland and Wales. Shakespeare had thoughts too about the notion of Empire, using imperialistic rhetoric in the play:

> ...London doth pour out her citizens.
> The Mayor and all his brethren in best sort,
> Like to the senators of th'antique Rome
> With the plebeians swarming at their heels,
> Go forth and fetch their conquering Caesar in
>
> (Chorus, 5.24–28)

For Shakespeare and his contemporaries, Empire was a concept that referred to English monarchical power just as much as it gestured towards the precedent of ancient Rome. A year after King James I came to the throne in 1603, Shakespeare's company performed *Henry V* at his court during Christmas. This speaks to the Jacobean King's own interest in cultivating a British political identity. Not just the final play in the history cycle, but all of Shakespeare's histories interrogate English entitlement, the divine right of kings and England's own burgeoning imperialistic ambitions, even while they create feelings of patriotic sentiment. When examined more closely, it becomes clear that those who feel Shakespeare's histories express only a longing for a purer English past or an imperial Roman one will be disappointed by moments of scepticism in the histories about such nostalgic ideals.

TRANSATLANTIC BARD

The Victorian writer Thomas Carlyle believed staunchly in England's Anglo-Saxon heritage and was a dedicated white supremacist. In an essay on hero worship published in 1841, he contends that there will be:

> a Saxondom covering great spaces of the Globe. And now, what is it that can keep all these together into virtually one Nation, so that they do not fall out and fight, but live at peace, in brotherlike intercourse, helping one another?... This King Shakespeare, does not he shine, in crowned sovereignty, over us all, as the noblest, gentlest, yet strongest of rallying-signs; indestructible... We can fancy him as radiant aloft over all the Nations of Englishmen, a thousand years hence... English men and women...will say to one another: "Yes, this Shakespeare is ours; we produced him, we speak and think by him; we are of one blood and kind with him".[38]

Shakespeare is imagined as a great uniter of English people throughout the British Empire, referred to here as 'Saxondom'. Shakespeare is 'King' of Saxons, rallying English patriots around the world who will identify him, own him and be of 'blood' and kinship with him. The image of a 'kingly' figure at a rally deliberately rousing nationalistic pride is one that is all too uncomfortably familiar to readers in a post-Trump world. And it is not how any of us wish to think of Shakespeare, his art, his words or his cultural 'soft' power. Carlyle's promotion of English racial bonds with Shakespeare has had more of a long-lasting effect than we like to imagine.

The International Society of Anglo-Saxonists (ISAS), a society of historians dedicated to the study of the pre-Conquest period, has changed its name. Its former vice-president, a Black female scholar, stepped down due to the rampant racism and sexism in the field of medieval studies. While the ISAS considered a name change, a fierce debate ensued and still continues, some believing the term 'Anglo-Saxon' simply refers to a period of time and that it would be erasing history or being 'woke' should the name of the field be altered. But people opposed to the term cite its racist connotations and its elevation as a racial differentiator in the eighteenth and nineteenth centuries. Matthew Gabriele and Mary Rambaran-Olm warn that modern conceptions of Anglo-Saxonism are based on a 'nineteenth century myth that centers on a false idea of what it means to be "native" to Britain'[39] and is the very basis of white supremacy. But this myth is incalculably powerful; it was essential to the founding of America itself. Unsurprisingly, the slave-owning Thomas Jefferson saw America as the culmination of Anglo-Saxon values. Jefferson philosophised that Americans were entitled to independence precisely because of their noble Saxon heritage; for him the English people and the framers of the Magna Carta were America's 'Saxon ancestors'.

This direct line from Anglo-Saxon heritage was, for Jefferson, evident in the English language itself and those who mastered it, particularly Shakespeare. His love of the Bard would be rooted in his admiration and pride in Anglo-Saxon history and culture. He read the works of Shakespeare avidly, attending plays in Williamsburg as well as on his many visits to London. Extolling the value of the poet's wisdom, Jefferson saw Shakespeare as a foundational giant of language and a source of great comfort. 'Shakespeare', he wrote to his prospective brother-in-law Robert Skipwith on 3 August 1771, 'must be singled out by one who wishes to learn' the 'full powers' of the English language. Jefferson saw a moral virtue in Shakespeare's works, musing to Skipwith that a 'lively and lasting sense of filial duty is more effectually impressed on the mind of a son or daughter by reading *King Lear*, than by all the dry volumes of ethics and divinity that were ever written'.[40] For Jefferson, Shakespeare was a generous repository of Anglo-Saxon wisdom, more effective than philosophy or even religious instruction.

The myth of Anglo-Saxon genius was essential to early Protestant America. As historian Nell Irvin Painter reminds us, 'to be American was to be Saxon'.[41] What is also true is that to be American means to claim Shakespeare as part of your Anglo-Saxon heritage and consequently part of your national curriculum. The American transcendentalist Ralph Waldo Emerson wrote beautifully about Shakespeare in the September 1904 issue of *The Atlantic* (the magazine he founded): 'wherever there are men, and in the degree in which they are civil, have power of mind, sensibility to beauty, music, the secrets of passion, had the liquid expression of thought, he has risen to his place as the first poet of the world.'[42] Values like aesthetic judgement, appreciation of beauty and civility, enabled the ideal of Shakespeare's genius to continue to flourish into the nineteenth and twentieth centuries.

Emerson's lesser-known book *English Traits* helps us understand why Shakespeare was of particular importance in the context of this Anglo-Saxon inheritance. It praises the whiteness and stature of English men, particularly the face and its 'fair complexion, blue eyes, and open and florid aspect'. Emerson aligned these features with a love 'of truth…fine perception, and poetic construction. The fair Saxon man, with open front, and honest meaning...is not the wood out of which cannibal, or inquisitor, or assassin is made, but he is moulded for law, lawful trade, civility, marriage, the nurture of children, for colleges, churches, charities, and colonies'.[43] The images of Shakespeare created in the eighteenth century would map rather neatly on to Emerson's own sense of English and thus American 'Saxon' perfection. Although the *First Folio*'s 'Epistle to the Great Variety of Readers' states that Shakespeare's 'hand and mind went together', meaning he committed his thoughts to paper with ease and largely without error, it would seem for Emerson, Jefferson and the writers and artists discussed here, it also implies that the Bard's *face* should match his fair mind.

Extremist nationalist groups still harp on the myth of Anglo-Saxon and align it more openly with white supremacist politics, such as the America First Caucus, a dangerous policy platform championed for a while in 2021 by Q-Anon fundamentalist and US congresswoman Marjorie Taylor Greene: the quoted rationale for the platform was a 'common respect for uniquely Anglo-Saxon political traditions'.[44] Shakespeare's construction during the height of the British slave trade and in the context of the creation of a biological racial theory enable claims upon him by those who consider white Anglo-Saxon culture superior, with Shakespeare being evidence of this superiority. As an icon, a national treasure, a native genius who wrote the 'greatest canon' in the world, Shakespeare speaks to whiteness in ways that can only be fully understood after examining his construction over two hundred years ago.

When the Capitol building in Washington D.C. was attacked on 6 January 2021, the extremist groups brandished an array of racist images, including swastikas and other Nazi symbols, confederate flags (some with assault rifles superimposed) and antisemitic slogans, to name a few. They had been planning the 'rally' for a while, as the 2022 congressional hearings established. The Folger Shakespeare Library sits on Capitol Hill and contains the largest collection of *First Folio* editions in the world, with accompanying volumes incorporating thousands of texts, images and sources relating to Shakespeare, theatre, performance and early modern culture. A group of extremists planned to forge a route around the Shakespeare Library; in fact the tunnel that led to the Capitol building emerged very near to the Library. In their conversations on the Donald/Win site (the conversation has since been taken down but survives in a series of screenshots) the insurrectionists discussed the Folger and actually composed a letter expressing reassurance to 'Folger Shakespeare Library and staff':

> This protest will include a 2.4-mile blockade surrounding all buildings to which the U.S. Capitol has underground tunnels to. Unfortunately, one of these buildings is the Library of Congress's John Adams Building, to which you share a block with…we will be blocking access to your building as well to prevent our persons of grievance from using you as a loophole. This is nothing personal to the library itself. We have no intention of damaging, trespassing, or otherwise altering your facility in anyway…We sincerely apologize in advance to any inconvenience this may cause you.[45]

The Folger were reassured they were not part of the dispute. The day after the attack, the Folger's director made the institution's response to the attack clear: 'the Folger – our staff, collection, and landmark building – remains safe. What's also safe is our commitment to engaging more and more of our fellow Americans in challenging conversations that elevate our shared humanity and strengthen our democracy.'[46]

Why was the Folger safe from the extremist rioters? Shakespeare, constructed as an icon of white excellence some centuries ago, still represents the very best of Anglo-Saxon culture to those that may never have read a Shakespearean word or watched a moment on stage. Decolonisation efforts would indeed have infuriated the rioters that day. Making Shakespeare anti-racist, diverse, opening up his canon to interrogation instead of sustaining its veneration, is precisely the kind of thing that such groups and others, like 'Save the Statues' in the UK, for example, are furious about. The hate mail and vitriolic tweets I receive because I dare to read Shakespeare in ways that help me and my students understand our current moment, that speak to the experiences and artistry of people from all racial and ethnic backgrounds, is further evidence that the Great White Bard is still with us. Tommy Robinson, the far-right, anti-Islam nationalist who spoke out against the toppling of slave trader Edward Colston's statue in Bristol in 2020, sums it up when he said in a video he released: 'Who gives a shit what it's about and what the man's done? It's part of British history.'[47] And that, for some, is that.

Two

BARBAROUS SPECTACLE

You've been on your feet for a while. The air feels stale because there's smoke or incense burning and little ventilation due to the temporary velarium roof covering the gaping hole of the amphitheatre. The soles of your feet are sore and your lower back is starting to ache, forcing you to shift your weight, though movement is limited by the many people around you. Then an actor charges through the crowd and you are shoved aside as he jumps up onto the wooden stage. Now you're irritated. Your body is telling you to leave but your curiosity is piqued. You hear the sound of an axe blade come thundering down onto the wooden stump, blood spurts in all directions and you can feel your gut twisting in dread. But you're afraid to move. More afraid to leave in case you miss what's to come. You see a person in front of you drop to the floor and stewards come rushing over, pushing through the crowd to help them up and out of the wooden doors. The actors keep saying their lines as if this isn't happening, and they will do so in every performance. Your heart beats faster, the adrenaline almost too much to bear.

DISCOMFORT

In 2006, Shakespeare's Globe staged a production of the playwright's first tragedy, *Titus Andronicus*, directed by Lucy Bailey.

The theatre reported an average of two to four fainters per performance, on a few occasions more. At one point, the paramedics sat just outside the theatre, waiting for audience members to drop. People felt nauseous and vomited inside and outside the theatre. The same production was revived in 2014, with even more intense physical effects amongst its audiences. *The Independent* headline read 'Globe Theatre takes out 100 audience members with its gory *Titus Andronicus*.'[1] The *Daily Telegraph* observed our trigger warning in its headline that the 'Globe audience faints at "grotesquely violent" *Titus Andronicus*'.[2] In 2017, Ian Hughes remarked in the *Stratford Observer* that 'Shakespeare still shocks', summarising research conducted by the Royal Shakespeare Company that monitored the emotional responses of the audiences who watched their own production, directed by Blanche McIntyre. Heart rates rose to 'the equivalent of a five-minute cardio workout – and men showed a slightly greater emotional reaction than women'.[3] *Titus* has been called Shakespeare's most 'brutal' play with its amputations, decapitations, rape, mutilations and cannibalism. Productions that stage this brutality honestly have been criticised for sensationalising Tudor violence. But a physical response to theatre is precisely what Shakespeare as a young dramatist counted on, and the playhouses of the time were designed for such gore.

In addition to being his first tragedy and revenge play, it is also his first to confront miscegenation and racial difference no holds barred. The play was written in the 1590s when Shakespeare was just getting started, inspired by the revenge sagas written by other Elizabethan dramatists and by the round open-air theatres that eventually made him. He was influenced by classical Roman sources such as Ovid's *Metamorphoses* (with its stories about bodily transformations, rape and assault) and Seneca's bloody

Thyestes (a tragedy that includes honour killing and cannibalism). Discomfort and trauma were foundational to his dramaturgical toolbox. This tragedy challenges contemporary political institutions as well as classical ideas, while objectifying racial difference and trauma in striking ways. No, Shakespeare is not comfortable. On the page *and* on the stage his works can even seem harmful.

The ire directed at academics and institutions looking to 'decolonise' Shakespeare or read his work in relation to its problematic qualities is rooted in the fear that problematising Shakespeare somehow makes him uncomfortable or unpalatable. I have worked at the heart of the beast for a long time and I know that Shakespeare was not concerned with his audience's comfort, at least not much. Not just because he wrote about love, loss, trauma, the destruction of the natural world, hate, suicide, murder, war, cannibalism, rape and bodily mutilation, but also because when audiences went to see his plays in the Tudor and Stuart periods, their emotional discomfort was paralleled by the physical discomfort of standing in the Yard of the amphitheatre for over two hours, or sitting on hard wooden benches with no back support. The same is true for audiences attending plays at the Globe Theatre today.

We do not know what input Shakespeare may have had in the design of the Globe, but we know that this theatre, for which he wrote many of his plays, informed his writing. When he was writing his plays, he was part of a troupe of actors known as the Lord Chamberlain's Men under Elizabeth I and the King's Men once James I ascended the throne in 1603. Being attached to this enterprise meant Shakespeare owned shares in the Globe Theatre itself, which made him a *house*holder as it was known then; he was also a sharer, meaning he owned shares in the company. He would have been there almost every day. He was intimately familiar with the shape, texture, size and capacities of the play-houses he worked in, literally and metaphorically. He makes this clear in *Hamlet*, for example, when the Prince of Denmark feels disenchanted with the world and the 'sterile' sky bounds him in:

> this most excellent canopy the air, look you, this brave
> o'erhanging firmament, this majestical roof fretted with
> golden fire, why it appeareth nothing to me but a foul
> and pestilent congregation of vapours.
>
> (2.2.265–69)

The stage of the Globe, where *Hamlet* was first performed in 1601 at 2 p.m. on a summer's day, was overhung by a roof held up by giant oak pillars; it had a stage roof – referred to as the 'heavens' and painted with stars and celestial imagery – to protect the actors from inclement weather; 'fretted' refers to the method of painting stars upon a ceiling. The playhouse roof, then, the very fabric of the theatre, gives Shakespeare the point of reference he needs to explore Hamlet's cynical rejection of a starry night.

If you can stand it, with exhaustion in your legs, pain in your back, the stiffness in your neck as you crane to see over someone's head, they'll echo the turbulent emotions you'll experience throughout a performance of tragedy. *Titus* would have been staged at the Globe, even if its first performances were in the Rose Theatre. Owned by theatre impresario Philip Henslowe, who worked closely with his son-in-law and star actor, Edward Alleyn, the Rose was made famous by the popular and Oscar-winning John Madden film, *Shakespeare in Love*. Elizabethan amphitheatres like the Rose (1587; re-modelled in 1592), and the Globe (1599), were not identical but they shared many basic structural features: the thrust stage, an architectural frame made of timber with lime plaster panels, galleries that rose like the skyscrapers of their time, and a Yard or pit for standing – where audiences were later referred to as 'groundlings', a term deriving from *Hamlet*. The Rose was quite a bit smaller than Shakespeare's wooden amphitheatre though, which meant audiences pressed in more closely as in a modern mosh pit. Why does this matter? Because intimacy makes the performance of bloodthirsty tragedy more viscerally charged. Shakespeare knew it was an uneasy experience, physically in the limbs and emotionally in the chest. For him, at the very core of theatre though was the constant beating heart of discomfort.

A FIRST STAB

Over the centuries, *Titus* has been praised and admired as well as criticised and attacked. In Shakespeare's own time, his friend and rival Ben Jonson was less than generous about the play, despite its popularity, calling it old-fashioned and suggesting it was too bombastic. In the eighteenth century the literary giant Samuel Johnson didn't think it held up due to the 'barbarity of spectacles' which could hardly be viewed as 'tolerable to any audience'.[4] Nineteenth-century critics like William Hazlitt referred to it as 'an accumulation of vulgar physical horrors'.[5] And in the early twentieth century, T.S. Eliot called it 'one of the stupidest and most uninspired plays ever written'.[6] Often, the authorship of this violent play has been denied altogether. It was, in fact, co-written with the playwright George Peele, known mainly for *The Battle of Alcazar*, a dramatisation of the Portuguese invasion of Morocco, with a 'Moor' called Muly Mahamet, at the centre. Some critics have suggested that it is the co-authorship that must explain the excessive blood and gore in the tragedy. Adaptations and retellings abound to suit the whims of directors, editors and actors. For example, Edward Ravenscroft's late Restoration reworking, *Titus Andronicus, or the Rape of Lavinia* (1678), cut crucial scenes, attempting to tone down the violence on stage. Notably, a fairly radical adaptation of *Titus* for the American-born Black actor Ira Aldridge, considered one of the first Black tragedians to make a successful career in Europe, harnessed a more sympathetic and dignified interpretation of the Moor as it was played at the Adelphi Theatre in Edinburgh in 1850.

It is now widely accepted that Shakespeare did indeed write much of this play, perhaps all of it except the first act. Regardless of who wrote which bit, however, clearly the playwright did not shy away from staging suffering and violence nor from positioning race front and centre. If we stand a chance of making race visible in Shakespeare, we must begin with his first Roman play.

Titus is neither stupid nor uninspired; gore is easy to dismiss. However, there is something unique about a play that, unlike much of Shakespeare's oeuvre – *Hamlet*, *King Lear* and *Macbeth* – does not glorify a singular white European experience. Instead it is a raging and at times chaotic narrative undergirded by passion and struggle. There is no genteel, civilising whiteness to speak of. Beyond the spectacle of body parts strewn on a stage, the play opens up some of the deepest questions of Shakespeare's age and dares to ask what happens when multiple identities converge in an imperial setting – questions we are still grappling with today.

The plot centres upon a warrior's triumphant return to Rome after his battle with the Goths, called back to the ancient metropolis because he has been elected Emperor. Accompanying him are the coffins of his sons lost in the war and his prisoners – Tamora, Queen of the Goths, and her three sons. Captured alongside them is Aaron the Moor, Shakespeare's first foray into black identity.

Their entrance was crafted by the playwright to be striking. In the Globe Theatre production, Titus bursts into the auditorium in a thrilling Latin *triumphus*, processing through the groundlings, who are temporarily transformed into a crowd of Roman citizens, revelling in the breath-taking pageant of Rome and its spoils. Upon a chariot, Titus greets the crowd as thunderous drums explode in their ears; the rising fog of incense left spectators gasping and in awe of the ancient story about to unfold.

Lucius, Titus's eldest son, insists that the Queen's eldest be sacrificed as is custom in Rome:

> Give us the proudest prisoner of the Goths,
> That we may hew his limbs and on a pile
> *Ad manes fratrum* [to the shades of our brothers] sacrifice his flesh
> Before this earthly prison of their bones,
> That so the shadows be not unappeased,
> Nor we disturbed with prodigies on earth.
>
> (1.1.99–104)

On her knees, Tamora pleads for her son Alarbus's life, staking her motherhood against Roman ritual in one of Shakespeare's most famous female supplication scenes. But Titus shows no mercy, declaring religious piety a priority, so Alarbus is hacked, hewn and thrown onto the sacrificial pyre. As to his imperial election, Titus turns it down and soon Saturninus assumes power with Titus promising his only daughter, Lavinia's hand in marriage to the Emperor, though she is already betrothed to

Bassianus. A fight takes place for this reason and Titus, out of loyalty to the Emperor, kills one of his own sons in the fray. Saturninus subsequently becomes attracted to Tamora; his private and overwhelming desire for her exceedingly white 'hue' is evident when he takes her as his wife in place of Lavinia: 'Clear up, fair queen, that cloudy countenance…he comforts you / Can make you greater than the queen of Goths' (1.1.266; 272–3) he promises. Now Empress of Rome, Tamora, her sons and Aaron the Moor are released from captivity.

Aaron and Tamora are lovers and both keen to wreak havoc on the Andronici. In the woods during a royal hunt, Lavinia and Bassianus come across them and taunt them with racist epithets about their sexual transgressions:

> Believe me, queen, your swart Cimmerian
> Doth make your honour of his body's hue,
> Spotted, detested and abominable.
>
> (2.2.72–4)

At Aaron's instruction, Tamora's sons murder Bassianus. Lavinia begs Tamora to kill or release her as her sons threaten to assault her, but, out of vengeful spite, the Empress refuses and allows them to proceed with the violent rape and mutilation. They cut out her tongue and amputate both her hands so she will lose the ability to communicate and name her attackers – a heinous crime *largely* borrowed from the ancient story of Philomel in Ovid's *Metamorphoses*. Lavinia later emerges, bleeding from her mouth and her wrists, traumatised and shellshocked. This is the point at which spectators feel queasy, particularly when staged convincingly as it was in the Globe – with stage blood pouring from the actor's mouth as opposed to more stylised red material, famously used in the 2004 Ninagawa production.

Once Lavinia is discovered by her family, they vow revenge. Things get worse, believe it or not, when Aaron convinces Titus that if he cuts off his own hand, Saturninus will release two of his sons previously taken prisoner. Titus willingly gives up his hand and we witness the amputation on stage, but instead of the lives of his sons, he is brought their decapitated heads.

It soon transpires that Tamora has given birth to Aaron's baby. The child is brought to him by a nurse who insists, by order of the Empress, that it be murdered because he is black. Aaron instead murders the nurse and threatens Tamora's remaining sons when they too threaten to murder the child. Lavinia, unable to communicate, is coached by her uncle to hold a stick in her mouth to write the names of her rapists. The revenge is nauseating – the throats of Chiron and Demetrius are slit, their blood drained from their bodies, their flesh baked into a pie and fed to their mother, who Titus then kills after telling her what she has just eaten. (We have the Ancient Roman tragedian, Seneca, to thank for this link between revenge, cannibalism and indigestion.) Aaron is eventually caught by Lucius and an army of Goths. Buried to his neck after confessing all the play's crimes and his part in devising them, he declares he'd do it all over again, and 'a thousand dreadful things' more. Titus sacrifices Lavinia to save her 'honour', is himself killed by Saturninus, who is in turn slain by Lucius, Titus's son. It's a bloodbath. Lucius, who started the cycle of violence with the opening scene's human sacrifice, becomes Emperor.

Brutality underpins the narrative: it opens the tragedy, becomes the engine of the play and then closes it. The kinds of slayings that take place seem absurd to a modern Western sensibility, but are rooted in the classical texts Shakespeare drew from as well as in the taste for violence amongst theatregoers of his day. It cannot be underestimated how formative classical texts were in the creation of Renaissance culture, drama and literature; they helped to frame ways of thinking about many aspects of life, from pedagogy to politics and philosophy, but crucially too they provided a template for Renaissance Europeans to imagine ethnic and national difference. This foundation becomes clear in *Antony and Cleopatra*, where we see the racialisation of the conflict between the Romans and the Egyptians.

In the midst of all the violence of *Titus Andronicus* is a grieving father, a warrior who has lost his purpose, his hand and all loyalty towards his nation. Also prominent is the 'Moor', but in his case audiences may wonder who he is, how he got there and why Shakespeare gave him so much stage time. He might be, and indeed has been, read as simply a symbol of evil, or architect of violence; perhaps he is a revenge *anti*-hero. If we want to discover what race has to do with Shakespeare, then we should start with his first Moor.

'BARBAROUS MOOR'

I still remember when my family received green cards – our permanent residency status in the USA. Across the top of the card and still burned into my memory were the words 'Resident Alien'. It made me feel as though genuinely belonging was never going to be available to me. I was on the fringes, othered by my own identification card. Language evolves over time. Perhaps it's harder to understand how race could be part of any analysis of Shakespeare, because the words we use to talk about it have changed. By examining the language that designated race and human difference in Elizabethan England, we can start to see just how preoccupied Shakespeare and his contemporaries really were with the concept. For example, if we trace the word 'barbarous' through the play we see a distinctly racialised term that becomes a way of critiquing Roman life too. The Danish theologian Niels Hemmingsen wrote in 1569 that 'barbarous' referred to 'he that is not a Greek or a Roman' in ancient times, but in the sixteenth century, the word was 'now applied to any that is in conditions and manners rude, fierce, cruel, uncivil, unnurtured, or in speech gross, unlearned, harsh, uneloquent. Also, it signifieth an Alien, Foreigner or Stranger born'.[7]

The word 'barbarous' is not used sparingly in this play: Marcus Andronicus tells us that his brother Titus has been 'accited [called] home / From weary wars against the **barbarous** Goths' (1.1.27–8); after Alarbus is sacrificed, his brother Chiron remarks 'Was never Scythia half so **barbarous**!' (1.1.134). Later, Marcus is trying to convince Titus to commit the son he killed into the family tomb: 'Thou art a Roman, be not **barbarous**' (1.1.382). This line is particularly interesting in light of the Roman poet Horace's understanding of blackness: 'This is a black Roman; beware thus.'[8] When Bassianus and Lavinia meet Tamora in the forest they goad her for her sexual relationship with a blackamoor: 'Accompanied but with a **barbarous** Moor' (2.2.77) and Lavinia shrieks after Bassianus is stabbed, 'Ay, come, Semiramis, nay, **barbarous** Tamora' (2.2.118). Barbarity is not exclusive to Rome's outsiders. No one really escapes this charge; they either exhibit 'barbarous' behaviour or are always on the edge of slipping into it. The distinctions between who is barbaric and who is civil are more blurred here because Shakespeare's estimation of our natures suggests there is a kind of precarious dance between humanity and 'barbarity' in every single one of us, 'civilised' or not.

'Barbarous' signalled the opposite to civil in the context of racial formation, something as true for the ancient Romans as it was for the Renaissance Europeans. During the Renaissance, 'barbarian' referred to those who hailed from the Barbary Coast of North Africa – the 'barbary Moors'. Curiously, another form of the word has long associations with language, seen in Elizabethan texts to assert the superiority of English and to identify a corrupt or inferior form of writing, communicating or speaking; in other words, 'lacking rhetorical eloquence'.[9] An analysis of the etymology of the word observes these key distinctions:

Barbarian,	belonging to.
Barbary, -ria	part of Africa.
Barbarism,	rudeness of speech or behaviour.
Barbarous,	cruel, inhumane.[10]

'Barbarous' is, clearly, Shakespeare's go-to word in *Titus*. Seemingly detachable from race or ethnicity, it can be assigned to most characters from across the range of ethnic groups represented in the play. It is a racialising tool, another way of describing savagery, and also a racially loaded term. The use of 'barbarous' in Shakespeare's time, no matter in what form, conjures racial identity because of the geographical region it identifies. Hence, when Titus is admonished by his brother to 'be not barbarous', he is warning him of the slippage into behaviour that associates him with a maligned race, telling him not to sink to the level of Goth, or worse, Moor. Tamora is also racialised when the word 'barbarous' is flung at her; she has behaved 'barbarous'-ly in Lavinia's eyes. We also hear from Bassianus that Tamora is spotted and marked by her sexual relationship with Aaron, his blackness transferring to her in an example of what Elizabethans might have seen as racial contagion. In this way, while no one escapes being labelled barbarous, it is nevertheless a term used to devalue blackness.

But what exactly is a Moor? Besides Aaron, Shakespeare's most famous Moor is Othello, known as 'the *Moor* of Venice', and in *The Merchant of Venice*, we meet a 'tawny *Moor*' in the Prince of Morocco. This explicit identification means Shakespeare wants us to take special note of these characters as outsiders in the white worlds he presents.

The word 'Moor' is English, shaped by the linguistic influences of European cross-cultural exchanges, particularly Spanish, Italian and Portuguese encounters, since these three European nations had a long and brutal history of relations with Africans, Arab Muslims and Turks.[11] The term derives from the Latin *maurus* – referring to the people of Mauretania, which is on the crossroads of the Maghreb and sub-Saharan Africa. *Mouro* is the Portuguese and *moro* the Italian designation; as the scholar of Italian grammar, William Thomas stated in 1550, 'Moro' denotes a 'Moore or black man'.[12] When used in Renaissance texts, 'Moor' can refer to Africans from Barbary or North Africa – the coastal area bound in by Egypt, the Atlantic, the Sahara and the Mediterranean, now Morocco, Algeria, Tunisia and Libya, a geographical region that England was familiar with having been involved in trade and commerce there since the mid-sixteenth century. While its etymology gestures to colour, it was also used to refer to Muslims or Arabian and Turkish moors, so it did not always signal a dark complexion; 'white moors', for example, are referenced by the sixteenth-century maritime venturer William Hawkins. John Pory's 1600 translation of Granada-born scholar, diplomat and converted Muslim, Joannes Leo Africanus' (born al-Hasan ibn Muhammad al-Wazzan al-Zayyati, 1494–1554)

Description of Africa, describes the 'Africans' as 'moors', identifying two kinds: white or 'tawnie Moores, and Negros or black Moores'.[13] Although we tend mainly to think of it as a term synonymous with dark-skinned 'Africans', we can see already that it was much more slippery and wide-ranging.

We may also come across 'blackamoor' or 'black moor' used frequently in parish registers, travel literature, plays and books on English grammar to designate more specifically black-skinned Africans: 'the Negroes…[are] call[ed] the Black-mores,' explains Sir Walter Raleigh.[14] Like many signifiers of identity today, the term 'Moor' is unstable: referring to skin colour as much as to geography, ethnicity and religion. This instability demonstrates the sheer challenge, and the absurdity, of reliably classifying humans in the first place. The lack of certainty around its precise meaning has led certain scholars to question the ethnic origins of Othello, for example, who, as Shakespeare's second representation of a Moor, is arguably the more sympathetic of the two. Even though the text of *Othello* calls attention to other racial markers, such as when he is referred to as having 'thick lips', there are those who suggest Othello may be of North African or Arab descent, particularly in light of the arrival of the Moroccan delegation to the court of Elizabeth I in 1600, four years before *Othello* was written.

Led by the Moroccan ambassador Abd el-Ouahed ben Messaoud ben Mohammed Anoun, the delegation was sent by the 'King of Barbary' or Sa'adian ruler of Morocco Mulay Ahmed al-Mansur to carry out talks with Queen Elizabeth I and her councillors regarding a potential military alliance that would bring England and Muslim Morocco into a partnership against their common enemy, Spain. People found them to be a spectacle of 'otherness', described by John Stow, the chronicler of London, as people who killed 'all their own meat within their house' and who prayed with beads.[15] They were treated well, however, because of the political gains England could make from such an alliance. The contact between the English and the Moroccans had been amicable for many years, and had led to the founding of London's Barbary Company in the 1580s. The visit in 1600 was a crucial moment in this relationship, coinciding with the peak in Shakespeare's writing career. It was also memorialised in an extraordinary painting (artist unknown) of the Moroccan ambassador, which was eventually sold to the University of Birmingham's Shakespeare Institute in 1955, where it still hangs.

Some believe that Shakespeare encountered the ambassador and the delegation because his theatre troupe performed at court each winter. We know that the visitors from 'Barbary' were there in November 1600, attending the Queen's coronation anniversary celebrations during that period. The visit wasn't successful in the end, as no great alliance between the two regions emerged,[16] but this event in Elizabethan history has led to speculations about Othello's identity as potentially Muslim-Moroccan rather than a sub-Saharan African. No doubt, the exchanges and encounters between England and the Mediterranean contact zones, which included Muslim powers, shaped dramatic performance in England quite significantly – there were over fifty plays from the 1580s on that dramatised Muslim characters or took place within Islamic settings. But while there are indeed striking similarities between Shakespeare's Moor and the Moroccan ambassador – both outsiders in a Christian white court – in my view, the likelihood of Shakespeare's Moor of Venice being of Moroccan Muslim descent is less convincing due to other phenotypical descriptions of Othello and his own self-identification and history – 'Haply, for I am black' – as well as Shakespeare's interest in exploring black identity in *Titus* using many of the same epithets.

There is no debate, however, about the identity of Aaron when it comes to skin colour and ethnicity. Like Othello, he declares it himself:

> Let fools do good and fair men call for grace,
> Aaron will have his soul black like his face.
>
> (3.1.205–206)

Of course, 'black' could be assigned to people who were simply not white, or to women who were not blonde and pale, as a term that constituted otherness and racial difference. This can challenge our ability to identify ethnicity precisely in these texts and leaves many conclusions we might draw open to dispute. However, it is notable that the only illustration we have of a Shakespeare play from the time is, remarkably, a composite sketch of *Titus Andronicus* by English artist Henry Peacham (above) that verifies Aaron's claims.

BLACKNESS AS ALLEGORY

Shakespeare deploys the word 'black' in *Titus* more than in any other of his plays. Associations between a negative symbolism of blackness and human difference developed through the Middle

Ages and the Renaissance, informing the process of racial formation. Shakespeare's first revenge tragedy registers this explicitly.
When Aaron proudly declares his face is black, and the actor
playing him emerges in blackface, the audience would think of
the 'troubling' connotations of black faces in the premodern era.

Popular in the medieval and early Tudor period, mystery cycles
were series of plays based on Biblical stories. Performances of the
fall of humankind symbolised Lucifer's lapsed state through a
painted black face: 'Now are we waxen black' says the newly
condemned Satan in *The Creation*.[17] Christian allegory routinely
linked blackness to the diabolical, ignorance, sin and mischief
and Aaron appears to embody these qualities through speech and
action. Conversely, white had the opposite associations – the light
of God, wisdom, purity, chastity and virtue were tied to whiteness
in texts, art and religious doctrine. Aaron is also a dramatic
descendant of the Vice figure, an allegorical character from medieval morality plays, also painted black.

While it was widely believed that all humans were born with
the black mark of sin on them and that baptism allowed a cleans-
ing or ablution that became ultra-symbolic, a proverb that
Shakespeare would have known well – 'to wash an Ethiopian
white is to labour in vain' – gestures towards biraciality in the play.
Literally, Aaron's blackness cannot be washed out. Even though
he breeds with a woman of the whitest 'hue', their baby is black.
Popular in Shakespeare's time, the proverb derived from Aesop's
Fables later reimagined through the Italian Andrea Alciato's *Book
of Emblems*. Reinterpreted more locally by English emblem artist
Geoffrey Whitney, it proved a stubborn adage that would not go
away. Whitney's emblem shows two white men attempting vainly
to wash a 'Moor' of his colour, the poetic motto underneath
declaring that one shouldn't attempt to do the impossible;

defeating Nature is a vain endeavour. It is mind boggling how long this proverb has hung around: eighteenth-, nineteenth- and twentieth-century books, magazines, advertisements and the minstrelsy tradition continued exploiting its iconography as a way of commenting on impossibility through this racist premise. It has echoes in the twentieth century 'one-drop' rule that asserted any person with any black ancestry, regardless of colour, was to be considered black.

Radically, Aaron's speeches and his self-presentation make the impossibility of washing away his blackness a virtue. The irony would not be lost on Shakespeare that the actor playing Aaron could, of course, wash his black face-paint off after each performance, since there were no black actors on the commercial stages that we know of. Here's a racial conundrum inherent in the way medieval and Renaissance Christians read the body from the outside in: if you were spotted or marked, it reflected the spots on your soul, but you could wash away your sins through religious salvation; not so if your skin was black.

The anti-blackness towards Aaron is entirely racially motivated, as is evident in Act 3 when Marcus kills a fly; Titus reprimands his brother for taking an innocent life, asking what 'if that fly had a father and a mother?' (3.2.61), but Marcus protests it was 'a black ill-favoured fly, / Like to the empress' Moor. Therefore I killed him' (66–7). Titus is quick to respond with, 'Give me thy knife; I will insult on him' (72). This scene allows for a brief moment the possibility of compassion towards a being that is imagined to have a whole life, but when Marcus reminds his brother that the fly's blackness simulates that of Aaron the Moor, the door to compassion closes. Why is this? Blackness? Aaron's particular villainy? It's both. Aaron's villainy is symbolically aligned with blackness and anything resembling Aaron, even a fly, becomes tainted with that same villainy. This type of transference is one of the engines of racism.

Aaron's hunger for power and revenge aligns him with the Elizabethan stock character known as the stage Machiavel, a term linked to Florentine writer Niccolò Machiavelli's treatise on political strategy, *The Prince*. The stage Machiavel was a malcontent, always plotting and strategising against his enemies, single-minded in his hunger for power or vengeance. You can see how Aaron has absorbed some of these features given the influence of popular playwrights and university wits like Thomas Kyd and Christopher Marlowe who reached fame before Shakespeare and were celebrated for their malcontents, Machiavels and avenging anti-heroes. Early on in the play, knowing his union with Tamora aids his own ambitions, Aaron intends to exploit it fully:

> Then, Aaron, arm thy heart and fit thy thoughts
> To mount aloft with thy imperial mistress...
>
> (1.1.510–11)

His thirst for revenge is shared explicitly in a soliloquy. The soliloquy, a form of direct address to the audience is usually, but not always, delivered by a character who is alone on stage or who believes themselves to be. It is striking that Shakespeare gave so many to his Moors.

Aaron is bold. He is unashamed of his ambition and upfront with the audience. In this way, he seems no different from Barabas the Jew in the antisemitic portrayal of inter-cultural conflict in Christopher Marlowe's *The Jew of Malta* (1589), the name of Marlowe's character punning on 'Barbarous' deliberately. Aaron has been viewed by some as a conflation of early modern boogeymen; his Jewish name alluding to the way medieval and

Renaissance anti-Jewish literature harnessed the imagery of anti-
blackness to stoke xenophobia and religious fear.

Some of the stereotypes that still haunt us today were around
in the sixteenth century and earlier; for example, black Africans
were believed to be excessively libidinous, sexually indiscriminate
and incapable of restraint. Even Leo Africanus's authoritative
account of Africa, its geography and its people, helps shape this
narrative. Although he gives a more balanced account of Africans
than most, he nevertheless judges that the 'Negros...lead a beastly
kind of life, being utterly destitute of the use of reason... They
have great swarms of harlots among them', and that they like to
court 'divers maids' before they eventually get married.[18]
Shakespeare is aware of this perception and has Aaron use the
stereotype to his advantage when he begins imagining his future
with Tamora:

> Away with slavish weeds and servile thoughts!
> I will be bright, and shine in pearl and gold
> To wait upon this new-made empress.
> To wait, said I? – to wanton with this queen,
> This goddess, this Semiramis, this nymph,
> This siren...
>
> (1.1.517–22)

Tamora is now a vehicle for his ambition for revenge. He praises
her using elaborate comparisons – a 'goddess', a 'nymph' – but
sexualises and racialises her with 'siren' and 'Semiramis', a name
that recalls the ancient Assyrian queen notoriously beautiful yet
cruel, incestuously married to her son Nimrod, who himself,
legend has it, was black skinned. Aaron suggests Tamora desires
his sexual attention, but he will not wait upon her; rather he will

'wanton' with her. He will give her what she desires to fulfil his own. But while Aaron will *use* sex, he does not seem to need it himself or show an inability to restrain his appetites. Their union is intended to wrong-foot audiences with very clear preconceptions.

Aaron's motivations for revenge have long been considered one of the play's great mysteries. His backstory is not revealed to us, so we can only speculate. I sometimes ask my students to write his backstory and many of them imagine him enslaved, taken from his family, or having witnessed atrocities in his youth. It is also difficult to speculate because Shakespeare didn't rely on one source for the story of *Titus Andronicus*; there doesn't seem to be any one particular moment in Roman history that Shakespeare is homing in on either, so his method in the construction of this play is selective. His representation of the Goths, for example, is not specific either.

Aaron's history is not narrated to us the way Othello's is. But we know enslavement lies in both of their pasts; when Aaron first appears, it is in the garments of a slave; we see what this might look like according to the imagination of Elizabethan acting companies in the Peacham drawing. By now, we can start to see a pattern in the way Shakespeare presents Aaron – he is a Janus figure, and is as surprising as he is compelling. Simply stereotyping Moors as vindictive, as anti-Spanish writer Robert Ashley did in 1589 ('the Moores [are] perfidious and revengeful') isn't as dramatically or psychologically interesting for a playwright like Shakespeare.[19]

Although a label like 'barbarous Moor' might be easily taken to be villainous, Aaron is therefore intriguingly multifaceted. When reading *Titus* through the lens of race, we gain insight into Shakespeare's early imaginings of a raced identity within a white

Roman world. Despite the violence Aaron helps orchestrate, Shakespeare gives us much more to grapple with than symbolic villainy or a black foil for white virtue, which there really isn't much of in this play. In his Roman plays Shakespeare meditates on the antithesis between Roman *virtus* (or virtue) and its opposite, barbarity. But the summation of virtue that emerges from these plays is that its cultivation is complicated by human nature and the violence rooted at the heart of state power.

FROM LONDON TO ROME

The Roman world Shakespeare presents with its interracial dynamics, preoccupation with conquest and vengeance and sexual violence is hardly distant from our own, let alone Shakespeare's. Our playwright existed in perhaps a more overtly violent world, one that would have been woven into the fabric of his writing. Before buying a property in Blackfriars, Shakespeare likely lived near or in Southwark, outside of the city of London's borders. It was a manufacturing district and was also largely where the playhouses, bull rings, bear-baiting arenas, cock-pits and brothels were located, a place for entertainment, delight, hard work and hard play. People from a range of ethnic, religious and geographical backgrounds lived, worked and were entertained there. Even though London rarely served as a setting for his plays, which more often ask audiences to imagine territories beyond England's borders, his direct surroundings provided the sights, colours and textures of his work.

In 1598, the German lawyer and writer, Paul Hentzner, documented his tour of London, describing its oddities, architecture, customs, quirks and spectacles in telling detail. One of the observations he made was of London Bridge. At that time, it was the only permanent structural connection between the north and the south banks of the River Thames. Along the bridge were lined multistorey housing, businesses and market stalls; just at the end before reaching the environs of Southwark was the gatehouse. He recounts: 'upon this is built a tower, on whose top the heads of such as have been executed for high treason, are placed on iron spikes: we counted above thirty.'[20] So violence, dismemberment and severed heads were part of public life and not simply a fiction of the playhouses. For these heads of traitors to last a while, at least until the next batch came in, they needed to be partly boiled and coated in pitch, a resin derived from coal tar, which blackened them thoroughly. This would make for a rather macabre journey to the playhouse across London Bridge; the atmosphere of crime, punishment and terrifying state power, its sights and smells unquestionably informing the reception of plays in these theatres. Shakespeare would have drawn upon that, tapping into an existing unease amongst his spectators. The tarred heads with blackened faces were inextricably linked to treasonous criminality in the imagination of the Elizabethan playgoer before they even set foot in the playhouse.

As mentioned previously, the relationship between crime and race that Shakespeare's first Moor appears to embody has its roots in the Christian world's first ever criminal, the fallen angel Lucifer. The ancient fathers who helped establish the Church spoke disparagingly of blackness, linking it to the devil, but also made further connections between the qualities that blackness evokes and Ethiopians. St. Augustine, for example, who himself had been depicted in medieval iconography as darker skinned, called Ethiopians the 'remotest and foulest of mankind'.[21]

This is upsetting, particularly within a context of religious writing. The key idea here for religious clerics is 'remotest'.

Christian logic insisted that being the farthest from the light of God was what made the devil black. Medieval artists visualised this idea time and again. The Italian poet Dante Alighieri's famous *Divine Comedy* (1320) portrays his journey to God through hell, purgatory and heaven guided by his favourite Roman poet, Virgil. The first part, *The Inferno*, describes hell, its torments and the sinners encountered there in incredibly rich language and horrifying detail. Dante depicts Satan in the lowest circle, of course – literally the remotest from God. He has three heads, each of which bites and chomps a different sinner – Judas, Brutus and Cassius – in its 'black jowls'. Satan is not free to fly around and wreak havoc, but rather encased in a sheet of ice from the chest down, representing his unfathomable and incalculable distance from God, light, purity and salvation.

Dante's terrifying vision shaped ideas about hell and Satan thereafter and also influenced subsequent heavily racialised depictions of the devil in art and literature.[22] The idea of racial exclusion and isolation is tied to this network of ideas about the devil, blackness, remoteness and identity and may be rooted in the Christian fables that theorise about why the devil is black. In the final act of *Titus*, when Aaron is captured by Lucius and his army, they plan initially to hang him and his son, a threat of a lynching, be it ancient Roman or Elizabethan, that sends shivers down the spine of any post-civil rights reader. But Lucius changes his mind when Aaron promises he'll confess all if Lucius agrees to save his child:

LUCIUS
Bring down the devil, for he must not die
So sweet a death as hanging presently.
            [*Aaron is made to climb down.*]

AARON
If there be devils, would I were a devil
To live and burn in everlasting fire,
So I might have your company in hell
But to torment you with my bitter tongue.

(5.1.145–50)

Aaron questions the very existence of devils, proving that he doesn't buy into Roman belief systems, while suggesting too that if they do exist, he wishes to be one so he can torment Lucius in his hell. Hauntingly similar to Dante's devil, Aaron is ordered to be set 'breast-deep in earth' (5.3.178), where he will be denied sustenance.

Aaron is not concerned about being labelled a criminal or a devil though. While he is linked to the Goths, their own criminality being inspired by his goading, he is fundamentally a self-determining agent in the play; visually, he stands out (as we saw in the Peacham sketch) and socially he operates outside the margins of each group. Shakespeare cannot be absolved for his obvious and, at times, hammering participation in the racist stereotyping of blackness, but his portrayal of Aaron does not neatly comply with the fanciful racial stereotypes of the age, or with his literary and biblical predecessors mentioned above. Aaron's displays of Black pride, a self-love that no other character in the play exhibits, not even Titus, are striking. This is not to say pride was considered a virtue in Shakespeare's time – quite the opposite. But pride in one's outsider status is nonetheless unusual in Shakespeare and it's a different emotion from the sort of pride linked to vanity in medieval and Renaissance Christian thinking. It is far more radical than that.

LOVING BLACKNESS

No one is innocent in *Titus Andronicus*. Just about every character in the play is accountable for the atrocities that occur, from Titus to Saturninus, Titus's sons, all the Goths, as well as 'the Moor'. Lavinia may sit outside the circle of responsibility, but if we are to consider her and Bassianus's racist slurs as a factor that contributed to their own demise – for example, when Bassianus refers to Aaron as Tamora's 'swart Cimmerian', and suggests that Tamora will be infected or 'spotted, detested, and abominable' through her dalliances with Aaron – even they can be said to be complicit in the ancient world of xenophobic violence that Shakespeare (and Peele) depicts. Yet the violence Lavinia endures is one of the central horrors of the play; she becomes a spectacle of trauma.

Because she was attacked by the Goths at Aaron's devising, for centuries viewers have struggled to see the 'Moor' as anything besides villainous. Indeed, Shakespeare presents Aaron as a black devil full of stratagem and mindless vengeance. But these stereotypes are simultaneously undermined by his outlook and agency; the meaning he assigns to his actions centres upon his self-knowledge about his race.

In Act 2, when Tamora asks Aaron why he looks so gloomy given they are finally free to spend time together in the forest while the others are hunting, he replies that while Venus dominates her desires, Saturn dominates his, meaning he's self-determined. It is at this point that he asserts his blackness as an outward sign of his inner self:

> What signifies my deadly-standing eye,
> My silence and my cloudy melancholy,

My fleece of woolly hair that now uncurls
Even as an adder when she doth unroll
To do some fatal execution?
No, madam, these are no venereal signs;
Vengeance is in my heart, death in my hand,
Blood and revenge are hammering in my head.

(2.2.32–9)

Aaron's speech makes us think of another famous malcontent. When Hamlet's mother Gertrude questions why her son seems so disproportionately upset about his father's death, he replies,

"Seems", madam—nay it is, I know not "seems".
'Tis not alone my inky cloak, cold mother,
Nor customary suits of solemn black,
Nor windy suspiration of forced breath,
No, nor the fruitful river in the eye,
Nor the dejected haviour of the visage,
Together with all forms, moods, shapes of grief,
That can denote me truly. These indeed "seem",
For they are actions that a man might play.
But I have that within which passes show,
These but the trappings and the suits of woe.

(1.2.76–86)

The speeches are structured alike, a device known as parallelism. We can see the similarities between Aaron's cataloguing of his features – 'my deadly-standing eye, / My silence and my cloudy melancholy, / My fleece of woolly hair' and Hamlet's 'not my inky cloak... / Nor customary suits of solemn black, / Nor windy suspiration of forced breath'. Compare also Aaron's 'No madam,

74

these are no venereal signs' with Hamlet's, "'Seems", Madam? Nay, it is. I know not "seems". / ...No, nor the fruitful river in the eye'. Both avengers use a rhetoric of blackness, Hamlet's linked to funerary symbolism and melancholy and Aaron's to his skin colour. Both soliloquists declare that their bodies express a single truth within. The fundamental difference is Hamlet's privilege and his status as a prince. He has time to contemplate his emotions, to rouse his anger at injustice, to weigh and consider his singular mission of revenge. Hamlet can remove his 'inky cloak'; indeed, he can play or perform or even pretend to be insane. Aaron's contemplations are expedited; at the fringes of the Roman empire, he has work to get on with and his purpose is aligned with an identity that he cannot change. He essentially says to Tamora and to all of us, 'all the things you think I am because of my black skin, indeed I am. So what?' In other words, he is the play's legible text and he is fine with that.

Black scholar and activist bell hooks argued for 'Loving Blackness as Political Resistance'. In her book, *Black Looks: Race and Representation*, she claims that racial integration is not possible until cultural attitudes about Blackness and Black people are radically different. The very value of being Black is often negated by the promise of success within the structures that favour whiteness; hooks, therefore, calls for an *active* political resistance to white power by *loving* Blackness; this kind of 'self-love' would be radical, revolutionary, undermining the core of 'white supremacist logic'.[23]

In addition to Aaron's bold affirmation of self, Shakespeare stages a scandalous relationship between a black man and a white or 'fair' (1.1.267) queen-turned-empress, the 'goodly lady...of the hue' the Emperor prefers (265). Aaron surprises us all when he shows he is the most compassionate parent in the play and

demonstrates race as something related to lineage when he repro-
duces a child that shares his complexion. Interracial coupling
fascinated Shakespeare throughout his career and we will come
across it at various points throughout this book. Most notably,
the example of miscegenation we witness in *Titus* results in a
biracial child that is brought out on stage, yet cursed by a nurse
for being black. Aaron's affection for his son has been talked
about as either an example of his humanity or an expression of
his narcissism. The truth probably lies somewhere in between.
But this further emphasises a pride in Blackness that indeed cuts
through the 'white supremacist logic' of the Elizabethan racial
stereotypes, voiced vehemently by the Nurse when she first brings
news of the birth:

NURSE
A joyless, dismal, black and sorrowful issue.
Here is the babe, as loathsome as a toad
Amongst the fair-faced breeders of our clime.
The empress sends it thee, thy stamp, thy seal,
And bids thee christen it with thy dagger's point.
AARON
Zounds, ye whore, is black so base a hue?

(4.2.68–73)

The baby is threatened by his half-brothers for the same reason,
but rescued and adored by his black father: 'Sweet blowze, you
are a beauteous blossom, sure' (4.2.74). Here Shakespeare
presents his audience with a dangerous dilemma. The child is a
threat to whiteness and to the lineage of the throne, as the
nurse suggests. But the so-called solution to this threat is difficult to stomach. Elizabethan society was largely xenophobic,

fearful of foreign customs, fashions, diseases, religions and the effect of otherness on English identity, but the attitudes towards biraciality that prevailed in the auditorium of the Rose Theatre during those first performances of *Titus* is nevertheless hard to know. There is evidence of racial, religious and ethnic anxiety in the period's literature and archives but there is also archival evidence of interracial relationships and biracial children in this period. The evidence of the presence of black people is demonstrated in parish registers in early modern England, a fact uncovered by the towering research of historian Imtiaz Habib. It may even suggest their presence was felt at the theatres, not just as characters blacked up on stage, but as members of the audience.

When Tamora's sons Chiron and Demetrius offer to 'broach the tadpole' on a 'rapier's point', Aaron threatens their lives with his scimitar (a short sword with a curved blade), asserting blackness to be superior to whiteness. He invokes the old adage that hovers in the play – you can't wash an 'Ethiopian white' – but turns the proverb to his favour:

> What, what, ye sanguine, shallow-hearted boys,
> Ye white-limed walls, ye alehouse painted signs!
> Coal-black is better than another hue
> In that it scorns to bear another hue;
> For all the water in the ocean
> Can never turn the swan's black legs to white,
> Although she lave them hourly in the flood.
>
> (4.2.99–105)

These white 'boys' are too easily changeable, as sanguine refers to their complexions which, according to Elizabethan humoral theory, can alter too readily with their moods. They are also like painted signs, 'white-limed', artificial and most inauthentic. Aaron's authenticity is the source of his strength and his exclusion. His status as alien enables him to move between these groups and attempt to destroy the destroyers – the Romans themselves.

Shakespeare keeps us on our toes with Aaron's unapologetic declarations of selfhood, his displays of sexual restraint, his eloquence and far superior paternal instincts, which are not at all devil-like. You could even assert that Aaron delivers the first ever Black power speech.[24] While it's appropriate to apply to the characters' identities classical and Elizabethan labels, 'Romans', 'Goths', 'Moors', rather than skin colour or modern racial tropes, the fact is, all the characters are white except Aaron and his son – some like Tamora and Lavinia are exceedingly white and aesthetically pleasing in the world of the play – and Shakespeare wanted us to see this difference. Skin colour is commented upon often. There are degrees of whiteness and of blackness too. In Act 5 scene 1, a Goth soldier reports to Lucius how he found Aaron; he heard the baby cry and then Aaron as he 'controlled the baby with this discourse':

I heard a child cry underneath a wall.
I made unto the noise, when soon I heard
The crying babe controlled with this discourse:
'Peace, tawny slave, half me and half thy dame!
Did not thy hue bewray whose brat thou art,
Had nature lent thee but thy mother's look,
Villain, thou mightst have been an emperor.
But where the bull and cow are both milk-white,
They never do beget a coal-black calf.
Peace, villain, peace!' – even thus he rates the babe –
(23–32)

Discussions of racial mixing were emerging mainly in scientific discourse during the eighteenth and nineteenth centuries, but biraciality is something that has occupied or concerned Europeans for many more. When Lucius threatens to kill Aaron's child, Aaron tells him not to touch him because 'he is of royal blood'. But the child would not, as the Goth soldier says above, ever rise to be an emperor because he is of the wrong hue. This is an acknowledgement of the belief in the essential physical inferiority of the child and his repeated disassociation from whiteness. Earlier, in Act 4, to keep his son safe, Aaron instructs Chiron and Demetrius to buy the child of another interracial couple who live outside the perimeter of Rome and whose baby is 'fair' like its mother. This baby will serve as the heir to Saturninus:

> Not far one Muly lives, my countryman:
> His wife but yesternight was brought to bed;
> His child is like to her, fair as you are.
> Go pack with him and give the mother gold,
> And tell them both the circumstance of all,
> And how by this their child shall be advanced
> And be received for the emperor's heir,
> And substituted in the place of mine,
> To calm this tempest whirling in the court;
> And let the emperor dandle him for his own.
>
> (4.2.157–66)

Extraordinarily, in a speech that is often missed, another interracial couple is referenced and a second baby – though white – will act as Aaron's son's photonegative counterpart, demonstrating the visible legitimacy of whiteness in a world that values the appearance of purity of imperial lineage.

Titus Andronicus is not a play for the faint-hearted. It is not just the violence and brutality at its heart, but also the play's blatant anti-black language, cruel stereotyping and allusions to the foundations of white supremacy that create challenges for modern directors to stage. Audiences will be literally struck down by the play's violence, yes, but how else might they feel when forced to face the racist structures represented through an ancient lens which continue to shed a light on our own racial divisions?

Three

MYTHOLOGISING THE
TAWNY QUEEN

Shakespeare's Cleopatra isn't wrong when she tells her attendant Iras at the close of *Antony and Cleopatra* (1606) that if she surrenders herself to Octavius Caesar,

> …I shall see
> Some squeaking Cleopatra boy my greatness
> I'th' posture of a whore.
>
> (5.2.218–220)

In the Renaissance commercial theatres, adolescent boys between the ages of fourteen and twenty-one played women's parts. Through wigs, makeup, gesture, voice and costume, boy actors performed women as virtuosos, regularly and convincingly. Cleopatra predicts some boy who squeaks in a breaking prepubescent voice will excessively stereotype her, representing her as a 'whore'. But Shakespeare's Queen of Egypt is without doubt one of his most striking and powerful female characters, an intensely demanding and oratorically complex part. It is astonishing to think that a white English teenage boy was the very first actor ever to inhabit the role. The famed actress Janet Suzman who played Cleopatra to great acclaim for television in 1974 could not really comprehend it, musing sceptically, 'I find it hard to think he wrote [Cleopatra] for a boy…it could never have been acted by a boy.'[1] But of course it was.

Cleopatra's lines quoted above are simultaneously prophetic and self-reflexive. The ancient queen in Shakespeare's fictional world imagines her portrayal in future years, while the boy actor speaking the lines comments ironically on the prospect of one such as himself impersonating her. Dizzying. Implausible illusion was the foundation of early modern performance, though, and Shakespeare's audiences, accustomed to mass entertainment with some artifice but no modern technology, readily accepted what we might deem too unrealistic today. Theatrical costume worked more symbolically in the Tudor and Stuart periods than now: in the same way that a simple Roman toga slung over a Jacobean ruff, doublet and hose signified a Roman setting, a fifteen-year-old boy in a wig gestured to womanhood. But the skills they needed to convince audiences were far more complex than the costumes they wore. Boy actors were in fact celebrated for the believability of their feminine portrayals. When the seventeenth-century travel writer Thomas Coryat was in Venice, he was shocked that women were allowed to perform on stage there, remarking, pleasantly surprised, that they were just as good as the excellent boy actors in England: '[these women actors] performed it with as good a grace, action, gesture and whatsoever convenient for a player, as ever I saw any masculine Actor'.[2]

When we think of that boy actor who played Cleopatra, it is tempting to wonder what costume he wore, how he moved, what gestures he deployed to play such a woman. What did his voice sound like? We might ask to what extent he spoke naturally or in a higher register. This depended upon whether or not his voice had broken, of course, which, according to Hamlet, when he meets the travelling players in Elsinore, potentially disqualifies the boy from playing the female part: 'Pray God your voice, like a piece of uncurrent gold, be not cracked within the ring' (*Hamlet*, 2.2.365). More crucially, did the boy who played Cleopatra wear white facial makeup as was the custom in the theatres of the time to portray white women, or did he perform the part in brown or blackface? The answer to this question depends upon whether or not we think Cleopatra was imagined to be black, brown or white. Oddly, many scholars and directors don't acknowledge that Cleopatra might have a racial identity other than white, even though Shakespeare provides us with more than a hint in the text. It is safe to say, however, that the boy actor playing this part had to be skilled not only in female impersonation but in racial impersonation too.

MISOGYNOIR

In 2010, the Black feminist Moya Bailey coined the term 'Misogynoir' to refer to the particular brand of misogyny that targets Black women. Bailey says herself that it 'has to do with the ways that anti-Blackness and misogyny combine to malign Black women in our world'.[3] Why is this term relevant to our understanding of Shakespeare's Egyptian queen? It is largely because, regardless of Cleopatra's racial ambiguity, she is racialised and as such has been aligned with black feminine stereotypes for centuries. Scholar Francesca T. Royster makes a useful parallel between the Cleopatra 'icon' and the way in which Black women have been portrayed or talked about across the centuries; for example,

> over the years, African American performer Josephine
> Baker has been compared to a bicycle, a machine gun, a

kangaroo, a perpetual motion machine, a leopard, a savage, a clown and a man as well as 'that contrary character about whom Shakespeare wrote, "Age cannot wither her, nor custom stale her infinite variety" – the "Jazz Cleopatra".'4

Set in ancient Egypt and Rome, *Antony and Cleopatra* (1606) is a timeless story derived from classical sources and revealing that ancient ideas about identity and difference were culturally inherited values. We saw evidence of the influence of ancient texts and myths in *Titus Andronicus*, but in this later Roman play the focus is on the intersection of gender and racial identity through the presentation of the dichotomous queen of Egypt who is at once real and imagined, at once boy and woman, at once black, brown and white.

Shakespeare lifted the plot from *The Parallel Lives of the Noble Greeks and Romans*, a series of biographies of ancient historical figures such as Julius Caesar and Mark Antony. Penned by the Greek historian Plutarch (AD 46–c. AD 120), it was a stonking hit during the Renaissance period, having been translated into English by an Elizabethan lawyer, Thomas North, in 1579. Plutarch's *Lives* revealed to Shakespeare, as did many other classical texts, early attempts in Western civilisation to define ethnic and cultural superiority through the extolment of Greek and Roman men of valour; as if to say, there is a noble or superior breed of men and much to be learned from their examples. Not just Plutarch's but many ancient tales about Greek and Roman empires, battles and nation-building are full of ideas and images that marked human difference in a variety of ways. While the opposition between 'noble' and 'savage' or 'civilised' and 'barbarian' is not solely rooted in skin colour in the ancient period, by the time Shakespeare is writing his plays, ways of identifying social, cultural and ethnic inferiority had already been established. For the literary scholar Ian Smith, the classical use of the term 'barbarism', for example, provides a clear 'cultural division of insiders and outsiders' in the Renaissance which becomes increasingly focused on colour-based racial difference.[5]

Shakespeare's play tests our tolerance for binaries. We witness the austere, masculine 'civilised' world of ancient Rome very deliberately pitted against the sensuous, feminine, 'barbaric' world of Egypt. Here white power stands in opposition to one more 'tawny' and the dichotomy is deliberate. The women in the play seem to be characterised merely as either pale, virtuous and saintly or black, amorous Jezebels, though to reduce Cleopatra to a mere Jezebel would be foolish. How she has been viewed, read, interpreted, talked about, represented and staged since that first performance at the Globe or the Blackfriars (Shakespeare's indoor theatre) in 1606–8 adds centuries of meaning that inevitably colours our modern perspective. But what is consistently evident in Shakespeare's text is that her ethnicity and the portrayal of her sexual behaviour are inextricably entwined. Plutarch's rendering of Cleopatra carries hints of the kinds of prejudices that continue to plague her representation:

> the love of Cleopatra lighted on him, who did waken and stir up many vices yet hidden in him…and if any spark of goodness or hope of rising were left him, Cleopatra quenched it straight, and made it worse than before… [S]he subtly seemed to languish for the love of Antonius, [starving herself to get slim]…she every way framed her [looks], that when Antonius came to see her, she cast her eyes upon him, like a woman ravished

for joy. Straight again when he went from her, she fell a-weeping and blubbering, looked ruefully on the matter... and when he came suddenly upon her, she made as though she dried her eyes, and turned her face away, as if she were unwilling that he should see her weep. All these tricks she used...[6]

Manipulative and deceptive, it is, of course, this foreign woman that stirs up the 'many vices yet hidden' in Antony. Accused of using her 'sumptuous' feminine wiles to seduce her lover, she keeps stringing him along as he literally sacrifices the world for her. Plutarch's presentation of her isn't all bad; in some moments he mentions her 'grace' and her pleasant 'voice'. But this doesn't really explain the intensity of Antony's much judged passion. Still, Plutarch's own bias is evident when he laments Antony's addiction to loving Cleopatra. In his other writing about Egypt and its customs he was far from complimentary, calling the religious worship of animals 'brutish' and stereotyping Egyptians as frivolous and inconstant.[7] The qualities of frivolity and inconstancy resonate in the moral condemnation that often accompanies representations or accounts of Cleopatra; in other words, anxieties about her in Shakespeare's time were not disconnected from her cultural and geographical origin. In his descriptions of Africa Joannes Leo Africanus reveals a much-recited stereotype about the women of Egypt, who apparently liked being expensively 'attired, adorning their foreheads' with chains of pearl, and were known for being so 'ambitious and proud, that all of them disdain either to spin or to play the cooks'.[8]

The frequent effeminising of Antony in the play and in Plutarch echoes the popular view of Egyptian culture in both eras, that women ruled the roost while the men were doormats. Shakespeare's play seems reluctant to challenge these cultural beliefs, fusing female sexual behaviour and dominance with ethnicity, drawing our attention to the very long history of misogynoir.

Mark Antony, the powerful orator we first meet in *Julius Caesar* (1599), along with Lepidus and Octavius Caesar, is a member of the triumvirate – the leaders of the Roman Empire – but he is spending an awful lot of time in Egypt and is condemned as doing so rather too decadently. His affair with Egypt's queen is no secret even though at the beginning of the play he is married to Fulvia. After Fulvia dies, Antony returns to Rome, where Octavius has recently learned of Pompey's threat to the triumvirate. In Rome, Antony, who is less influenced by his emotions, makes the political decision to marry Octavius's sister, the chaste Octavia – 'Whose virtue and whose general graces speak / That which none else can utter' (2.2.137–8).

The will no doubt strengthen the union of Antony and Caesar, but when news of this marriage reaches Egypt, Cleopatra flies into a spiteful rage, histrionics considered typical of this queen. One can imagine beating the messenger would be physically demanding for any actor given the part of Cleopatra:

MESSENGER
Madam, he's married to Octavia.
CLEOPATRA
The most infectious pestilence upon thee!
                              Strikes him down.

MESSENGER
Good madam, patience!

CLEOPATRA
What say you?

Strikes him.
(2.5.60–2)

First, she *strikes him down*, then *strikes him* again, then '*hales him up and down*', eventually drawing a knife to threaten him 'Rogue, thou hast lived too long!' (73).

A truce is agreed between Pompey and the triumvirate, but it's soon revealed that Caesar has broken the truce, and furthermore is plotting against Lepidus. Antony sends Octavia to Rome to help intercede, but to no avail: they end up at war. A sea battle at Actium proves disastrous for Antony; his impassioned act of following Cleopatra's retreating ships leads to his reputational demise, so he blames her, rages at her, condemns her, but then forgives her. Such is love. He hears Octavius is planning a truce with Cleopatra and feels betrayed, so he prepares for a second battle – and is triumphant. However, in the third battle, Antony's men, including his most trusted ally Enobarbus, desert him. (Enobarbus eventually feels so much shame for his betrayal, he dies of a broken heart.) Antony thinks Cleopatra has betrayed him to Octavius. The queen is so angry, she goes to her monument and pretends she has committed suicide – in this gesture, Shakespeare's Egyptian queen lives up to the ancient and Renaissance critiques of her as the consummate performer. Antony asks one of his servants – suitably named 'Eros'– to kill him, but the servant refuses and kills himself. Antony falls on his sword (not very expertly – a source of humour in many productions) before he is taken up to Cleopatra's monument, reuniting with her before he dies in her arms.

Having convinced Caesar she'll surrender, privately she admits she'd rather die than be publicly humiliated in Rome where, you may remember, 'squeaking Cleopatra [will] boy my greatness'. Famously, she kills herself with two asps – one at her breast, which, while the most iconic scene, is a challenge to stage effectively; not many can pull off the epic significance of this tragic death with a rubber snake clipped to their chests. While the legacy of Cleopatra is fraught with negative stereotypes, the emotional complexity and passionate power of this queen complicates this perception, as does her relationship to race, which, in performance, goes strangely unremarked upon.

Antony is struck by fierce jealousy and a sense of betrayal when he walks in on Cleopatra, offering her hand to Caesar's servant to be kissed in a courtly gesture, that makes it seem she is accepting Caesar's proposition to betray Antony. Incensed, he asks:

> Have I my pillow left unpressed in Rome,
> Forborne the getting of a lawful race,
> And by a gem of women, to be abused
> By one that looks on feeders?
>
> (3.13.111–14)

Shakespeare's fascination with the ease with which passion bursts through regulated and cultivated temperaments is evident in Antony's tirade in this scene – just before he demands that Caesar's servant be whipped. Courtly gestures are just that and can be misread easily, a device Shakespeare uses often in his works to show how hard unregulated human passions can clash against the overly practised courtly rules of the day.

Antony's anger provokes him to remark negatively upon Cleopatra's difference. He uses the word 'race' to refer to lineage or breeding since in Shakespeare's time it was defined loosely as belonging to the same family; descending 'from a common ancestor... kindred'.[9] These connotations are inherent in the formation of race in this era, which also incorporated culture, religion and skin colour into its meaning – distinctions Europeans encountered more regularly from the Middle Ages on. Attributing difference to groups, distancing 'others' from 'pure' whiteness or 'fair' complexions, and generally marking out groups in ways that subject them to oppression and alienation are part of a linguistic and rhetorical process known as *racialisation*. It occurs when gender, nationality, indigeneity and class are viewed as markers of difference in racial terms, such as the Irish being called by the early modern English barbarians or savages. In 1611, for example, cartographer John Speed published *The Theatre of the Empire of Great Britain*, containing a map of Ireland that pictured a 'Wilde Irish man' with untamed hair and wearing an Irish mantle; he is presented as 'strange' (or foreign) and designated racially different, even monstrous, compared to the more civilised English.[10] Dissociating the Irish from whiteness was a way of racialising them and justifying the colonialisation of Ireland and asserted the distinctiveness of the English as virtuous, civilised and a purer breed.

Not just by being referred to as 'black' and 'tawny' in the play, Cleopatra is also racialised by the entwined descriptions and references to her sexual character and the customs of her country. Perhaps the most famous moment, largely pinched from Plutarch, is when earlier in Act 2, Antony's closest friend Enobarbus describes Cleopatra on her barge. It's a breath-taking image and, though steeped in orientalist language, has continuously captivated the imaginations of filmmakers, theatre designers and visual artists over the ages:[11]

The barge she sat in, like a burnished throne,
Burned on the water; the poop was beaten gold;
Purple the sails, and so perfumed that
The winds were love-sick with them; the oars were
silver,
Which to the tune of flutes kept stroke, and made
The water which they beat to follow faster,
As amorous of their strokes. For her own person,
It beggared all description: she did lie
In her pavilion, cloth-of-gold of tissue,
O'erpicturing that Venus where we see
The fancy outwork nature. On each side her
Stood pretty dimpled boys, like smiling cupids,
With divers-coloured fans, whose wind did seem
To glow the delicate cheeks which they did cool,
And what they undid did.

(2.2.201–214)

Full of playful evocativeness, the language nonetheless reflects the 'exotic' perception of Egypt at the time, its references to gold denoting the overwhelming and unimaginable wealth and luxury that attends the legend of Cleopatra and the glorious Egyptian past. Shakespeare uses bold consonants – 'burned on the water'; 'beaten gold'; 'purple the sails'; 'beat to follow faster', 'amorous as their strokes' – to hint at a sexual danger, perhaps violence, in this notoriously lusty love affair. As beautiful as it has been deemed, this description racialises Cleopatra, making her seem 'strange', exotic, and, therefore, a threat.

Race and gender are interwoven categories of identity, and it is hard to separate one from the other in the way Cleopatra is presented. We see, for example, how Shakespeare draws on artistic and poetic tropes and symbols aligning white woman-hood with purity, modesty and chastity, while blackness is linked often with excess, sexual boldness and sensuous luxury. Whether he does so to challenge such binaries or reinforce them is hard to know from one moment to another. But it would be nice to think Shakespeare is critiquing the limiting, harmful symbolism and racist stereotypes of his day.

These distinctions have a long history, seen in religious instruc-tion through the Middle Ages and well into the seventeenth century. For example, the Virgin Mary versus Jezebel is a common opposition; it rehearses the timeless comparison between the virgin and the whore, which doesn't allow for much in the middle. The relationship of this opposition between virgin and whore to race becomes more explicit by the Middle Ages, as evidenced in the adoration of Mary in pre-Reformation art where we see the link between her whiteness and her powerful virginity. These were associations that were easily transferrable to Elizabeth I, within what was known as the cult of 'Gloriana' – the worship of the Virgin Queen through poetry and art that took place in post-Reformation England. But Queen Elizabeth's excessively whit-ened face not only symbolised her untouched body, it became an assertion of whiteness as an identifying feature of English iden-tity and the legitimacy of the country's ambition to become the world's most powerful nation, something James I's reign was wholly committed to as well. In the literature and public discourse of the time, white women who sexually transgressed were condemned in ways that attributed blackness to them. The English moralist, William Gouge, insisted that 'the sins of women are to be cast as dirt on their faces that they be more ashamed'.[12] So blackness or swarthiness is still aligned with white woman-hood when it comes to sins of the flesh.

In Antony's reference to 'Lawful race' in Act 3, he evokes not just the ancient setting of the play, but a shaping sense of English nationhood. 'Lawful' implies legitimacy and superiority. In Western Europe at this time Antony's adulterous affair with Cleopatra was unlawful indeed. Nor would the intermingling of their blood be lawful in a world with such clear cut cultural and ethnic divisions. Antony's fury continues: 'You have been a boggler ever' (3.13.115), he claims, using the term 'boggler' to accuse Cleopatra of inconstancy, of wavering in her loyalties (remember Plutarch drew the same conclusion about Egyptians in general). He's calling her a whore. The term seems to be a Shakespearean invention, probably deriving from the noun 'boggle', which referred to a 'goblin or spectre, an undefined creature of superstitious dread. (Usually supposed to be black, and to have some human attributes).'[13] During the Elizabethan and Jacobean periods, images of monsters, spectres, demons, witches and animals were used regularly to assign a racial character to someone; the language of strangeness, foreignness, or blackness was also weaponised to demonise entire groups. By associating Cleopatra with 'boggling', Antony demonises her, exploiting her ethnicity or race specifically by accusing her of sexual excess.

In a softer mood, Antony once refers lovingly to her as his 'serpent of Old Nile' (1.5.26). Thus, sometimes charmed by the serpent, sometimes resentful, he oscillates between the pleasure and the agony of his relationship with Cleopatra. Serpents, linked to cunningness and sexual excess, embody the traits Antony seems to celebrate and condemn in his lover with equal vehemence. But a centuries-old stereotype about black female sexuality is what can be felt in such allusions as 'boggler' and 'serpent'. Shakespeare's use of allusion, popular emblems and symbols that gesture to larger ideas in his age, are partly what make his plays rhetorically complex, dazzling and ever readable.

The blending of race and gender in the play speaks powerfully to the present moment, reminding us of the kinds of stereotypes and perceptions still projected onto women of colour. In a study of white masculinity conducted within the context of a white extremist group and a white anti-racist group, Matthew W. Hughey found that perceptions of blackness were quite similar between both. Most relevant is a discussion with a white suprem-acist named 'Joey' who liked to watch pornography featuring Black women:

> **Joey**: I tried white porn for a while but I just didn't get as much out of it… Man, those black girls do some crazy stuff; they are so much more free and expressive… I like it because, they are just more sexy and voluptuous.
> **Author**: So, that's the kind of woman you are looking to settle down with one day?
> **Joey**: Oh hell no! I would only marry a white girl… But I can take some tricks…that will surely liven up my ordinary sex life and whatever normal white girl I settle down with.[14]

Antony's love for and sexual obsession with the tawny queen and his politically safe marriages with virtuous Roman ladies are evidence enough that the virgin/whore binary and its relation-ship to racialisation is a tale as old as time, whether it's told in the history books or on stage. Reading this play through the lens of race means being aware of the long history of misogynoir that influenced and shaped this magnificent queen's representation over the centuries.

MISCEGENATION

The opposition between Antony's Roman wife, Octavia – the 'gem of women' – and Cleopatra is apparent in Antony's accusations. (It was not terribly original of Shakespeare to think about the clichéd trope of 'the virgin versus the whore' in racial terms.) It is significant that Antony uses the phrase 'lawful race' in a speech in which he shames and debases the sexuality of a woman of colour. Moreover, he speaks about breeding and lawfulness in the context of this racialisation, underscoring the anxieties surrounding interracial mixing or miscegenation. In this play, Shakespeare presents another interracial love affair against the backdrop of an emerging empire where this time crucial distinctions between the lawfully-breeding Rome and the boggling Egypt are made visible.

In the same act of the play, the soon-to-be Roman Emperor, Octavius Caesar, mentions the couple's 'unlawful issue that their lust / Since then hath made between them' (3.6.3). This refers to illegitimate and biracial children they may have had but also is a metaphor for the outcome of their union, such as Antony giving Cleopatra excessive power. Their relationship jeopardises the future hopes of Rome and poses a threat to the vision of a hyper-masculine Roman purity that underpins Caesar's ambitions. Anxieties about miscegenation have been extraordinarily powerful in sustaining white supremacy through the ages. Asserting and protecting white womanhood in order to stabilise white patriarchy is ever the goal. We see it in Octavius's suggestion that Antony stay away from Egypt and marry Octavia, his sister, to stabilise their power. Closer to home, we need only recall the dramatic exit of Prince Harry and Meghan Markle from the British monarchy to see that it is still with us even in our progressive society; there are many who will ever bristle at the idea of interracial families.

The suspicion of interracial relationships is surprising when we think that people from different ethnicities and varieties of skin colour were present in Britain since the early Tudor period and perhaps much earlier. The very fact that Shakespeare wrote about it often should give us pause. In the sixteenth century, black men married white women and white men married black women, as the English traveller George Best describes in 1578:

> I myself have seen an Ethiopian as black as coal brought to England who taking a fair English woman to wife, begat a son in all respects as black as the father was, although England were his native country, and an Englishwoman his mother; whereby it seemeth that blackness proceedeth rather of some natural infection of that man, that neither the nature of the clime, neither the good complexion of the mother concurring, could anything alter...[15]

This is an extraordinary suggestion that genetics rather than climate produce different skin colours. Best also makes it clear that even the 'good' complexion of the mother didn't make a difference. Archival records reveal marriages between 'blacka-moores' and white English people throughout the country: 'Joan Marya a Black Moore' married 'Thomas Smyth Byllsmaker [weapons manufacturer]', for example.[16] But such facts of history can get overused to suggest that race and racism were not issues of contention for the Tudors. While historical records can help us to reconstruct a picture of society, the art, literature and drama are what fill in the gaps when it comes to lived experience. The atti-tudes governing the experience of being a different skin colour, ethnicity, or religion in Shakespeare's England don't necessarily emerge from parish registers alone.

Not only did interracial marriages take place at this time, but also pre-marital and extra-marital relationships between white men and black women are documented. In some cases, records show white English men impregnating black female servants. In March of 1606 'Marey a negroe' explained to the court in Bridewell that 'one John Edwards...had the use of her body twice & she is with child by him'.[17] Shakespeare even addresses this kind of encounter in *The Merchant of Venice* when Lancelot Gobbo (servant to Shylock the Jew) alludes to the fact that he himself has made a black woman pregnant, as the young Venetian Lorenzo reminds him: 'I shall answer better to the commonwealth than you can the getting up of the negro's belly: the Moor is with child by you Lancelot!' (*The Merchant of Venice*, 3.5.32–33).[18] So there is evidence, literary as well as archival, that women in sixteenth-century England had children out of wedlock and that some of these women were African. It tells a story about white male entitlement and the sexual exploitation of black and working-class women throughout history.

Shakespeare's literal and metaphorical interest in interracial coupling began well before he sat down to pen *Antony and Cleopatra* in 1605–6. *Titus Andronicus* places an interracial couple front and centre and this relationship serves as a nucleus of the violence in the play. *Othello* (1604) shows us what happens when interracial and clandestine marriage occurs in a world where the continuation of purity and whiteness is *de rigeur*. But *The Tempest* (1611) hints at it too by way of rejection, first when Sebastian criticises the nobleman Alonso for letting his daughter get married to 'an African' (2.1.123), and again in its celebration of *proper* marital mingling. Prospero, the exiled duke who has occupied an island, uses magic to raise a storm, causing a shipwreck that will toss his usurping brother and other dignitaries ashore so that he can exact his revenge. Prospero's daughter Miranda famously hasn't met anyone other than her father and the indigenous Caliban, whom Prospero has enslaved. When she sees Ferdinand, the Prince of Naples, she falls head over heels. This is all part of Prospero's plan and he embraces Ferdinand's hopes of his union with Miranda: 'fair issue and long life' (4.1.23). This time, not only would the issue be lawful, but 'fair' too; in other words, virtuous white children will come from this sanctioned marriage. It is perhaps a moment of relief for the audience and Shakespeare would have been well aware of why.

BLACK QUEEN/WHITE QUEEN:

CLEOPATRA DIVIDED

She is Shakespeare's most captivating, illustrious, passionate dark lady. The nineteenth-century academic F.J. Furnivall referred to Cleopatra as 'the dark woman'. In the same essay he laments the fact that Antony fell to his ruin under the 'vicious splendour of the Egyptian Queen; makes us look with admiring hate on the wonderful picture he has drawn, certainly far the most wonderful study of woman he has left us... [I]n her, the dark woman of Shakespeare's "Sonnets", his own fickle, serpent-like, attractive mistress, is to some extent embodied, I do not doubt'.[19] The feeling of simultaneous anxiety and wonder Furnivall expresses mirrors Antony's own attraction to Cleopatra and sums up conventional attitudes towards the seductive power of so-called dark women throughout history, even in literary criticism.

Shakespeare's Queen of Egypt is full of paradoxes: a possessive, at times, insecure lover but a sexually confident woman;

empathetic but with a heart full of fury. In Act 2, she is described by Enobarbus as unable to fully satisfy even as she satisfies:

> ...she makes hungry
> Where most she satisfies; for vilest things
> Become themselves in her...

> (2.2.247–8)

But such qualities are not virtues in Roman eyes, nor were they in the eyes of many who saw the boy actor play her on the Globe stage in 1606.

I opened this chapter with the question of whether or not the boy actor who performed the role first wore white, black or brown makeup. The historical Cleopatra is being rewritten by feminist biographers and is now said to have been far more multidimensional than even Shakespeare chose to portray. Shakespeare's impact upon our imaginations over the centuries is so immense, however, that we might struggle to comprehend that there may have been an actual person behind Shakespeare's creation, as is the case with Richard III. Shakespeare's Richard is 'deformed' but history tells us the real Richard III probably was not. Likewise, looking back, it is hard to distinguish Egypt's Queen from Shakespeare's. A recent biography of Cleopatra calls her an exceptional military strategist and a 'capable clear-eyed sovereign...[who] knew how to build a fleet, suppress an insurrection, control a currency, alleviate a famine'. But 'she nonetheless survives as a wanton temptress, not the last time a genuinely powerful woman has been transmuted into a shamelessly seductive one'.[20] Historically speaking, Cleopatra VII was possibly Greek – the Greeks having ruled Egypt in the first century BC – so it is argued by some classical historians that she was white due to her Macedonian heritage. Does this mean that she was not black? Perhaps she was brown. In either case, it is unlikely that she was as white as an English lily, especially if, as it has been surmised, her mother was African and the Queen herself identified as Egyptian. Cleopatra's family had been in Egypt for at least three hundred years by then. Bewildering as it seems, debate continues to rage about Cleopatra's racial identity. In the West, there is still an investment in her being white. The insistence to this day on Cleopatra's supposed whiteness demonstrates the way in which the study of the past is diligently Eurocentric.

In Shakespeare's time, her identity was an amalgamation of perceptions. Cleopatra turned up in several poems and plays, mostly private plays known as closet dramas that were written for audiences of aristocrats or university students. In most of these plays, such as Samuel Daniel's *The Tragedie of Cleopatra* (1594), she is white, but as Kim F. Hall reminds her readers in her literary analysis of racial tropes, she is nonetheless described in terms that suggest her outsider status: '[i]n Daniel's version, Cleopatra is very much the unruly female whose sexuality destroys not only Antony but Egypt as well'.[21]

In other literary works from the period, such as Robert Greene's 1589 *Ciceronis Amor*, she is a woman of colour. The famous woman writer Aemilia Lanyer's poem *Salve Deus Rex Judaeorum* (1613) also depicts Cleopatra as black. At the time, Egyptians were thought, like Africans, to be dark-skinned – Andrew Boorde, for example, claimed in 1555 that the people of Egypt were 'swart', meaning swarthy or dark. Yet, most of the *visual* representations of Cleopatra during the European Renaissance through to the late seventeenth century depict her as pearly white. This attention to the eroticised white body is captured in Giovanni Pedrini Giampetrino's 1538 depiction.

In the portraits that emerged at this time in Europe the emphasis is on Cleopatra's whiteness as well as the eroticism associated with her death, but I look at these paintings and think, this can't be what Shakespeare imagined. Just because Cleopatra is depicted this way by artists and writers catering for an elite European clientele does not mean that the sources that Shakespeare consulted told the same story. While Plutarch may have insisted that Cleopatra was Greek, Herodotus, in his *History of Egypt*, translated into English in 1584, uses the theory of climate to declare that the blackness of Egypt's inhabitants is due to the 'vehement heat and scorching of the sun'. There in Egypt, he continues, 'people are in countenance alike black, in hair [a] like frizzled'.[22] We can't really deny this link between Egyptians and blackness and how it may have informed Jacobean perceptions of the Queen of Egypt on stage.

Another timeless quality found in most representations of Cleopatra is her sexual allure and capacity to use it; the portraits above certainly exploit this aspect of her legacy. But Shakespeare does too. The opening scenes of the play paint an unambiguous picture when two of Antony's followers, Philo and Demetrius, gossip about the effect she has upon the now effeminate Antony. His 'dotage' surpasses limit; his 'goodly eyes' that once observed the assembled ranks of soldiers in war now only gaze 'Upon a tawny front'; his proud 'captain's heart' has become merely a fan to 'cool a gipsy's lust' (1.1.1, 6, 10). Sexual power is tied in Shakespeare's language to difference. She is 'tawny' or brown. The word 'gipsy' conjures a host of associations in Shakespeare's time with the gypsy or traveller population who were heavily legislated against and racially abused, linked as they were to the Egyptians in the cultural imagination of the day. Outsiders, other and foreign, gypsies were troublesome and, as such, highly racialised in English eyes. Gypsies were perceived even then as being con-artists, a stereotype Shakespeare incorporates stealthily into the play through the famous palm-reading scene: Charmian gives '*her hand to the Soothsayer*' and asks 'Good sir, give me good fortune…forsee me one' (1.2.15–16).

The seventeenth-century satirist Thomas Dekker demonstrates just how racialising works in one of the period's most damning descriptions of an entire group:

> They are a people more scattered than Jews, and more hated: beggarly in apparel, barbarous in condition, beastly in behaviour, and bloody if they meet advantage. A man that sees them would swear they had all the yellow jaundice, or that they were tawny Moors' bastards, for no red ochreman carries a face of a more filthy complexion.[23]

A 'filthy' complexion was not inherent as Dekker suggests, but linked to vagabondage and the 'mad' and 'wild' men who lived nomadic lifestyles. There was little trust in the travellers, the homeless and their unhousedness in general. It is not that 'gipsy' and 'Egyptian' are synonymous as we understand it, but the lines were blurred in the Tudor and Stuart popular imagination.

We feel the sexual and racial tensions surrounding Cleopatra more acutely in Act 1 when she ruminates on her lover's whereabouts after he has returned to Rome. She is reminiscent of the youthful Juliet in her wistful and urgent longing for the man she loves, but with a somewhat more experienced note to her erotically charged imaginings:

> O, Charmian,
> Where think'st thou he is now? Stands he, or sits he?
> Or does he walk? Or is he on his horse?
> O happy horse, to bear the weight of Antony!
>
> (1.5.19–22)

She then wonders rhetorically, as if questioning the absent Antony, does he:

> Think on me
> That am with Phoebus' amorous pinches black
> And wrinkled deep in time?
>
> (28–30)

Here is a flash of the Queen's insecurity as a middle-aged woman 'wrinkled deep in time'; her skin is darker than the so-called virtuous white women of Rome, like Antony's first wife, Fulvia, and his second, Octavia. Shakespeare once again shows his knowledge of the climate or 'heliotropic' theory – that people who live in hotter climes are naturally darker than those in cooler ones – but here he gives us a rather erotically charged image of Phoebus, the sun god, pinching Cleopatra's flesh amorously until it turns black. We are to imagine that the sun makes passionate and even painful love with the Egyptian monarch. Her sexual allure and her skin colour are remarked upon in the same breath.

When it comes to Cleopatra's infamous beauty, the problem for Western depictions of her is she must conform to the European *ideal*, which for centuries has been fair-haired, with lustrous pearly-white skin and a bit of a rosy blush in the cheeks. This presents a problem for Shakespeare's Cleopatra who is called both 'tawny' and 'black'. The easiest thing for artists and directors to do has been simply to ignore these traits physically even if the racial language continues to resonate metaphorically in her sexual confidence and temperament.

CLEOPATRA, RACE AND PERFORMANCE

Doña Croll was the first Black woman to play the part of Cleopatra on the British stage. It was 1991. This was a step-change moment in theatre history as she herself acknowledges:

> White actresses play her as a sexy queen. I play the politics and power. Any woman that runs a country and turns it around is not a bimbo. She is somewhere between Maya Angelou and Tina Turner… [T]he fable of the white Cleopatra is just another way of bleaching out history, cutting the nose off the sphinx.[24]

This production, staged by the renowned all-Black Talawa Theatre Company, was directed by Yvonne Brewster, the company's founder, at the Everyman Theatre in Liverpool and then at the Bloomsbury Theatre in London. Actors Touring Company did another, shortened adaptation of the play, *Cleopatra and Antony*, in 1989, which premiered at the Swan Theatre in Stratford-upon-Avon. With a cast of only four, much of the play was cut so that Cleopatra could dominate the performance even more than she already does. Starring Pauline Black (pictured here), it could be argued that *this* was the first time that a Black woman played the part in Britain.

And so, in the final decade of the twentieth century, we begin to witness a turn in the perception of Cleopatra and her racial heritage. When Doña Croll made history in 1991 with her

© David Corio

performance in a full production, it should have become more difficult for directors to consider casting only white Cleopatras thereafter. Indeed, Yvonne Brewster had hoped that would be the case – that 'it might just be the beginning'.[25] But between 1989 and 2018, there have been only around seven Black actresses cast as Cleopatra in major British theatres. Even now, directors continue to think of the Egyptian Queen as white. You may be thinking, 'well, that is fair enough because we don't really know what Shakespeare imagined'. That would be understandable. But the fact is that Cleopatra is explicitly, though not frequently, referred to as dark and she is repeatedly talked of as the very embodiment of Egypt itself, which in the minds of Shakespeare's contemporaries was a place of people with darker complexions: 'Egypt', 'false soul of Egypt', 'Great Egypt', 'royal Egypt', 'foul

Egyptian', 'Egyptian dish'. Antony describes her allure for him as 'strong Egyptian fetters', again invoking their proclivity for bondage (1.2.123). For Shakespeare this Queen, with all her majesty and sexual allure, was synonymous with Egypt. In the English imagination Egyptians were dark-skinned – 'swart' as Andrew Boorde had told us. So why has it been so hard to embrace her racial identity on stage?

As of 2022, the Globe has only ever cast white women and one white man in the role in the three productions it has staged since opening in 1997. Sir Mark Rylance was lauded by critics for playing the part so convincingly in 1999 in the Globe's famous 'Original Practices' style, a method which requires all-male casting in an attempt to recreate the practices of Shakespeare's original theatres. This performance style was radical in the 1990s in its use of historic methods for performance, music and costume-making. Original Practices (OP) productions, therefore, aimed to replicate as far as possible the acoustic and visual aesthetic of Tudor and Stuart performances, and were revelatory in their rich and illustrious presentation of the English Renaissance theatre.

The problem faced by the artists at the Globe, however, was that to be absolutely rigid in the method, an OP production of *Othello*, *Titus Andronicus*, *The Tempest*, *The Merchant of Venice* or *Antony and Cleopatra* would have required the use of blackface; cosmetic paints and powders made of various organic and mineral ingredients were available in the sixteenth century and used heavily by theatre companies in order to achieve racial and gender distinctions in the staging of these plays. This was a welcome problem because Rylance didn't want the Globe to be a museum, but instead a living, working theatre; it needed the pulse of modernity to keep it alive. It would have been hugely problematic, therefore, for Rylance to portray Cleopatra in black or brownface. Thus there was no gesture in the 1999 performances towards the play's references to her complexion even in the Globe's desire to stay as true to early modern practice as possible.

In 2005, Josette Bushell-Mingo played the part at the Royal Exchange in Manchester and in a 2013 co-production, the Royal Shakespeare Company and New York's Public Theater cast down the middle of the racial line – for the most part, the Egyptians were played by black actors and the Romans by white actors in order to create a visual picture of the play's preoccupation with racial difference. In this black and white production adapted and directed by African American playwright Tarell Alvin McCraney, Joaquina Kalukango played Cleopatra opposite Jonathan Cake's Antony.

This casting was plotted against the backdrop of a Caribbean setting and was more conceptual than a traditional production, but it was not a modern or conceptual intervention to cast a black Cleopatra. Josette Simon performed the part for the RSC in a full production, finally, in 2017, and to great acclaim Sophie Okonedo stepped into the role at the National Theatre in London opposite Ralph Fiennes's Antony in 2018.

Across the Atlantic, casting women of colour as Cleopatra has been an equally sporadic practice. Festival theatres such as the Oregon Shakespeare and Stratford Ontario have been known to cast in response to Shakespeare's racial cues; while in the Folger Theatre, Washington D.C, Shirine Babb played the part in 2017. This handful of examples can only tell us so much, but there is an increasing tendency for directors to envision Cleopatra as a woman of colour. So, is the tide changing and if so, is it still embracing misogynoir tendencies in the portrayals? Why has it taken so long, we might wonder, to acknowledge the skin colour of Cleopatra? Perhaps due to white academics and directors failing to see inequalities where they exist in the study as well as the performance of Shakespeare's plays, Cleopatra's racial identity is continually denied and she is presumed to represent the default position: whiteness.

Shakespeare imagined Cleopatra to be a dark lady and his portrayal consistently invites anti-black responses, creative and academic. But such responses are complex, and like the Roman attitudes towards her, interwoven with fascination, awe, fear and unrelenting desire. They reflect the responses to black people in Shakespeare's time – the double-edged sword of marvel/attraction and rejection. In Cleopatra, Shakespeare presents us with a fulsome portrayal of a non-white racial identity, not a tokenistic superficial show of diversity. She incites empathy in us; we are enraptured by the colossal emotions she expresses for Antony. We are whiplashed by her quick switches between wit and anger. But perhaps most of all, it is the fractious, complicated relationship between her heart and her words, rare in Shakespeare's other female characters. If you've lost someone close, this impassioned, aching tribute to lost love may resonate:

> His face was as the heavens, and therein stuck
> A sun and moon which kept their course and lighted
> The little O, the earth.
> ...
> His legs bestrid the ocean; his reared arm
> Crested the world; his voice was propertied
> As all the tuned spheres, and that to friends;
> But when he meant to quail and shake the orb,
> He was as rattling thunder. For his bounty,

There was no winter in't; an autumn it was
That grew the more by reaping. His delights
Were dolphin-like; they showed his back above
The element they lived in. In his livery
Walked crowns and crownets; realms and islands were
As plates dropped from his pocket.

....

Think you there was or might be such a man
As this I dreamt of?

(5.2.77–92)

The eloquence and muscularity of Cleopatra's language is what attracts the greatest actresses of our time to the part. English actress Dame Harriet Walter's performance was, she said, motivated by this very aspect of the role. She sees Cleopatra as a 'complex character who uses her sexuality as a political weapon. I decided I was going to play Cleopatra as someone with a brain... [T]he play contains very few references to what she really looks like'.[26] Walter makes no reference to Cleopatra's complexion but she does allude to the over-sexualised impression that people have had of her over the years. To mitigate this effect, she decided to inject some intelligence into the role, though Shakespeare had already done so. Unconsciously, Walter seems to suggest that the intelligence is linked to the actor's whiteness rather than to the Queen herself.

There aren't enough roles for women in Shakespeare without gender-fluid casting. So why wouldn't great actresses of all ethnicities want to take a stab at this titanic Queen? But there is something particular about Cleopatra and the imaginative escape she offers for white performers. She presents a fantasy of a stately queen with an erotic power that white actresses can inhabit and take pleasure in without facing any of the difficulties faced by Black women. Like white European colonial settlers, they occupy her character though only briefly. And this is nothing new. In the seventeenth century, one aristocratic woman had her portrait painted as Cleopatra – a performative act in which it was possible to pretend to be the kind of woman she could never actually be within the chaste and virtuous bounds of Renaissance white womanhood. The sitter is identified as Lady Anne Clifford. A Jacobean lady in Egyptian regalia, according to seventeenth-century orientalist notion of national costume, holds an asp above her breast, iconically invoking Cleopatra.[27] For a long time, it seems, white women have stepped into the fantasy of the dark queen.

It seems odd that *Antony and Cleopatra* was not always viewed as one of Shakespeare's 'race' plays. That is changing, finally. If theatre directors continue to centralise whiteness in their readings of the play, however, it in many ways replicates Caesar's triumph over Egypt. We relive Cleopatra's defeat every time we watch a white woman play her – due respect to Dames Judi Dench, Helen Mirren, Harriet Walter and Eve Best. But we begin to see more clearly the Egyptian Queen's own prophetic vision as she chose to end her life on her own terms. She imagined herself being performed for years to come by actors who do not resemble her in any way – and that is, for the most part, what has happened. The denial of this phenomenal role – requiring powerful acting, speed of breath, clarity of voice and athletic lung capacity – to actresses of colour is a denial of race in the play, of race in Shakespeare's imagination and a denial of the capacities of performers of colour.

Four

MODEL MINORITY

An African American actor walks out on to a stage to audition for the part of Othello; the director can't be seen; he's just a 'disembodied voice' from the stalls:

Actor: *Her father loved me; oft invited me;*
Still question'd me the story of my life,
From year to year, the battles, sieges, fortunes,
That I have passed.
I ran it through – Fuck me!! ... Shit, Sorry,
I'm sorry...

Director: You were doing great. You can pick it up right there...

Actor: *I ran it through, even from my boyish days,*
To the very moment...
Any gift of oratory that he has...

                              He tosses the book to the floor.
If we're quoting lines here? ... He says, when he's first brought before the senators, he says,
"...Rude am I in my speech,
And little bless'd with the soft phrase of peace..."

He says,
"...little shall I grace my cause
In speaking for myself..."

Shit, don't *I* know it...in other words, "If I tell you mugs what's really on my mind – sans the soft phrase of peace – y'all are gonna get your noses all outta joint and say, 'Oh oh! This n____'s gettin' all obstreperous n'shit.' Any scant communication, is gonna break right down, and I ain't gonna get nothin done here..." He knows his purpose for these men, *and* his value *to* them. The combination of humility and the knowledge of one's own worth is called "self-possession." If anything, it breeds composure, stillness, and it too has forever been disquieting to white men when they see Black ones wearing it, so, yes, it is...pragmatic for him to "mind his place..." He's here to do a job he knows he's damn good at if folks would just get over themselves and let him... But meanwhile he stands here, in front of you, having to play this game of civility and field your stupid comments with a look of interest and a smile while wanting nothing so much as to slap you knowing, if he did, that the ages of ancestral animosity accumulated in that single stroke would probably kill you dead.

In this moment from *American Moor*, a play by African American actor and playwright Keith Hamilton Cobb, we feel the modernity of Othello's experience. Interspersed in the extracts from *Othello*, are the protagonist's thoughts as he auditions. As he swings sometimes gently, sometimes hard, between Shakespeare's words and his own, he offers thought-provoking, emotional commentary on a play that speaks to his own painful experiences of playing Shakespeare in a white-dominated profession. The anger is palpable, the passion for Shakespeare powerful. Reflecting on his play and its many performances, Cobb says that he

> spoke back to Shakespeare. I spoke back to the white-owned and operated American Theater and to Shakespeare in his safe, unassailable fortress within it. I spoke back to the obliviousness of the obliviousness of white Americans who perceive everything that I am and do from within a framework of ancient, intricately wrought privilege so meticulously constructed that I can barely blame them for not being able to see beyond it. I spoke back – a cardinal transgression of the American order since the time slaves first learned English. I was honest, adamant, and indicting – and I apologized for nothing.[1]

Nor should he. Cobb's play shows how the encounter with Shakespeare for a Black man can be a wholly different, more alienating experience than for a white person. The power of *American Moor* lies in its direct confrontation with Shakespeare's original and Cobb's deep affinity with its title character. Later in the play, Cobb shows just how profoundly he identifies with the Moor:

> First up, a little white man is asking me if I have any questions about being a large Black man, enacting the role of a large Black man in a famous Shakespeare play about a large Black man which, for the last fifty, sixty

years or so has been more or less wholly the province of large Black men…

No…I ain't got no questions… But you should.

American Moor offers a challenge to the structures of racism entrenched in the theatre industry. It speaks honestly to whiteness and the ways in which the construction of Shakespeare as the Bard – or what Cobb calls 'the framework of ancient, intricately wrought privilege so meticulously constructed' – can be oppressive to people who can't possibly fit the mould. Not only is *Othello* a play about race because it centres upon a racialised figure, a Moor, but it is also a play about race because it centres upon *whiteness* and the white spaces that Othello is employed to defend.

Othello is a painful play, as Cobb's emotional journey through it makes clear. Many Black actors who perform the role feel traumatised during the production and even for a while afterwards. In a festival on Shakespeare and Race I curated in 2018, I gathered together a panel of four actors who had played the part to speak about their experiences. The word 'trauma' was used often throughout the conversation. But why is this? The Nigerian poet Ben Okri reflected upon what it feels like to watch the tragedy unfold from his perspective. Race becomes inescapable even if it isn't for the white spectators: the 'black person's response to *Othello* is more secret, and much more anguished, than can be imagined. It makes you unbearably lonely to know that you can empathise with them [whites], but they will rarely empathise with you. It hurts to watch *Othello*.'[2] Cobb corroborates this view in his play as he describes how it feels to be locked into that role as a Black man:

No! No, Gotdammit, no! What brand of credulous, self-loathing baboon, I thought, must such a man be?…

And why?! I was ashamed of him. I was ashamed that any reasonable person could look at me and see him, and I could no sooner portray him than I could show up for one of those Black urban dramas...

Okri's perspective does not define how all Black actors feel about the role. Cobb's play shows how complicated the actor's journey really is through *Othello*, realising that as dignified and self-possessed as the character seems, the white world he finds himself in objectifies his difference so relentlessly that it makes him un-incorporable into that world: 'I have a brother who can't defend himself... [N]ow I'm here. And I'm gonna defend and protect this much maligned, misunderstood, mighty character... my brother's dignity...or maybe my own'. Hugh Quarshie, who played Othello in 2015 for the Royal Shakespeare Company, had wondered almost a decade before whether '[o]f all parts in the canon, perhaps Othello is the one which should most definitely not be played by a black actor'. In a lecture delivered at the University of Alabama Hudson Strode Theater, he argued that,

> if a black actor plays Othello does he not risk making racial stereotypes seem legitimate and even true? When a black actor plays a role written for a white actor in black make-up and for a predominantly white audience, does he not encourage the white way, or rather the wrong way, of looking at black men, namely that black men, or "Moors", are over-emotional, excitable and unstable...[3]

Quarshie offers a completely valid response and important provocation. What partly fuels the reproduction of centuries-old stereotypes is that white directors cannot fully comprehend what it feels like to be a black person in a white-dominated society, as Cobb's play attests to in the exchanges between the white director in the dark and the Black actor auditioning onstage. In the centuries that followed its first performance, the play has been a favourite of white directors, theatre critics and scholars. The question of race, however, even now, is not seen as central to the play even though the well-known twentieth-century Shakespeare scholar G.K. Hunter stated in his British Academy lecture in 1967 that Othello's skin colour was a tangible force in the play and 'significant to our understanding of it'. Despite very rigorous scholarship on race in Shakespeare, many white directors and scholars still argue race is just 'one of' the playwright's themes, and that military bonds, jealousy, domestic abuse or misogyny are far more prominent. I do not need to echo that *Othello*, as with all Shakespeare's oeuvre, has many strands. One of the playwright's extraordinary gifts is his capacity to weave together a multiplicity of the perspectives, emotions and concerns of his day, as well as our own in intersecting ways. But race is the very motor of *this* play.

We do not meet Othello in the opening scene. Instead, he is introduced through rhetoric by the army's ensign, Iago. Adapted from one of the tales in Giovanbattista Giraldi Cinthio's *De Gli Hecatommithi* (*One Hundred Tales*; 1565), the protagonist of the source story is referred to as simply 'the Moor', whereas Shakespeare gives his Moor a name, a deep history and complex identity. Other key characters in the source are 'Disdemona', the evil 'Ensign' and the 'Corporal'. In Cinthio's version, the Ensign has a very clear motive for his actions: he is in love with Disdemona so he plots to poison 'the Moor' against her, persuading him that she has been unfaithful with the Corporal. A handkerchief is stolen and placed in the Corporal's house to dupe the Moor. Together the Ensign and Moor scheme to murder the adulterous couple. The Corporal is only wounded, but they both beat Disdemona to death with a sand-filled stocking, a more brutal method of dispatch than in Shakespeare's version. While Cinthio's text is limited by facile caricature, our playwright saw the dramatic potential in centralising the complexities of race on stage.

Shakespeare's play jarringly opens in a way that feels comedic when Iago and his dupe, the Venetian fop, Roderigo, wake up Brabantio in alarmed tones, all the while keeping the audience entertained. Brabantio's daughter has secretly married 'the Moor' and this seems to be the stuff of scandal. Brabantio is a patrician of Venice; in other words, he is of the ruling, elite class. In Renaissance Italy, patricians were notorious for their dedication to keeping their bloodlines 'pure'. Clandestine marriages would therefore have been dealt with punitively. The social and racial purity of patrician families were non-negotiable, since daughters of these mega-elite households were viewed literally as property and commodities to be exchanged in the game of power. In the opening scene from Shakespeare's play, we learn very little about Othello from Iago at first, except that he is black. Iago hammers this point home through a performance of extreme racism; he deploys familiar racialising strategies of evoking the opposition between black and white and using dehumanising rhetoric to set the stage for the tragedy to come. In modern performance, the comic effects of this scene work against what we deem acceptable given that its racist humour and stereotypes tend to elicit laughter from majority white audiences. Humour always lives on the edge of palatability and Shakespeare is still testing us four hundred years on.

Iago refers repeatedly to Othello by pronouns – 'him', 'his', 'he' – before we learn anything else about his person or identity; as he describes how the Florentine Michael Cassio has been promoted to Lieutenant, Iago becomes increasingly and strategically specific to draw us in: 'the Moor', a phrase that appears over forty-five times in the play lest we might forget his 'otherness' for a brief moment. Once at Brabantio's window, Iago tells the patrician that Othello is 'an old black ram' who is 'tupping your white ewe!' (1.1.87–8); he is 'the devil' that may make a 'grandsire' of him. The fear-mongering crescendos when Iago threatens, 'you'll have your daughter covered with a Barbary horse; you'll have your nephews neigh to you, you'll have coursers for cousins and jennets for germans!' (110–112). Invoking 'Barbary' of North Africa and the notion of barbarousness, Iago agitates Brabantio's elitist anxiety about miscegenation. Animal/horse imagery dehumanises Othello and any prospective offspring of the couple and is a final flourish to Iago's racist rhetoric. It lays bare his hostility to sex itself; for him, sex is bestial and interracial sex is barbaric. If Iago were real and alive today, he'd spend most of his time in a Reddit chatroom provoking misogynistic, racist and homophobic involuntary celibates to deepen their fear and hate.

MODEL MINORITY

We finally meet Othello in the Doge's court, where he explains his actions after being accused by Brabantio of witchcraft, of using 'spells and medicines' to seduce his only daughter. Othello's eloquence is evident in his stirring narration of the origins of their love:

> I will a round unvarnished tale deliver
> Of my whole course of love, what drugs, what charms,
> What conjuration and what mighty magic –

For such proceeding I am charged withal –
I won his daughter.

(1.3.91–5)

Bewitchment was a common anxiety in this period, being associated with the unknown and unfamiliar. We saw the fear of witchcraft in the characterisation of Cleopatra's seductiveness. We'll
see it in *Macbeth*'s weird sisters, those 'secret, black, and midnight
hags' (4.1.48). Witchcraft lore was, of course, popular during the
European Renaissance. Linked to the devil, witches were given to
extreme and perverse sexual impulses, shapeshifting and trans-
forming others, known to trick, poison, infect, maim and murder.
In *The Triall of Witch-craft*, the seventeenth-century physician
John Cotta tells the story of the King of France hunting in the
forest with noblemen who heard the 'devil' – or 'cry of hounds'; as
they approached the sound, '[A]t length a big black man presented
himself in the thickest of bushes, and speaking unto the Earle
some few words, suddenly vanished.'[4] Othello, the 'extravagant,
wheeling stranger' ('wheeling' meaning turning or compassing –
swinging about, wavering – unreliable, roaming, travelling) or
'erring barbarian' ('erring' meaning full of error, but also wandering, going astray) as Iago calls him, similarly carries with him an
exotic history and a body presented as threatening insidious
poison able to bewitch, transform and infect a pure, white
Venetian woman.[5]

At court, though, it seems that tolerance for ethnic minorities,
particularly those who contribute to the health of the city's economy, is the standard. Othello, captain of the Venetian army, for
example, is there to protect the city state's interests in the
Mediterranean against the enemy, the Turk, a looming threat that
hovers in the play, but also gestures toward the fear of Muslims,

one of the religious and racial enemies premodern Christian Europe was defining itself against. But is tolerance enough to claim that racism in *Othello* only resides in Iago's extreme language? Why is tolerance enough? We have heard Boris Johnson and other statesmen deny claims that Britain is racist in the twenty-first century, asserting that Britain is a 'tolerant' society. As an ethnic minority, I don't wish simply to be tolerated. The Duke of Venice and the Senate feel Othello's explanation is clear enough and are willing to overlook his apparent unsuitability as a husband to Desdemona; his 'round unvarnished tale' actually charms them. Besides, he is useful to them, particularly as we learn that the Turks are closing in on the Venetian outpost of Cyprus – Othello is to be sent there immediately to stave off any attack. Desdemona and her gentlewoman/attendant Emilia, Iago's wife, will join him and Iago there.

Microaggressions characterise the day-to-day experiences of so many minorities. They can be verbal or non-verbal, hardly visible, making it easy for people to suggest that attitudes like racism exist only in extreme individuals or cases, or indeed that the offended individual is only imagining their abuse. Meanwhile, a successful person from a racially diverse background is pointed to as an example of how systemic racism is, in fact, a fantasy. But this is what is known as the 'model minority' myth. If there is a British South Asian Prime Minister or Home Secretary in the UK, or a Black President of the United States, for example, surely that means success and opportunity are available to *everyone*? This type of thinking has influenced readings of Shakespeare's play for decades. Similar arguments have been made about whether or not race is a central theme of a play subtitled 'The Moor of Venice'! Some have interpreted the play through this model minority lens, which is, in fact, skewed by the idea that white experience frames *all* experience; such a perspective would indeed lead to the conclusion that race might be incidental or even a trivial concern of the play and that tolerance is the ideal that produces opportunity. 'Othello can't be a victim of institutional racism because he's a Captain of the Venetian army'; 'Othello is successful; he has dined with the elite Brabantio, admired by the very Duke'; 'Othello is a trusted leader protected by the state.' He is tolerated, so what's the problem? These readings seem valid, but only for the briefest of moments.

SIXTEENTH-CENTURY TOLERANCE

Venice was famous for its tolerance of 'strangers'. As the sixteenth-century German tourist Sebastian Munster reported, 'this superlatively magnificent, beautiful, and rich city has become Queen of the Sea, and is inhabited by huge throngs of people of various races, indeed from virtually all nations, come together in that place to trade',[6] a description that could serve as the caption to Carpaccio's masterpiece, *The Miracle of the Relic of the True Cross on the Rialto Bridge*, painted in 1494.

It really should not surprise us, then, to meet a Moor *in* Venice, nor is it surprising to find him described as the Moor *of* Venice in the play's title and commanding the Venetian army, since, as sixteenth-century Italian diplomat Cardinal Gasparo Contarini tells us:

> some foreign men and strangers have been adopted into [Venetian citizenry], either in regard of their great nobility, or that they had been dutiful towards the state, or else had done unto them some notable service.[7]

This is a sentiment hauntingly echoed in Othello's final speech: 'I have done the state some service, and they know't' (5.2.337).

Despite this 'tolerance' demonstrated in the play, Shakespeare's Duke of Venice shows us the way racial thinking works in this white ruling-class society, where prejudice is buried deep in minds that appear, on first glance, more enlightened. To calm Brabantio, the Duke tells him,

> And, noble signior,
> If virtue no delighted beauty lack
> Your son-in-law is far more fair than black.
>
> (1.3.289–91)

In his mind, the Duke is being fair in the other sense of the word. But by saying this, he is asking Brabantio to see how *white* Othello can be. He may be black on the surface, but, according to the Duke, Othello doesn't *act* black, and that should suffice for now. The Duke banishes blackness as it manifests in attitude and behaviour, even if he cannot banish Othello's complexion. Othello flickers between white mind and black skin. Such oscillations will feel familiar to the global majority today for whom code-switching is part of life. What the Duke expresses here is not an archaism, nor is it anachronism; this connotation of 'tolerance' is still with us and was ever thus. Legal scholars Devon Carbado and Mitu Gulati observe the difference between 'status' and 'conduct' in the way employers tend to reward 'racial performance'. In modern workplace environments, discrimination is prevalent based not purely on phenotype or skin colour, '(for example, whether a person is discernible as black) but also on racial conduct or performance (for example, whether the black person is perceived to be "too black")'.[8]

President Obama was considered much more palatable to conservatives because he seemed more white than black. This became publicly obvious because of the 'private' comment made during the 2008 presidential campaign by then Democratic Senate Majority leader Harry Reid when he insinuated Obama's success was due to the fact that he was 'light-skinned' and was without a 'Negro dialect, unless he wanted to have one'. If not attributed directly to whiteness, excellence must be found in proximity to it. This is a problem detectable four hundred years ago in Shakespeare's Moor and the so-called tolerance or niceness of the Venetian Duke when he sees Othello's virtue as a white attribute acquired through his career in white spaces and which supersedes his skin colour. When Desdemona speaks to the Senate about her reasons for marrying Othello, she too looks beyond the surface of his skin, claiming that she saw his 'visage in his mind' (1.3.252), that his internal beauty negates his natural blackness. But does it? He tells her stories about being enslaved, about his adventures in foreign lands, experiences that are a product only of his racial identity. Desdemona fell in love with Othello *because* of those stories, the heart that endured the experiences related in them and the extraordinary capacity for recounting them: with 'greedy ear', she 'devour[ed] up [his] discourse' (1.3.150–1).

IAGO'S BEWITCHING TONGUE

If there is witchcraft in the play, its source is its most adept liar. Iago sees how his plans can unfold, how, in effect, he can entrap the 'Moor' with a 'web' of lies – the imagery of a spider illustrating Iago's capacity to weave together lies and confusion and 'enmesh them all' (2.3.357). Spiders were linked in the Renaissance imagination to the sense of touch, to weaving, as well as to black-ness. The handkerchief as Othello describes it has 'magic in the web of it', after all. Iago decides to convince Othello that his beloved wife, Desdemona, is having an affair with Cassio, the newly appointed lieutenant. It's hard to know if Iago is more jeal-ous of Othello's relationship with his wife or his lieutenant; we never really get to the real motivation for his lies – even the overt racism he expresses seems to be a deflection tactic from what motivates his actions.

Once in Cyprus and secure in the knowledge they have neutralised the threat of the Turks, Iago convinces Cassio to have a drink. Knowing the straight-laced lieutenant can't hold his liquor well, Iago sends Roderigo to provoke him so he'll lose his temper. A fight breaks out, and when the governor of Cyprus, Montano, tries to stop it, he gets injured in the fray. When Othello enters to break it up, he dismisses Cassio and demotes him, which drives him to despair, lamenting the loss of his repu-tation. Cassio's grief gives Iago the opportunity to manipulate him further. He convinces him to pursue a pardon through Desdemona, who will have some sway over her husband, Iago presumes. This allows Iago to infect Othello's perception as he gestures towards an affair at first subtly – such as when they are seen talking together in 3.3. At the end of their conversation Cassio leaves hastily as they walk in; Iago claims, 'I cannot think it that he would steal away so guilty-like seeing you coming.' Such opportunities prove useful in making Othello think he has the 'ocular proof' (3.3.363) he demanded as the seed of doubt is planted in his imagination. Iago is clever, strategic and danger-ously charming. This 'honest Iago', as he is referred to, needles and admittedly spins one of the most elaborate webs of deception in all of Shakespeare.

He convinces Othello that Desdemona gifted the handkerchief to Cassio. Handkerchiefs, gloves and other personal items were highly meaningful objects of exchange symbolising intention, desire and promises of love in Renaissance courtship. Iago knows that if he can get his hands on that handkerchief, he can dominate Othello's perception. Othello asks for 'ocular proof' of his wife's infidelity, which Iago manipulates to be *tangible* proof. Emilia steals the incriminating handkerchief – perhaps to gain favour with a husband who neglects her – and Iago places it in Cassio's tent. This seemingly trivial object has been agonised over by critics for years; as far back as the late seventeenth century, the grumpy historian and wannabe playwright Thomas Rymer criticised the excessive attention it had received:

> So much ado, so much stress, so much passion and repetition about an Handkerchief! Why was not this call'd the *Tragedy of the Handkerchief?* What can be more absurd [...] Had it been Desdemona's Garter, the Sagacious Moor might have smelt a Rat: but the Handkerchief is so remote a trifle no Booby on this side of *Mauritania* could make any consequence from it.[9]

Yet the handkerchief is no trifle. It has power in this play and it is an 'outsider within' just as much as Othello is. Its story is one that transcends geography, culture and time. As Othello says,

> That handkerchief
> Did an Egyptian to my mother give,
> She was a charmer and could almost read
> The thoughts of people. She told her, while she kept it
> 'Twould make her amiable and subdue my father

Entirely to her love; but if she lost it
Or made a gift of it, my father's eye
Should hold her loathed and his spirits should hunt
After new fancies.

...

'Tis true, there's magic in the web of it.
A sibyl that had numbered in the world
The sun to course two hundred compasses,
In her prophetic fury sewed the work;
The worms were hallowed that did breed the silk,
And it was dyed in mummy, which the skilful
Conserved of maidens' hearts.

(3.4.57–65, 71–7)

The handkerchief was an 'antique token' that Othello's father gave to his mother. Its provenance is Egypt, endowed with magical properties that can make a woman faithful, thereby keeping her husband 'subdued'. Tracing the actual narrative of the handkerchief's origins, a more complex and unexpected history emerges. The handkerchief has traditionally been thought of as white with red strawberries, a design which has come to represent Desdemona's virginity as well as her complexion – 'fairness' – the Renaissance white and red beauty ideal. In its very creation, however, it is more likely to be black. A sibyl – an ancient Greek prophetess – was the original maker of the cloth. When she wove it in a 'prophetic fury' she did so using the silk produced by sacred worms, then it was dyed in bitumen or 'mummy' – a substance taken from corpses – which would give it the blackened colour of pitch (like the heads on London Bridge). Othello tells us clearly it was 'dyed', therefore it *cannot* be white. The literary scholar Ian Smith has argued convincingly that the handkerchief is not white and red as many have assumed, and therefore not linked to Desdemona's body at all. Instead, the handkerchief was very likely to have been conceived of as black in the playwright's mind, thus more representative of Othello. This plausible theory should influence more productions, as it did the Globe's in 2018, starring André Holland as Othello, directed by Claire van Kampen. It was the first major commercial production to incorporate this theory and stage a black handkerchief rather than a white one. [10]

By Act 4 scene 1, the torment is too much for Othello, when he hears Iago describe Cassio talk about Desdemona in his sleep – more lies, of course. Othello's emotional devolution is matched by a verbal one. This loss of English eloquence reinforces the racist dismissals of African speech in the period. Sixteenth-century rhetorician George Puttenham commented on the 'rude and barking language of the Africans now called Barbarians', seeing it as a sign of irrationality.[11] Though Othello's language sounds more like despair rather than Puttenham's crass devaluation of African speech:

> I tremble at it. Nature would not invest herself in such shadowing passion without some instruction. It is not words that shakes me thus. Pish! Noses, ears, and lips. Is't possible? Confess! handkerchief! O devil!
>
> [He] falls in a trance.
>
> (4.1.39–43)

Othello falls to the ground in a dramatic fit, probably an epileptic seizure, temporarily losing consciousness. Though Julius Caesar suffers the same affliction in his eponymous play, only Othello's experience is racialised. He is watched chillingly by Iago, who delights in what he sees, doing nothing to help him: 'Work on, / My medicine, work!' (4.1.44–5). Iago's reluctance to help Othello has been compared to contemporary examples of anti-black police brutality in which a disabled black man (Othello's epileptic fit may suggest he suffers regularly from this disability) suffers because of the harm done to him, and the bystander and actor of the violence does nothing, which stages the other ubiquitous stereotypical view that black men are irrational, criminal, 'unruly' and, often, 'insane'.[12]

Shortly after Othello's fit we witness an eavesdropping scene astutely choreographed by Iago, in which he questions Cassio in earshot of Othello about his love affair, but under his breath whispers that he'll ask Cassio about Bianca, his courtesan lover. Othello of course thinks that Cassio is referring to Desdemona as his lover, and with a little more encouragement from Iago he first resolves to 'chop her into messes!' (4.1.196), then decides to poison her. Iago encourages a gentler and gruesomely more erotic approach – 'strangle her in her bed – even the bed she hath contaminated' (204–5). Desdemona enters with the Venetian, Lodovico, but Othello is in such a rage that he does the unspeakable and smacks her in public, his erratic behaviour witnessed by the very state itself – 'Is this the noble Moor whom our full senate / Call all in all sufficient?' (264–5). This marks the beginning of the end for Othello as he slips into stereotype.

In the final act, Iago manipulates Roderigo into attacking Cassio in the street; Iago secretly stabs and kills Roderigo, but Cassio lives. Othello enters Desdemona's chamber, creating the play's most iconic scene in which he praises her beauty, only to smother her in her bed. Emilia enters and is horrified at what has happened, accusing Othello of brutality and aligning it with his blackness. He tells her why he's killed Desdemona, but Emilia reveals the truth – that his wife was faithful, the handkerchief taken from her room by Emilia's own hands. The penny drops in the most heart-breaking way. Iago is brought in for questioning by Cassio and the Venetian noble, Lodovico, but he says nothing. Othello, broken by the revelations, kills himself.

In the 2015 Royal Shakespeare Company production starring Hugh Quarshie as Othello, Iago was played by British-Tanzanian/Zimbabwean actor Lucian Msamati. A black Iago was a bold and provocative choice; it perhaps brought the 'black villainy' motif to the fore. We might think of the literary affinities that Iago has with the medieval Vice or the cunning devil in mystery plays – 'When devils will the blackest sins put on / They do suggest at first with heavenly shows / As I do now' (2.3.346–7) – but Iago is no paradox. As he says himself very early on, 'I am not what I am' (1.1.64)'; his white skin and 'heavenly shows' conceal his true designs. The director of the RSC production, Iqbal Kahn may have had no intention of objectifying the racism in the play, having cast a Black actor as Iago to decentre race. However, the dynamic did not shift away from race at all, as the racist associations with blackness harnessed by the play's language were heightened by Iago's villainy and the historic symbolism of blackness it invokes. It also shone a light on intra-racial colourism – the belief that a lighter skin tone is superior to a darker one, a phenomenon that 'has stratified the black community for generations'.[13] Khan's casting choice highlighted the *internalised racism* – the adoption of beliefs about one's race absorbed from the dominant culture – that is a devastating effect of systemic racism. Othello suffers from this phenomenon, as do some of the actors who have stepped into the role and found themselves at the bottom of the pecking order in a rehearsal room even though they are playing the chief part.

'VIRTUE INTO PITCH'

This play can be traumatising for viewers too. Some are more moved by Desdemona's story than Othello's. In 1610 when the King's Men performed the tragedy at an Oxford college, the scholar Henry Jackson reported on the effect of the performance on the audience: 'the celebrated Desdemona slain in our presence by her husband…entreated the pity of the spectators by her very countenance'.[14] In 1660, Samuel Pepys had noticed that 'a very pretty lady that sat by me cried out to see Desdemona smothered'. In the eighteenth and nineteenth centuries, audiences continued to weep, while trembling with fear at the force of Othello's brutality:

> In mid-nineteenth-century London, even the relatively restrained oriental Moor of William Charles Macready produced so "thrilling" an effect that when, after the murder, he thrust "his dark, despairing face through the curtains of the bed", a female spectator is said to have "hysterically fainted" at the sight.[15]

This stage picture epitomises the colour-coded ways of thinking about race that stayed with the play well after Shakespeare's company first staged *Othello* at the Globe in 1604. The image is iconic: a white, luminous Desdemona lies on the bed, while the tortured darkened face of Othello hovers over her sleeping body. He approaches his wife as she slumbers, poised to murder her. But he pauses suddenly, distracted by her shimmering complexion:

> Yet I'll not shed her blood
> Nor scar that whiter skin of hers than snow

And smooth as monumental alabaster:

(5.2.3–5)

Artists have rendered and directors have staged this heart-breaking tableau in multiple ways, but unmistakably, the contrast of complexions is more often than not the central focus.

The reader will recall hearing about John Boydell's Shakespeare Gallery in Pall Mall. This drawing was based on a painting by

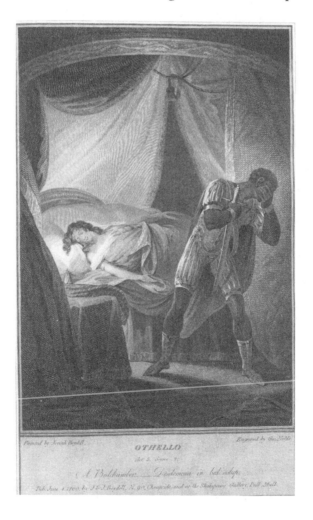

Josiah Boydell – his nephew. The danger, the terror and the despair of this domestic tragedy is more often than not expressed in interweaving tropes of dark and light, highlighting visually Shakespeare's fascination with interracial love but often to racist effect.

More often than that, the emotional power of the scene for early spectators rested upon their fear for the assailable white female body. Comparing Desdemona's skin to the smooth whiteness of a statue or monument, Othello indulges in sixteenth-century conventional praise of female beauty. But the playwright's inclination to unite tragic irony with poetic beauty comes to the fore in a moment that houses some of the finest, and most disturbing, lines in the play:

> Yet she must die, else she'll betray more men.
> Put out the light, and then put out the light!
> If I quench thee, thou flaming minister,
> I can again thy former light restore
> Should I repent me. But once put out thy light,
> Thou cunning'st pattern of excelling nature,
> I know not where is that Promethean heat
> That can thy light relume: when I have plucked the
> rose
> I cannot give it vital growth again,
> It needs must wither. I'll smell thee on the tree;
> [*He smells and then kisses her*]
> O balmy breath, that dost almost persuade
> Justice to break her sword! Once more, once more:
> Be thus when thou art dead and I will kill thee
> And love thee after. Once more, and that's the last.
>
> (5.2.6–16)

The actor playing Othello would be holding a single candle, or 'taper' until he blows out the 'flaming minister' that represents the spark of life within Desdemona. Shakespeare paints the scene with shades of light and dark, black and white to illustrate the contradictions that sit within Othello's psyche, his very identity – the man who we are constantly reminded is black but who has been enabled to succeed in white spaces and act white. Imagining the scene on stage, we see Desdemona's luminous, candle-lit pallor. It dazzles next to Othello's dark skin, painted on to white actors until the late twentieth century when it became standard for Black actors to play the part. On historic candlelit stages, the juxtaposition of painted blackface and cosmetically enhanced whiteface was designed to entrance as the flickering light danced and the audiences' attention was drawn inexorably to the horror painted in an utterly deliberate contrast of black and white.

The scene is distressing not just because a woman gets murdered by her husband, but also because of the way colour itself is hyper-objectified in a blatant act of racial formation – colour being positioned as *the* crucial factor in the murder. Othello looms even today in many productions and illustrations as some sort of terrifying spectre of darkness, while Desdemona presents a glimmering beacon of passive, white fragility and property. Powering the narrative is the jealousy and violence that audiences were led to believe only a black man possessed. In Shakespeare's own day, claims were made in books on travel and emotions suggesting as much and this enabled a Jacobean audience to rationalise their xenophobic yet fascinated responses. For example, Leo Africanus reported that '[N]o Nation in the world is so subject unto jealousy; for they will rather lose their lives, than put up any disgrace in the behalf of their women.'[16] The sixteenth-century Italian historian Benedetto Varchi thought people hailing from warmer regions were more inclined to the emotion, particularly if their wives or mistresses were 'tainted with the foul blot of unchastity'.[17] Directors who think that race isn't central to the play can therefore end up creating another layer of oppression for Black actors, making it all the more intolerable to watch. Cobb's play articulates this tension for the actor:

> So what do I do? Do I paint Othello's dignified countenance as a façade which so easily crumbles, turning a great and graceful Black man into a monster, thus suggesting that we are never really that great and graceful at all?

The credit won becomes the credit lost for Othello because the social structure depicted, the colour binary set up by the language, and the casual denial of race in the play by directors, all conspire against both Othello and Desdemona even as the interraciality of their union is fetishised.

Othello illustrates the colour-coding culture of sixteenth-century Venice and of early seventeenth-century England. An Italian artist's manual translated into English in 1598 describes the meanings of colours. About black, it states that 'some think it is a sign of madness and folly...because fools and madmen are over-charged with black choler', while whiteness represents 'simplicity, purity, and elation of the mind'; a 'white man is interpreted to be a good and sincere man'.[18] The issue of colour symbolism and its relationship to race in the seventeenth century is captured perfectly by Peter Erickson: 'the concept of color as an ethnic marker is present [in this period] even if the word race is not used to denote it'.[19]

Whiteness had many symbolic meanings too. I sometimes ask my students to consider just how white Desdemona is meant to be and to what extent her whiteness is vulnerable. This seems like the least obvious way to think about race, but it's an important avenue in light of Renaissance conceptions of ideal womanhood, conceptions that Shakespeare harnesses as well as critiques. Race runs deep within the structures of Venetian, and by extension European/English society. It is part of the psyche of the play and it permeates the experience of each character. But pausing upon whiteness and the meanings attached to it illuminates Shakespeare's depiction of a Renaissance European crisis: to be a wealthy, global centre of commerce and trade, a metropolis or nation must come to terms with racial mixing, the perceived threat of foreign infiltration and the danger that 'strangers', as useful as they are, pose to ethnic, religious and cultural purity. This crisis is more urgent given the development of the African slave trade during this period, inaugurated by the Portuguese and the Spanish. This crisis motivates and drives the fear of miscegenation and the destructive, torturous behaviours that characterise white resistance to it. But this crisis, sadly, is not just a premodern crisis. We still navigate our way through racial divides. While biraciality is more common nowadays, rather than being celebrated, mainly it feels like it's just tolerated.

WHITE PROPERTY

The primacy of whiteness had already been articulated through classical philosophy, but religion, art, poetry and drama were also important media for the assertion of whiteness as a standard of human beauty and aesthetics and a symbol of virtue. White

Christian women's bodies became the central focus of this ideal. The burden of the purity of the white race placed upon white women for centuries is captured lucidly in the play's voyeuristic attention to Desdemona's body. The academic Richard Dyer observes that white women are the 'indispensable means by which the group – the race – is in every sense reproduced'; their very role in reproduction, for Dyer, 'makes them at once privileged and subordinated in relation to the operation of white power in the world'.[20] As an elite woman in Venetian society, Desdemona is property, like Othello once was when he was a slave. Her transgression against her father is a transgression against her racial group and the state itself. Her death thus feels punitive on more than one count.

Ideals of beauty for white women established long before Shakespeare wrote this play were inherited from ancient Greek and Roman philosophers who proposed that symmetry, proportion and the perfect harmony of colour on the face were crucial markers of perfection. When the Italian spiritualist Marsilio Ficino revived Plato's philosophy in the 1400s, he added Christian piety to the classical definition, claiming that beauty reflected the light of God shining from within the body: 'beauty is a kind of force or light, shining from Him through everything'.[21] Beauty became a powerful manifestation of virtue and purity too. Premodern writers and artists firmly established a glistening whiteness as the preeminent complexion and primary signifier of perfection. A fifteenth-century Florentine manual on beauty insisted that the perfect woman's cheeks should be 'fair', which for the author meant a 'colour that besides being white, also has a certain lustre, as ivory does; while white is that which does not glow such as snow'.[22] Being white isn't really enough then. Skin had to *glow*. Thus what 'fair' means in

Shakespeare's time is white + luminous = virtue. Desdemona glows, dazzlingly, like 'monumental alabaster'. Italian philosopher Thomas Buoni remarked on the glow or lustre of perfect white skin resembling 'the clear light of the moon' or the 'bright beams of the sun, the whiteness of silver, the splendour of gold, the purity of marble'.[23] White women were to embody the riches of the cosmos and the earth, treasure only white men were entitled to.

If you have visited galleries in Europe, you'll have noticed many Renaissance portraits of women that celebrate this glistening whiteness, often emphasising the erotic interplay of light and colour on faces and hands. In admiring these portraits over the years, I never fully understood until recently how much I had internalised this ideal, how at odds I felt about my darker features. The media of the present as well as the white-idealising media of the past shape how we view ourselves through the lens of perfection and these expectations continue to sit heavily on girls and women of colour. *The Portrait of a Woman in White* (c. 1556) by the Italian Renaissance painter Titian showcases this European exemplar of beauty. The shimmering whiteness evident in her face, neck, hands, dress and pearls reflect contemporary definitions of beauty as something that shines or radiates naturally through whiteness.

The curious relationship between virtue and fairer skin tones had been consolidating for centuries before it was further established in Shakespeare's own moment. By the thirteenth century, white skin had become synonymous with Christian virtue and piety.[24] Medieval and Renaissance art illustrate this literally. Images of Mary, Christ, God, saints and angels are generally depicted with light using white pigments, while the devil, demons and death are often shown as black. Apart from being the religious 'export' of

Europe, as Dyer suggests, Christianity has been thought about and practiced in 'distinctly white ways for most of its history'.[25]

The genre of poetry – known as 'mistress worship' – was another medium that contributed to the creation of the beauty ideal. A woman's skin might be compared to lilies in one poem, crystal, moonlight, or alabaster in the next. Significantly, ivory was a particularly alluring material to poets – 'The lovely arched, ivory, polished brow', writes John Drayton in his Sonnet 33 'To Delia'. Elizabethan William Goddard's Sonnet 2 ruminates on how his lady's 'white excels the ivory', while Sonnet 39 by lesser-known poet B. Griffin relishes in his mistress's hand 'of ivory the purest white'. Ivory, a precious material brought to England through its mercantile ventures in Africa and India, is even used in some of the cosmetic recipes of the period. For example, and ironically, to make a black pigment, herbalist Nicholas Hilliard recommends a powder 'manufactured from ivory burnt in a crucible, ground with gum water'.[26]

One of the most admired writers of the sixteenth century was Edmund Spenser, known for his epic poem *The Faerie Queene* as well as for his anti-Irish sentiments.[27] His verses celebrating the virtue and beauty of his soon-to-be wife often utilise the poetic blazon – a form of verse that uses exaggerated comparisons to create a picture of female perfection by dissecting and describing each body part individually. The result is similar to today's techniques of air-brushing and of camera filters which make faces seem cleaner, whiter, prettier than they are in real life, producing an impossible fantasy of womanhood:

> Her goodly eyes like sapphires shining bright,
> Her forehead ivory white,
> Her cheeks like apples which the sun hath rudded,

Her lips like cherries charming men to bite,
Her breast like to a bowl of cream uncrudded,
Her paps like lilies budded,
Her snowy neck like to a marble tower,
And all her body like a palace fair,
Ascending up with many a stately stair,
To honour's seat and chastity's sweet bower.
(Epithalamion, Stanza 10, 171–84)

Shakespeare struggled with this, but he indulges in it too. Throughout his plays, the language of lilies, roses, snow, alabaster, ivory, etc. emerge to gesture towards female beauty, or at least the conventional ideal of it. When Othello stands over Desdemona's sleeping body, the image he selects in his poetic devotion to her is very similar to other moments in Shakespeare's work; for example, in his narrative poem, *The Rape of Lucrece*, the sleeping lady is watched and admired by Tarquin, the rapist:

The silent war of lilies and of roses,
Which Tarquin viewed in her fair face's field…
(71–2)

The 'fair' picture of a sleeping beauty provokes his violence. Shakespeare, and in fact many other writers of the time, would keep coming back to this disturbing trope. In Shakespeare's late play *Cymbeline, King of Britain*, Giacomo, who has snuck into Imogen's chamber by hiding in a trunk, spies her sleeping and is attracted to her vulnerable white femininity:

How bravely thou becom'st thy bed. Fresh lily,
And whiter than the sheets! That I might touch,

But kiss, one kiss. Rubies unparagoned,
How dearly they do't. 'Tis her breathing that
Perfumes the chamber thus. The flame o'th' taper
Bows toward her, and would underpeep her lids,
To see th'enclosèd lights, now canopied
Under these windows, white and azure laced
With blue of heaven's own tinct.

(2.2.15–23)

The spectacle – centred on Imogen's alluring lily-like whiteness – is made grisly, and its whiteness somehow more precious and delicate, by the prospect of rape by a hidden intruder. Recall too, within the Capulet tomb, Romeo approaches what he thinks is the dead Juliet, but she is actually in a sleep-like state that mimics death. Upon seeing her, he can't help but admire her white complexion and her stillness:

Ah, dear Juliet,
Why art thou yet so fair?

(5.3.101–2)

Like so many sonnet mistresses of the Elizabethan age and so many female characters in Shakespeare, Desdemona's virtues are registered by her skin; but the 'fairness' of a woman – the combination of white, glistening complexion and internal virtue – is precarious. Advice written into sixteenth- and seventeenth-century books instructing Christian women how to behave shows just how fragile female virtue was. A conduct book translated into English and widely circulated reminded women that 'chastity is the principal virtue of a woman'. It was the measure by which all of her other qualities were judged. But how were people supposed to know if a woman was chaste? It offers an answer: 'she that is chaste...fair, well favoured, rich, fruitful, noble and all best things that can be named'. The author also tells us that 'nothing is more tender than is the fame [reputation]...of women, nor nothing more in danger of wrong'.[28] Once a Renaissance woman is accused of adultery or called a 'whore', whether it is true or not, she is, well, cancelled. It becomes impossible for her to make a good match or to recover her husband's or father's reputation or her former beauty.

As with Othello, our impression of Desdemona is partly determined by what other people say about her throughout the play. Crucially, the first thing we learn is that she is young and white; remember, 'an old black ram is / Tupping your white ewe', as Iago snidely spits out under Brabantio's window. In the early acts, she is a 'fair lady' (1.3.127), 'gentle mistress' (1.3.178), 'jewel' (1.3.196), and according to Iago a 'super-subtle Venetian' (1.3.357); for Othello, she's a 'fair warrior' (2.1.179); to many she is 'virtuous Desdemona' (3.1.35), but then as Iago works on twisting Othello's imagination and our own, we notice an alteration in Desdemona as she begins to change colour. Iago admits he wants to turn her 'virtue into pitch' (2.3.355), meaning literally turn her from white to black. She is also like a text, a blank page that Iago has written 'whore' upon in black ink; the 'fair paper' (4.2.72), the 'goodly book' (73). Her face which was 'as fresh / As Dian's [the moon = symbol of chastity] visage, is now begrimed and black' as Othello's 'own face' (3.3.389–91); as she's transitioning on this racial spectrum, she is momentarily in limbo – a 'fair devil' (3.3.48); but then she transitions completely to 'Devil!' (4.1.239), judged ultimately to be the 'Impudent strumpet' (4.2.82), the 'cunning whore of Venice' (4.2.91).

Black and white are unstable notions in Shakespeare, transfer-rable between characters as the meanings become detachable

141

from skin, as we'll see in both tragedies and comedies not typi-cally linked to race. Desdemona is initially bathed in language praising her whiteness, but we witness her gradual permeation with blackness as Othello's perception of her shifts. He projects on to her the colour he himself associates with the label 'whore': his own skin colour, revealing the scarring, weathering effects of internalised racism. But the way Shakespeare plays with this colour binary is even more complicated. Iago is an example of a 'white devil' – a figure in the Elizabethan period that presented as 'fair' but was actually rotten to the core. The seventeenth-century preacher Thomas Adams felt 'haunted' by this figure in his sermon called simply *The White Devil*, aligning it with an insidious decep-tion and hypocrisy; in 1612 the Jacobean playwright John Webster of *Duchess of Malfi* fame penned a tragedy *The White Devil* along similar lines. Iago is the white devil of Shakespeare's play, though he'd have you believe Desdemona is. According to the racist logic of Elizabethan colour symbolism, he is metaphorically as 'black' in his purpose as Othello is in his complexion.

Conversely, as we have seen, Othello is called 'far more fair than black' as someone who has acquired success in the white, elite spaces of Venice. It's intriguing that this transference of symbolic colour is materially realised in the staging of race *and* gender in the original performances – Othello played by Richard Burbage in blackface and Desdemona by a boy actor in whiteface – the facial makeup used might have been literally transferred or stained the other during the couple's more intimate exchanges.

The play reaches a startling and tragic climax. Once Othello decides to kill himself, he delivers a speech comparing himself to the 'base Indian' (5.2.345) who, unable to recognise true value, throws away a 'pearl', an unforgiving stereotype about non-Euro-peans that Othello succumbs to in his final realisations. In 1585

Thomas Harriot described the indigenous people he encountered in Virginia, asserting the superiority of the civilised English: '[I]n respect of us they are a people poor and for want of skill and judgment in the knowledge and the use of our things, do esteem our trifles before things of greater value'.[29] The image of the Indian holding a white pearl thus animates the colour trope of black/white binary that the play's language consistently evokes. We tend to think of race in the play constellating around Othello's body, as many characters remind us: whether he is the 'lusty Moor', or the 'noble Moor'. But race is represented by the other characters too; whiteness emerges in the play as a racial category that is ethereal, vulnerable, permeable and powerful. It is the default position, which Shakespeare renders visible.

In the last twenty years, we have learned more about the demographic of Tudor England than we could have previously imagined. 'Black Lives Matter' is an idea finally taking root when it comes to setting the *historical* record straight. Historical as well as artistic and dramatic projects are emerging with the aim of bringing to life forgotten voices showing how Black and ethnic minorities have been part of English history for centuries. For me, this body of knowledge has given rise to questions about the extent of Shakespeare's own interracial encounters. What true knowledge did he have of Africans, Asians, Muslims and Jews? What was in his star actor Richard Burbage's mind if he stepped out onto the Globe stage in blackface, gesturing in ways that felt 'Moorish' to him, with Black men and possibly women in the audience? Perhaps it should be in our minds, as we try to really know Shakespeare, that his world was not racially homogenous. Given the way some Black actors view Othello – as a racist portrayal and over-fictionalised fantasy of how a black man might behave under pressure – I wonder could Shakespeare have created such a deep and biting portrayal *without* having a more than anecdotal awareness of race? Perhaps he 'held a mirror up to nature', explicitly reflecting on the complexities, tragedies and social tensions that can occur when different cultures converge, where so-called 'strangers' attempt to belong within a 'tolerant' society that just isn't willing or ready for racial cohesion and perhaps never will be.

Five

STAGING HATE

It is 1605 and a play recently performed at the court of King James I is being restaged at the Globe Theatre. Spectators make their way by boat across the Thames or by foot over London Bridge if arriving from the north side of the river; those closer to densely inhabited Southwark (population: 20,000 by 1600) haven't as far to travel to catch the 2 o'clock performance. Playbills litter the city's posts and tavern walls announcing that the tale of 'Shylock the Jew of Venice' will be told by the King's Men at their grand amphitheatre on the south bank of the Thames.

Some audience members arrive having seen the play before, keen to re-experience the story of Shylock whose brutal demand for a pound of Christian flesh brings about his own conversion and the tragic loss of his fortune. Others look forward to seeing the virtuosic boy actors who played the crafty and unforgiving Portia and her gentlewoman Nerissa, as they outwit not only Portia's dead father, her suitors and Shylock himself, but also their own husbands. And there are those who simply love watching and listening to plays set in exotic locales, like Venice and the fantastical Belmont.

This audience knows something about Venice and are about to have their expectations either met or surpassed by a play that will make them see that Shakespeare's Venice was much closer to

London than they dared to acknowledge. The multicultural, multi-ethnic character of Venice fascinates Shakespeare's audience, who are flocking to the theatre to see Moors, Jews and Spaniards performed in ways that will make them laugh, marvel or shudder.

At this 1605 performance, actors are preparing backstage as the Yard is filling up with groundlings consisting of the citizenry of London. The galleries begin teeming with mercantile and upper-class patrons. Groundlings purchase their bottles of ale and munch on hazelnuts, dropping the shells right where they're standing as they wait for the prologue to begin. In the tiring house or backstage area, it is frenetic as the actors prepare for the performance. There is a large trunk or two filled with props of all descriptions, hooks around the walls where various items of costume are draped. Wooden tables with looking glasses are set up to help the actors put on their makeup, after stage hands have ensured the cosmetic pots, concoctions and brushes are prepared, mixed and ready in enough time. The plot or 'platt' of the play is posted to the wall near the doors to the stage so the actors can see when their exits and entrances are, and remember which props to bring out and when. In this repertory theatre with potentially over twenty plays to perform in a season and never the same one two days in a row, there is very little time for detailed or extended rehearsals, so the plot is their crucial game plan for the performance.

Richard Burbage, the star of the King's Men, is preparing to play the part of Shylock. Being an actor in the early modern theatre, he is accustomed to performing or seeing his fellow actors across London play a variety of racial identities in many plays, donning costumes that invoke foreign worlds and painting their faces black or brown. He recalls the playwright Ben Jonson's scandalous *Masque of Blackness* at the court earlier that year, in which Queen Anna of Denmark and her court ladies performed with their faces, necks, and arms painted with glistening black makeup! He is an actor, however, and knows how to shift his voice, alter his accent, adapt his gestures and deportment to impersonate any ethnicity (something early modern audiences would not have winced at in the way modern audiences should), having just played Othello to great crowds in the Globe the year before.

A tirewoman approaches and smiles at him, perhaps takes a prosthetic nose and helps him apply it to his face, Jewish stereotypes having been well established by this time. Another actor to his left is smearing a concoction of burnt walnut shells, oil and cork onto his skin in preparation for acting the part of the Prince of Morocco. Burbage recalls donning blackface often himself to play Othello and knows he will do so again.

The lines from yesterday's play keep popping up in his mind, getting in the way of Shylock's words. But Burbage is a professional. He wanders over to the platt to jog his memory, having already learned his lines from the 'part' – written on rolls of paper consisting only of his speeches and the 'cues' or few lines heard just before.

His cue comes! He walks out onto the stage to present Shylock the Jew. As the play begins, and develops before the eyes of his audience, Burbage's performance is far from stylised; he shifts seamlessly between naturalistic and symbolic as and when the words and emotions require. The audience loves it – no, not the character, but sadly, the characterisation. But Shakespeare has written this one very well indeed and has provided the people crowded around the stage with a Jew of unexpected (to them) breadth and depth. At the end of the play, though, most of the audience will emerge into the evening sunshine feeling more racial prejudice than when they walked in and started crunching those hazelnuts.

*

The Merchant of Venice was originally staged in 1596 and printed in Quarto format as a single edition in 1600, its title page calling it

> The most excellent History of the Merchant of Venice.
> With the extreme cruelty of Shylock the Jew towards
> the said Merchant, in cutting a just pound of his flesh:
> and the obtaining of Portia by the choice of three
> caskets.

We know it had been 'divers times acted by the Lord Chamberlain his Servants', which would have given the play credibility and more saleability in its book form. Because its comedic genre and structure tend to mask the more disturbing elements within the plot and language, it is classified as one of Shakespeare's 'problem plays'. But for Shakespeare's original audiences, it was hardly a problem.

RACIAL IMPERSONATION

Early performances would not have presented a portrayal of race grounded in much reality. Myth, stereotype and fantasy were the building blocks of staging racial identity, particularly as it was then the domain of white Christian actors for largely white Christian audiences. In her history of blackface, Ayanna

Thompson reminds us that one of the factors that drive racial performance is 'a belief that virtuosity in acting can be expressed through cross-racial impersonations'.[1] Richard Burbage's inaugurating performances received great accolades, many accounts suggest. One elegy composed upon his death in 1619 remarks on his Othello:

> But let me not forget one chiefest part,
> Wherein, beyond the rest, he moved the heart;
> The grieved Moor, made jealous by a slave,
> Who sent his wife to fill a timeless grave,
> Then slew himself upon the bloody bed.[2]

Over the years since the 1600s, white Christian actors have been praised for their portrayals of Shylock and Othello. It's reasonable to assume that most audiences in the twenty-first century would recoil from exaggerated, stereotypical racial performances in the theatre. However, in a January 2022 *Guardian* article, Orson Welles's film of *Othello* in which he wore blackface was referred to nostalgically as 'the best screen outing' of that play.[3]

We might wonder to what extent white fantasies of 'otherness' in Shakespeare's time were actually problematised by the fact that Shakespeare and his contemporaries encountered ethnicities and even religions different from their own. As discussed earlier, there is ample evidence of early modern racial diversity across the country, evidenced in parish records, government papers and personal correspondence.[4] This makes us stop and reconsider the composition and demographic of early modern theatre audiences. Surviving testimonies already show us that playgoers came from Germany, Italy, Spain, Holland, Switzerland and elsewhere; the addition of black people and other minorities to the visual picture of a Tudor audience is not fanciful. Black Africans such as the silk weaver known as 'Reasonable Blackmore' resided with their families in Southwark, where Shakespeare's theatre was located. What encounters did they have with the theatrical community on their doorstep?

It wasn't just Shakespeare who was staging the lives and adventures of non-Europeans; for example, between 1588 and 1637, there were over thirty plays featuring Moors or characters described as Moors. Audiences therefore anticipated and relished these fanciful portrayals of 'otherness', and there was even the possibility they stood in the Yard with people of the same ethnicities as the characters being exaggeratedly performed on stage. We only need to think of the minstrelsy tradition in the United States to note how blackface became the performance property of white men who lived amongst black people and recall the exaggerated performances of blackness by celebrated actors such as Laurence Olivier in the 1960s.

But how would such performances be possible in Shakespeare's time? The stories of racial 'others' were told through visual, aural and verbal cues: costume, face-paint, wax prosthetics, textiles, props, music, accents, movement and gesture as well as through language. These mechanics of theatrical performance added meat to the bones of white English people's imaginings of cultures, ethnicities and religions different to their own. Representing Jews on stage would have been almost an entirely fantastical affair given that there were only a few Jews living in England at that time, including converted Jews such as the notorious Portuguese physician to Queen Elizabeth I, Dr Roderigo Lopez. Most in Shakespeare's audience would not have met an outwardly practising Jew.

Christopher Marlowe, famous for his tragic tale of pride and the occult in *Doctor Faustus*, also wrote *The Jew of Malta* (1589–90) about the Machiavellian stage villain Barabas the Jew. The play begins with him in his counting-house, invoking stereotypical associations between Jews, greed and moneylending. Like Aaron the Moor and Iago, Barabas speaks directly to the audience, sharing his ambitions and how he intends to achieve them. He seeks revenge on the Christian state for seizing the wealth of the nation's Jews but ends up on a murderous spree, taking his revenge too far; he is thus associated both with 'barbarism' and – like all Jews since the twelfth century – the devil himself. Barabas is a precursor to Shylock, though Shakespeare's Jew is more complex and sympathetically written than Marlowe's.

At one point, Barabas's slave Ithamore says to him 'Oh, brave, master! I worship your *nose* for this', leading to the speculation that Elizabethan actors relied on the age-old stereotype that Jewish people had big noses. The very first rendering of a Jew in English records dates to 1277 and seems to launch, at least graphically, this myth in England.

We might even credit Marlowe with inventing the trope for the stage Jew – and maybe actors cast as Jews on the Elizabethan stage wore some sort of prosthetic nose. It's debatable. We do know, however, that theatre companies were adept at acquiring or producing fake body parts. Elizabethan staging practices required the use of prosthetics for actors to impersonate a range of characters. So when Burbage got ready for a performance of Shylock, what did he wear? A prosthetic nose, as would have been possible? Perhaps a red beard? There was a long-established trope that Jews had red hair and beards because it was believed Judas did, and false beards were a staple of any Elizabethan theatre company's props store. Did Shakespeare's actors believe Jews were recognisably red-bearded and try to represent it on stage? In the mid-seventeenth century the actor Thomas Jordan composed a ballad that summarised *The Merchant of Venice* suggesting they might have:

> His beard was red; his face was made
> Not much unlike a witches.
> His habit was a Jewish gown,
> That would defend all weather;
> His chin turned up, his nose hung down,
> And both ends met together.[5]

Written long after the King's Men had ceased operating, the racist ballad may not actually reflect what Burbage wore but rather a Restoration actor's impression.

When Shylock reminds Antonio and the others that they have spat on his 'Jewish gaberdine', it indicates a specific costume that would have immediately signalled to an audience that the character was Jewish. But what would that have looked like? An intriguing anonymous sixteenth-century painting of the King's Fountain in the Lisbon Alfama (*Chafariz d'el-Rey*) shows Africans and Jews together, the Jews depicted with long beards, greenish cloaks, red hats and yellow circles fixed to their clothing.

Clearly in Portugal Jews wore red hats; by some accounts, in sixteenth-century Milan they wore yellow hats and badges, while in Venice, depending on their geographical origins, they are said to have worn turbans. Historically across Europe, Jews were expected to be distinguishable from the Christian population for fear that they might stealthily convert people to their religion. For instance, in 1215 at the Fourth Lateran Council, Pope

Innocent III decreed that Jews and Muslims needed to be distinguishable by their clothing, though he left it up to individual nations to decide how.

We may never know Shakespeare's reference point, the extent of his travels being undocumented. Travel and illustrated books suggested there were visual ideas about the dress and customs of

MORO DI CONDITIONE.

other nations and cultures, however. A 1590 book consisting of over four hundred woodcuts by Italian artist Cesare Vecellio depicts people from many geographical locations, providing several examples of Moors and Turks.[6]

The author Nicholas de Nicolay's *The Navigations into Turkey* (1585) provided images of 'a Merchant Jew', a 'Physician Jew' and female Jews, which also revealed that in some parts of the Renaissance world, Jews were able to practice a number of professions.

But since Jews had been expelled from England, there wouldn't have been a prescribed style of dress contemporaneous with Shakespeare's audiences. The Italian writer Orazio Busino stated in his diary on a visit to England that 'Foreigners in London are little liked, not to say hated, so those who are wise take care to dress in the English style…and make themselves understood by signs whenever they can avoid speaking, and so they avoid mishaps'.[7] Even if Busino saw little evidence of foreign dress on the streets of London, the mass entertainment venues of the time were a different matter. Signalling difference on stage was crucial and the outward markers of identity were essential to early modern English society as a whole.

Costumes were drawn from different pieces in a theatre company's inventory. The theatrical impresario Philip Henslowe, made famous by John Madden's 1999 film *Shakespeare in Love*, left behind a theatrical ledger documenting the activities of his company, The Admiral's Men; this alongside papers surviving from their star actor Edward Alleyn (the first actor to play Marlowe's Faustus and Tamburlaine the Great) list pieces of costume and props in their store. Some items speak to the presentation of foreign people and settings, such as Italian legwear and Spanish jerkins (a tight-fitting sleeveless men's jacket). But it goes beyond the continental in items like 'a Mores lymes', which may have been black leggings or long black gloves for an actor playing a Moor. Henslowe's diary shows a payment of £3 to playwrights Thomas Dekker, John Day and William Haughton in 1600 for a play called 'The Spanish Moor's Tragedy', which may have been referring to the surviving play called *Lust's Dominion* in which characters disguise themselves as Moors by putting on 'moors habits' and painting their faces with 'the oil of hell' (*Lust's Dominion*, 5.2.167–72). Concoctions for face paints comprised white lead and vinegar for whiteface – when boys played white women – and burnt walnut shells, cherry stones or burnt ivory or cork, mixed with an almond or poppy oil, for the staging of black Africans.

Although we don't have a surviving set of papers for the activities of Shakespeare's company, it is agreed that they would have operated in a similar way to the Lord Admiral's Men. Shakespeare would have wanted the Prince of Morocco to be identifiably a 'tawny' Moor, painted with black or brown makeup and dressed with costume pieces or adorned with props that best expressed his exotic difference. As for Shylock, he may simply have worn an identifying badge or a red hat. Literalism wasn't always necessary for the Elizabethan theatre audiences. A sign like a hat, a gown, a fake beard or a bit of makeup could be all that was needed to suggest an identity quite distant from their own even if it was built from fragments of myth, exaggerated illustrations or loose interpretations. But staging multiple ethnicities today is a more dangerous game.

ANTISEMITIC AUDIENCE?

A year after the reconstructed Globe Theatre opened in London, spectators booed and hissed at Shylock, played by German actor

Norbert Kentrup, presumably thinking in the new Globe Theatre audiences were expected to behave like Elizabethans and boo the 'villain', but the fact that it was considered okay to boo and hiss at a Jew in the late twentieth century is perhaps the most disturbing aspect of this reaction. To what extent is the play capable of stirring unconscious prejudices and deeply entrenched stereotypes even now? In 2010 the Swedish scholar Willmar Sauter published the findings of a study he and a colleague conducted in which they aimed to assess whether productions of *The Merchant of Venice* can reinforce or even provoke antisemitic feelings in their audiences. By asking audiences of three different productions in three different European countries (Sweden, Germany and England) to fill in a questionnaire before and after a performance, they were able to show the extent to which the performance may have influenced or changed their perceptions:

> The results were shocking. One out of four spectators believed that the statement "The reason for anti-Semitism is the behaviour of the Jews in history" was more correct after the performance than they had thought before. Moreover, 4% changed their opinion completely: before the performance they thought it was not correct, but after the performance they confirmed the same statement as being correct. Especially upsetting was the fact that youngsters under the age of 20 were affected the most, while spectators over 40 years increased their already high prejudices. The prejudices were also confirmed by other questions: Was Shylock portrayed as a "typical" Jew? 28% agreed, 39% disagreed, which means that

two thirds of the audience thought they could decide whether or not a stage character looks or behaves like a "typical" Jew.[8]

I probably needn't mention that while almost all of Shakespeare's plays were performed during the Third Reich in Germany, the most popular one by far was *The Merchant of Venice*. Between 1933 and 1939 there were over fifty productions. Historians agree that very few changes were needed to make the text rouse antisemitic sentiment in the audiences – though exaggerated performances of Shylock's physicality and discernible characteristics helped Shakespeare's play go even further in the service of Nazi propaganda.

Yet Shylock's character has been played much more sympathetically in productions since World War II. The Globe staged an anti-racist production of the play in its indoor theatre in 2022 precisely because its Jewish director Abigail Graham was acutely aware of Sauter's study and its findings on how audiences tend to receive the play. Directors should endeavour to explore the history of the play so as to navigate carefully the tightrope of Shylock's portrayal as villain or victim. The *Evening Standard* review felt it hit the right note for the time we are living in:

> Graham's delicate and artful rethinking of the portrayal of 'The Jew' means that we're on his side from the off; I feel a deep sense of sympathy with this gentle man who is perpetually on the receiving end of bullying and abuse. Schiller's embodiment of Shylock is delectably restrained; his being hums with the tension and rage that simmers just below the surface, threatening to overspill at any moment.[9]

But while there is ambiguity and complexity in his character, unquestionably, we can't get away from the echoes of medieval antisemitism in how he expresses himself, how others talk about him and in his assertion of his bond.

After seeing a performance or reading the play, how *should* we feel? Surely, we are not charmed by the Venetians and their comedic courtships punctuated by sexist jokes about marriage and racist jokes about non-Christians. Surely a modern audience is repulsed by the behaviour and artifice of the Christians in the play – their overreliance on material acquisition over and above compassion and the enactment of mercy. The bigoted behaviour towards Shylock is unpleasant to perform and to watch. But the play is too complex to designate Shakespeare's attitude as either antisemitic or philosemitic. Shylock is too multifaceted to simply reduce *him* to an Elizabethan stereotype. Whatever Shakespeare's views, he asks the audience to confront *their* own attitudes. Why do some view Shylock as a horribly antisemitic portrayal and others view him as sympathetic, emotionally evocative, a hero even? Shakespeare often challenges us to hold two contradictory views simultaneously. Contradiction and dichotomy often underpin questions of identity in his works.

THE MYTH OF THE JEW

Set in two locations, one very real (Venice) and one fantastical (Belmont), this problem play gives us a glimpse into the fascination with global-facing cities in which different ethnicities and religious communities could mingle in the common marketplace. An endless curiosity for Shakespeare was the question of what happens to human behaviour when such diverse cultures interact.

Shakespeare hints at the ambivalence of the play's genre in the opening scene. A solitary figure, the eponymous merchant, Antonio, feels melancholic but can't explain why. Venetian buffoons Salerio and Solanio toy with him, suggesting it is love or perhaps his ships and the potential loss of the merchandise they are carrying that have him on edge. After all, in the Renaissance period, the stakes were dangerously high in venture capital trading. Ships could be attacked by pirates, or be subject to tempests that might dash them against:

> ...dangerous rocks
> Which, touching but my gentle vessel's side,
> Would scatter all her spices on the stream,
> Enrobe the roaring waters with my silks...
>
> (1.1.31–4)

But all the risk was worth tremendous gains. We never seem to get to the bottom of Antonio's sadness. However, Queer readings of the play have illuminated that the same-sex bond between Bassanio and Antonio is deeply rooted in a love suppressed by the excessive value placed on heterosexual marriage and mercantilism under the banner of Christianity.

The economic theme is amplified by the play's setting but also by Venice's most prominent immigrant, Shylock, the money lender. With Shylock's friend Tubal and daughter Jessica, Shakespeare presents a community of Jewish people who, in the historical city of Venice, would have been able to move freely around by day, but who nevertheless had to return to the ghetto by dusk. (This was the world's first walled area designed to segregate Jews from the dominant Christian populace; there were in fact two ghettos in Venice, founded in 1516 and maintained for centuries: the Ghetto Nuovo and the Ghetto Vecchio, separated by a bridge.) There is very little emphasis on the Venetian ghetto in Shakespeare's play, which shows to some extent the lack of detail needed in representing the worlds he chose for his settings. The history of antisemitism in Europe is too long and complex to tell in one book, let alone one section of a book, but understanding some of the ideas that Shakespeare inherited about Jews will shed light on the play's creation of literature's most famous one.

The Venetian Solanio sees Shylock coming and says, 'Let me say amen betimes, lest the devil cross my prayer, for here he comes in the likeness of a Jew' (3.1.17). Aligning Jews with the devil was all too common in medieval and Renaissance Europe and one of the many dehumanising tropes seen in sermons, theological treatises, poems, stories and plays. The antisemitism of the medieval period dominated the cultural imagination well into the seventeenth century and beyond. Historians trace hostility towards the Jews to biblical narratives of Christ's sacrifice and the supposed Jewish conspiracy and hypocrisy – often singled out in the story of Judas, who betrayed Christ for pieces of silver. Over time anti-Judaic feelings sedimented into antisemitism – a deeper feeling of hate rooted in the belief that Jews are inhuman. George M. Fredrickson's history of racism contends that,

> Anti-Judaism became antisemitism whenever it turned into a consuming hatred that made getting rid of Jews seem preferable to trying to convert them, and antisemitism became racism when the belief took hold that Jews were intrinsically and organically evil rather than merely having false beliefs and wrong dispositions.[10]

By the twelfth century it was believed Jews routinely kidnapped Christian boys and murdered them as a way of re-enacting the killing of Christ. This 'ritual murder libel' led to terrifying superstition and an oppressive suspicion of England's own Jewish communities, encoding antisemitic mythology into law and leading to horrific massacres or 'pogroms' around the world.[11] The 'blood libel' myth, which maintained that Jews desired Christian blood for their own religious ceremonies, illuminates the references to blood, drams and liquid throughout Shakespeare's play. That Jews would re-enact the killing and torture of Christ underscores the play's positioning of Shylock poised with a knife over Antonio as sacrificial Christ figure: 'For if the Jew do cut but deep enough, / I'll pay it instantly, with all my heart', he says when he is close to giving up his pound of flesh to Shylock (4.1.275–6). That Jews were responsible for disease or 'poisoning the wells' (the Black Death of the thirteenth and fourteenth centuries was placed squarely on their shoulders, for example) sheds some metaphoric light on the allusions in the play to 'infection' and contagion – expressed, for example, in the clown's antisemitic anxieties about becoming a Jew if he continues to work for one.

Jews were thought to be cursed by God as a 'wandering' nation, but they resided in many European cities; after they were expelled from England in 1290 though, quite a few other countries followed suit. Conversion was seen as the alternative and those that chose not to embrace Christ as their saviour had to leave their homes and countries. Once allowed or tolerated, Jewish people were given limited opportunities to acquire wealth; the profession of usury (money-lending with interest) became an obvious option in most city-states because Christians were not permitted, by papal decree, to charge interest. For centuries it was one of the only professions or skills many Jews were allowed to

practice (in the most general terms of course) in Christian economies, which also meant many Christians were in debt to Jewish
moneylenders and banks, including nobles and merchants – a
shift in the hierarchy many Christians could not abide.

In the opening scene of the play, the gentleman, Bassanio,
approaches his melancholy friend, Antonio, for help:

> ...my chief care
> Is to come fairly off from the great debts
> Wherein my time, something too prodigal,
> Hath left me gaged...
>
> (1.1.127–9)

Bassanio needs money to woo and marry a 'lady richly left',
Portia. If he can marry her, he'll acquire her vast wealth and pay
off what he owes. Antonio's wealth is tied up at sea, however, so
they approach Venice's most famous moneylender. Shylock agrees
to the bond, enjoying the fact that Antonio is vulnerable and in
need of his help, because of their past history:

> Signor Antonio, many a time and oft
> In the Rialto you have rated me
> About my money and my usances.
> …
> You call me misbeliever, cut-throat dog,
> And spit on my Jewish gabardine,
> And all for use of that which is mine own.
>
> (1.3.101–103; 106–108)

Shakespeare clearly wants us to know that Antonio has been
hateful to Shylock in the past. Even though he needs a loan, he

does not apologise for his previous behaviour: 'I am as like to call thee so again, / To spit on thee again, to spurn thee too' (1.3.125–6). Earlier Antonio refers to him as the 'Devil', an 'evil soul', and a 'villain with a smiling cheek' when he suggests Shylock cites the Bible to justify charging interest. Other Venetians in the play also provide much of its hateful rhetoric. When Shylock's friend Tubal enters in Act 3 scene 1, Solanio remarks, 'Here comes another of the tribe. A third cannot be matched unless the devil himself turn Jew' (64–5). Throughout Shylock is called 'devil', 'wolf', 'dog' or 'cur', his heart compared to stone as a consequence of its Jewish blood.

When Shylock dares express his own dislike for Christians and their ways, it seems at first to vindicate them. Earlier in Act 1, Shylock tells Antonio that he'll do business with him but 'I will not eat with you, drink with you, nor pray with you' (1.3.30–2). Is this anti-Christian hate? Or are Shylock's sentiments perhaps more rooted in a resentment of years of oppression and racial abuse? I don't think I'd want to dine with people who think I should go back to Pakistan and only *tolerate* my presence in England.

Regardless of the problematic nature of his treatment, it may seem to some that Shylock's conditions for the loan seem disproportionate: he wants a pound of Antonio's 'fair flesh' if the terms of the bond are broken. The merchant's identity as a white Christian is emphasised in the designation of his flesh as 'fair'. Whiteness becomes a marker not just of beauty in this play but also of the promise of salvation linked inherently and explicitly with Christianity. A Tudor or Stuart audience may not have found such a story so shocking; the pound of flesh narrative was, in fact, quite familiar. Shakespeare's play was inspired by a story in a fourteenth-century Italian collection by Giovanni Fiorentino called *Il Pecorone*,[12] which tells the tale of a stubborn Jewish moneylender who refuses to release a merchant from his bond, demanding his pound of flesh.

TROPHY WOMEN

The sub-plot of Shakespeare's play revives yet another familiar narrative: a medieval tale of three caskets is told in a thirteenth-century collection known as the *Gesta Romanorum* (or *Deeds of the Romans*). In Shakespeare's Belmont, Portia and her attendant, Nerissa, entertain a series of suitors who must participate in a 'casket' test devised by Portia's late father, a sequence that some modern productions have staged like a game show. If a suitor guesses correctly which casket contains her portrait, the lucky man wins her hand in marriage plus all of her father's opulent estate and wealth. It's a pretty good deal. Perhaps it seems at first that this sub-plot has nothing to do with the 'pound of flesh' story, but actually Portia, like all high-status marriageable ladies, is a commodity to be traded between her father and husband, another 'pound of flesh' to be won or lost.

Portia seems at first like Shakespeare's other comedic heroines in that she epitomises the Elizabethan values attached to white womanhood: virtuous, beautiful and upper-class. Across the works we see the 'fair' ideal beauties pitted against darker-haired or darker-complexioned ladies: Helena and Hermia in *A Midsummer Night's Dream*; Octavia and Cleopatra in *Antony and Cleopatra*; Rosalind and Phoebe in *As You Like It*; the fair-faced young lad and the dark lady of the *Sonnets*. In this play, there is more of an opposition between the fair Portia and Shylock's daughter, Jessica, who with her Jewish heritage presents as the metaphorically 'darker' lady in the play. Bassanio tells Antonio about Portia, introducing her as:

> ...a lady richly left,
> And she is fair, and, fairer than that word,
> Of wondrous virtues.
>
> (1.1.161–63)

Apart from wealthy, she is not just 'fair', but 'fairer' even 'than that word...' Her 'sunny locks / Hang on her temples like a golden fleece' (169–70). The ancient Greek myth of Jason and the Argonauts, who went on a quest for the fleece of a ram with golden wool, is Shakespeare's reference point for the high stakes casket test. In the context of Shakespeare's Venice, the emphasis on Portia's whiteness is tied to her privilege, evident in this reference. A paragon of Renaissance beauty, Portia resembles Desdemona or Octavia in her value as a prize to be won, monetarily as well as in terms of power and status. The one who acquires this 'golden fleece' is the one who'll end up with everything a capitalist economy promises. Connections Shakespeare makes between wealth, female virtue, power and whiteness in *The Merchant of Venice* are unmistakable and not accidental.

The first suitor to try his hand at the casket test is the Prince of Morocco, Shakespeare's second portrayal of an African after *Titus*'s Aaron. Some productions portray him as an Arab, which is understandable when you see the stage direction announcing his arrival: *Enter* MOROCCO, *a tawny Moor all in white, and three or four followers accordingly* (2.1). Sometimes 'tawny' referred to brown, but in other contexts it referred to blackness. So he can be staged as either. Aware of his difference in the presence of the 'fairest creature', as he calls her, the Prince draws attention to his skin colour, paradoxically seeming to apologise for it, while showing pride in its appeal and power:

> Mislike me not for my complexion,
> The shadowed livery of the burnished sun,
> To whom I am a neighbour and near bred.
>
> (2.1.1–3)

He goes on,

> I tell thee, lady, this aspect of mine
> Hath feared the valiant. By my love I swear,
> The best regarded virgins of our clime
> Have loved it too. I would not change this hue
> Except to steal your thoughts, my gentle queen.
>
> (8–12)

Shakespeare alludes once again to the ancient theory that climate was a determining factor of racial difference, Morocco's skin being the 'livery' painted by the heat of the sun. His 'aspect' or complexion has frightened the bravest of his enemies, he says, but has also attracted the ladies of his own country. Like Aaron, the Prince values his skin colour, a powerful statement Shakespeare makes in more than one play. Indeed, Morocco is far more complex and interesting than most theatre productions give him credit for. Interpretations of him on stage and screen range from simplistic to stereotypical to painfully racist.

After some deliberating, the Prince guesses that the golden casket contains Portia's picture, as the riddle reads 'Who chooseth me shall gain what many men desire' – for him that is Portia herself, the 'mortal breathing saint' (2.7.40). Alas, he is wrong. The golden casket contains not Portia's portrait but a 'death's head' with a poem beginning with the line 'All that glisters is not gold' (65). As he departs, Portia remarks 'A gentle riddance… / Let all of his complexion choose me so' (2.7.78–9), exposing the anti-black racism at the core of elite society. The tolerance and multi-ethnic comingling of Venetian society doesn't extend to Belmont, I guess. As a result of choosing the wrong casket Morocco not only leaves empty handed, but he also has to forfeit his right *ever* to marry so he can never legitimately reproduce. The Prince of Morocco's 'aspect', 'hue' or 'complexion', his race, is wiped out of the future, while Portia relishes having dodged the bullet of an enforced interracial marriage.

In comes the second suitor, the Prince of Aragon of Spain, who chooses the silver casket incorrectly, so that he too must leave empty-handed. His portrayal would have allowed Shakespeare's audiences to have a raucous laugh at the expense of the great Elizabethan nemesis: Spain. The Iberian nation held an ambivalent position for the Elizabethans; fuelled by Hispanophobia and intermittent wars, including the infamous Armada in 1588, there was widespread hostility towards the Spanish at the same time as a distant admiration for their capacity for imperialism, something Elizabethans aspired to themselves.

The Spanish were imperial giants, who, along with Portugal, were successful slave traders and plantation owners in South America and the Caribbean. The way to deal with the growing sense of Spain's power was through literary propaganda – to mock and stereotype their people, which occurred regularly in religious literature, ballads, political treatises, poems, and of course, plays. The Prince of Aragon exemplifies this tradition but

Shakespeare takes it to a much more interesting level. Aragon calls to mind King Philip II of Spain who was originally married to Elizabeth's Catholic sister, Mary. Once widowed, Philip tried unsuccessfully to court the Protestant Queen when she ascended to the throne in 1558. Aragon bumbling around the caskets thick-accented and failing to win the hand of the virgin saint would have been a poignant joke for the time, and a veiled gesture to Elizabeth I's precarious status as the fair Virgin Queen.

Both of Portia's foreign suitors were written with a sardonic quill, so it is almost impossible to stage these roles today without making eyes roll. The cues in the stage directions and in their speeches don't help. The prince swears by his 'scimitar' and invokes popular Islamic tropes. It is painful to watch on the modern stage, as 'orientalist' interpretations tend to dominate.

A consequence of the portrayal of Portia's first two suitors is that the audience feels compelled to root for one of the least likeable comedic heroes in all of Shakespeare: the Venetian, Bassanio, who 'miraculously' chooses the lead casket – but let's not forget he was aided by Portia herself, who slyly requests a song to be sung while he is deliberating:

> Tell me where is fancy bred,
> Or in the heart, or in the head?
> How begot, how nourishèd?

$$(3.2.63–5)$$

Not so miraculous after all then. Rhyming the last word of each line subtly guides Bassanio's hand towards the lead casket. Once he chooses it, he finds Portia's portrait within. Such a triumph allows Portia to step fully into the role of guardian of the white patriarchy since the wealth of her father will now safely pass to a

Christian, Venetian gentleman, rather than to her. Sociologist Sarah J. Brazaitis's analysis of this white female guardianship of the status quo illuminates Portia's attitude and her eventual treatment of Shylock in the trial scene in Act 4:

> the pressure to preserve the existing power structure is exceedingly strong... Interrupting the status quo often feels nearly impossible, and costs much, particularly for those in power. White women who reject gender subjugation and denounce White privilege risk losing access to White male power, in addition to White male attention and affection.[13]

Portia's attachment to white privilege and the power afforded to white men on her social level defines the lengths she will go to in the service of keeping things as they are.

She may not win our sympathies when we notice how she registers her hidden biases. So who do we root for, if not for her or Bassanio or even Antonio? Shakespeare hasn't given us a lot to work with in the Christian Venetian community here. Shylock's daughter, Jessica, is Shakespeare's only representation of a Jewish woman. She says very little in the play, but we know that she wants to leave her father's house, which feels oppressive to her, as does their condemned religion. Her desire for belonging is symptomatic of being a minority in a white Christian society, but is also tied to the desire she feels for the Christian Lorenzo.

Shakespeare's fascination with interracial relationships emerges again here, though this time the promise of conversion aims to erase their difference. Together they plot for her to escape disguised as a boy, but only after stealing her father's jewels and money. While she is the darker lady in the play because she is Jewish, she is spoken of by the Venetians as 'fair' and 'sweet', which increasingly aligns her with white Christian womanhood. At one point, when Solanio is talking to Shylock he draws deep distinctions between him and his daughter using anti-black language: 'There is more difference between thy flesh and hers than between jet and ivory' (3.1.32–4). This is not the first time one of Shakespeare's ladies changes colours meta-phorically through the course of a play. Most memorably Desdemona's face was said to be 'begrimed' and 'black' by her supposed adultery. But Jessica never quite crosses the colour line. Shylock's reaction to her leaving seems startling. We are told by Solanio that Shylock was witnessed having an emotional breakdown:

> I never heard a passion so confused,
> So strange, outrageous, and so variable
> As the dog Jew did utter in the streets.
> "My daughter! O my ducats! O my daughter!
>
> (2.8.12–15)

Shylock's outcries confirm for the Christians his greed, that he shouts about his ducats with the same passion he shouts about his daughter. If this eye-witness testimony is true, of course… The reason Shakespeare places it within a report is so that we will doubt its veracity, perhaps suggesting all the so-called 'eye witness' accounts of Jewish practices and behaviour, which amount to centuries of hearsay, can be called into question as well.

It is unclear where early audiences' sympathies might have fallen regarding Jessica. Was it a relief or even funny to witness a Jew betrayed by his own flesh and blood or would Elizabethans have harshly judged a disobedient daughter? Given the way sympathies tended towards Juliet, Shakespeare's other disobedient daughter, through the centuries – 'For never was a story of more woe / Than this of Juliet and her Romeo' (5.3.309–10); or towards Desdemona where we have an audience account from a 1610 performance in Oxford that refers to the pity she raised – my hunch is Jessica might have been seen to be making the right decision to convert and marry a Christian. Despite the play's seeming celebration of Jessica's conversion, Lancelot Gobbo, Shylock's servant, throws doubt over the move when he raises a popular racist myth of the sixteenth century: whether converting to Christianity really could purify Jewish blood. He invokes the antisemitic myth that the sins of Jewish ancestors (the crucifixion of Christ and Judas's betrayal) cursed their entire people:

> the sins of the father are to be laid upon the children, therefore I promise you, I fear [for] you.
>
> (3.5.1–3)

Lancelot worries that her conversion will make no difference to her soul. All Jews are cursed by the act of deicide that Christian doctrine asserts they committed. It might be better to hope her mother was unfaithful, a 'bastard hope'. By this logic, she is damned no matter what. If her mother is a whore she is metaphorically blackened by her sin; if her father is Shylock, she is tainted by his faith. In saying so, Launcelot dissociates her from pure whiteness. While he is fond of Jessica, he embodies the inherited antisemitic beliefs of his country; he is a conspiracy theorist, like a modern-day Q-Anon sympathiser who trades in racial absurdities which lead to divisive hate. Upon his first appearance in the play, Launcelot is deciding whether or not to leave his 'Master' Shylock and join the Venetian Bassanio's household to serve him instead:

> To be ruled by my conscience I should stay with the Jew
> my master who, God bless the mark, is a kind of devil;
> and to run away from the Jew I should be ruled by the
> fiend who, saving your reverence, is the devil himself.
> Certainly the Jew is the very devil incarnation...
>
> (2.2.18–22)

Such a view reveals the close relationship between anti-black racism and antisemitism in the play's language and in the broader cultural imagination. We learn in the later scene with Jessica and Lorenzo that Launcelot has callously impregnated a black woman and the jokes that ensue allow Shakespeare to pun with energy. Lorenzo reminds him he has enlarged a 'negro's belly: the Moor is with child by you, Lancelot!' In response, Lancelot quips, 'It is much that the Moor should be more than reason, but if she be less than an honest woman, she is indeed more than I took her for' (3.5.34–6). Allusions to his interracial sexual encounter draw our attention to the multi-ethnic character of Renaissance Venice, but also to the binary of womanhood that is commonly linked to colour in Shakespeare. If Portia is the virtuous white woman, the unnamed, unseen African woman is the opposite, with Jessica lost in the middle.

Characters like Lancelot Gobbo or Iago in *Othello* trade in the vocabulary of extremism linked to a deeper narrative of superiority in European institutions such as religion, law and government. This play was written against a mired history in which Jews were condemned, vilified, periodically massacred, forced to wear markings that distinguished them from

Christians, made to live separately and their way of making a living heavily regulated. Indeed, when Shakespeare was writing the play, Jews had long been expelled from England altogether, while Elizabeth I was issuing warrants, the first one in 1596, the year Shakespeare's play was written, expelling a group of Moors from her shores, albeit unsuccessfully.[14] As Europe identified that to be European meant being Christian and white, many of those who didn't fit the mould, regardless of the levels of tolerance, could be subject to abuse, prejudice, persecution, isolation, expulsion or all of the above.

JUSTICE OR MERCY

Attempting to justify his insistence on the bond, Shylock speaks the most famous lines in the play, a speech that has made scholars and actors celebrate Shakespeare's extraordinary expression of equality and shared humanity:

> He hath disgraced me, and hindered me half a million; laughed at my losses, mocked at my gains, scorned my nation, thwarted my bargains, cooled my friends, heated mine enemies, and what's his reason? I am a Jew. Hath not a Jew eyes? Hath not a Jew hands, organs, dimensions, senses, affections, passions; fed with the same food, hurt with the same weapons, subject to the same diseases, healed by the same means, warmed and cooled by the same winter and summer as a Christian is? If you prick us do we not bleed? If you tickle us do we not laugh? If you poison us do we not die? And if you wrong us shall we not revenge?
>
> (3.1.46–53)

Remarkably, Shylock suggests there is no biological difference between races or religions – long before the idea of racial genetics was invented in the eighteenth century. And his insistence upon his humanity encapsulates Shakespeare's brief flirtation with a utopian ideal yet to be realised: *valuing difference* can lead us to what it truly means to be equal. But the speech is problematic too. He uses these promising equivalences to justify revenge. But revenge was not and is still not a Christian teaching.

To help Bassanio, Portia uses her influence and wealth to disguise herself as a lawyer and infiltrate the male space of the trial. For many, she is a feminist hero able to outwit Shylock using a simple legal loophole. Entering the courtroom she asks, 'Which is the merchant here, and which the Jew?' Does she ask this to show the objectivity of Justice, that they are both the same in the eyes of the law? How many of us believe that they could be? Perhaps this tells us that Richard Burbage didn't dress that differently to play Shylock. Perhaps it is simply to identify the plaintiff and the defendant. In my view, it signals the pretence that the legal system is objective; like Portia's disguise and her own awareness of who is who, the promise of objectiveness is merely an illusion.

Portia gives Shylock several opportunities to drop his case against Antonio, particularly as he can be paid even more than he is owed. Throughout the trial scene we hear the hateful interjections of Bassanio's friend Gratiano – 'inexecrable dog' (4.1.128); 'currish spirit'; 'currish Jew' (287); the Duke's apology to Antonio at the top of the trial scene – 'I am sorry for thee. Thou art come to answer / A stony adversary, an inhuman wretch' (4.1.3–6); and Antonio's suggestion that trying to reason with a 'wolf' is pointless, showing how the rhetoric of the court is biased towards Shylock's demise. But he remains resolved, seeing the law on his side. And, in the strictest terms, it is. Or so we think. Both Portia and the Duke, who represents the state, ask Shylock to show mercy, a very Christian value, contrasted with Shylock's attachment to justice and revenge. Portia's speech has been upheld as one of the most profound expressions of our capacity to forgive:

> The quality of mercy is not strained.
> It droppeth as the gentle rain from heaven
> Upon the place beneath. It is twice blest:
> It blesseth him that gives, and him that takes.
> 'Tis mightiest in the mightiest. It becomes
> The thronèd monarch better than his crown.
> His sceptre shows the force of temporal power,
> The attribute to awe and majesty,
> Wherein doth sit the dread and fear of kings;
> But mercy is above the sceptred sway.
> It is enthronèd in the hearts of kings;
> It is an attribute to God himself,
> And earthly power doth then show likest God's
> When mercy seasons justice...
>
> (4.1.179–92)

'When mercy seasons justice' we are most godlike. But which god? Portia rightly points out the relationship of power to mercy, but what if you're the one *without* power? What can mercy achieve then? Portia is playing a subtle game. Shylock never had the power to show mercy. He is delivered the cold reminder that he may be allowed to practice his religion and his trade, but only for as long as the Venetian state lets him.

When Shylock refuses to relent, Portia has a final trick up her sleeve. The bond says nothing about Antonio's blood. If the blood of a Christian is spilled by an outsider, then the consequences will be grave. Shylock urgently relents. But it is too late. The legal system, seeming to have been on his side, is rigged against him, against all 'aliens' in fact. After lecturing him about the quality of mercy, Portia shows none herself, devising a harsh punishment, with approval from the state. Shylock must give up his wealth – half going to Antonio and half absorbed by the city – reminding us of the precarity of his 'alien' status in spite of the so-called tolerance of the law. Worse still than losing his wealth, he must convert to Christianity. Shylock fades from the play with a multitude of losses and humiliations to bear: his community, his child, his faith, his trade, his wealth – all are gone. Would Shakespeare's audiences have cheered? Maybe. Most of the time, the end of the court scene elicits sympathy from a modern audience. But as research has shown, even now the antisemitic language of the play taps into an ingrained trepidation of Jews that endures. Pinpointing Shakespeare's exact feelings about Jews would be impossible. Instead, we are asked to look inwards. What will we find there?

When the Globe was inviting actors to audition for its production in 2021, the casting team sent the script to an actor, whose agent promptly came back saying the actor refused the role because they did not wish to say the hateful things the text required. Prominent scholars have even argued that it should no longer be staged because of the potential harm it can do or the subtle influence of its antisemitic tropes and anti-black racism upon audiences. If Shakespeare is going to be ossified in his position as the Great White Bard, if his moral superiority and special kind of genius continue to be asserted, then I can see why more progressive thinkers might want this play to disappear. But perhaps we shouldn't avoid it altogether.

To stop performing, teaching or talking about it would be the same as hiding away from the past. When staging it now, we have opportunities to find brave ways of unpacking the difficulty the play so definitively and unashamedly contains. Ugliness is as much a compelling, attractive and fascinating spectacle as is beauty and a deeper awareness of its presence, of its depth and of its complexity provides directors, actors – and audiences – with an opportunity to see more keenly the subtleties – the interleaving golden threads – of a play too easily dismissed as simply 'a problem'. Dispensing with the play entirely would produce more harm than good in the long run. It would mean pretending anti-semitism only emerged in the twentieth century, which might be comforting for those who look at premodern history through golden-age-tinted glasses. But it would be a lie.

Six

SHAKESPEARE'S WHITE SETTLER

[A] dreadful storm...began to blow from out the North-east, which swelling and roaring as it were by fits, some hours with more violence than others, at length did beat all light from heaven, which like an hell of darkness turned black upon us, so much the more full of horror... [N]ot only more terrible, but more constant, fury added to fury, and one storm urging a second more outrageous than the former...the Sea swelled above the Clouds, and gave battle unto Heaven. It could not be said to rain, the waters like whole Rivers did flood in the air. And this I did still observe, that whereas upon the Land, when a storm hath powered itself forth once in drifts of rain, the wind as beaten down and vanquished therewith, not long after endureth: here the glut of water...was no sooner a little emptied and qualified, but instantly the winds spoke more loudly, and grew more tumultuous, and malignant. What shall I say? Winds and Seas were as mad as fury and rage could make them; for mine own part, I had been in some storms before, as well upon the coast of Barbary and Algiers, in the Levant, and...in the Adriatic Gulf... It pleased God [on this occasion] to bring a greater affliction upon us...

William Strachey, 1610[1]

Sea Venture, a ship owned and operated by the Virginia Company of London – established by King James in 1606 with the purpose of colonising the east coast of North America and which founded the Jamestown Colony a year later – was on its way to the English colony in America in July of 1609 but found itself caught in a 'dreadful Tempest', finally wrecking off the cost of Bermuda. A member of the company and friend to poet Ben Jonson, William Strachey was on board – the description above comes from his letter to a 'noble Lady'. After describing the terrifying storm that ravaged the ship as well as the hearts and minds of those aboard, Strachey reveals that there was no hope to save the vessel so they ran 'her ashore'. With the aid of 'God's mercy', they spied an island: 'we found it to be the dangerous and dreaded island, or rather Islands of the Bermuda...because they are so terrible to all that ever touched on them...such tempests, thunders, and other fearful objects are seen and heard about them that they be called commonly, The Devils Islands, and are feared and avoided of all sea travellers alive'.[2] We learn all the passengers survived and lived on the island for ten months as new ships were being built that would eventually transport them to Virginia.

It is possible that Shakespeare came across the manuscript of Strachey's narrative, which was in circulation from 1610. But even if he didn't, there were other accounts of the event, such as the voyager Silvester Jourdain's *A Discovery of the Bermudas, Otherwise Called the Ile of Devils* (1610). The story of *Sea Venture* was in the ears of all at court. Shakespeare's theatrical troupe, the

King's Men, were acquainted with various members of the Virginia Company; the actors – sometimes called 'His Majesty's servants' – visited the court of the royal household seasonally at Greenwich, Hampton Court and Whitehall to put on plays and entertainments, and there they would have been privy to the latest maritime gossip.

Stories of brave seafarers, accounts of coastlines explored, territories discovered and the habits, appearances and customs of the people encountered were inestimably popular at the time Shakespeare was writing his plays. Not only that, but the popularity of travel books throughout the sixteenth and seventeenth centuries cannot be underestimated. Highly influential was the work of geographer and scholar Richard Hakluyt, who collated numerous accounts of voyages and edited them together in *The Principall Navigations, Voyages and Discoveries of the English Nation* (1589 and re-printed in several editions). Hakluyt's travel tome may even have sparked a greater impetus for colonial travel and trade, as his work sought ambitiously to promote and advocate for England's position as 'stirrers abroad, and searchers of the remote parts of the world', while 'compassing the vast globe of the earth'.[3] No doubt audiences hankered after dramatic tales of worlds unknown, and *The Tempest*, Shakespeare's last solo-authored piece, charts the experiential journey of sea travellers and their extraordinary, fantastical adventures of exile, shipwreck and eerie magic. Remarkably, the play articulates the perspective of indigenous people as well as that of the European castaways.

Beginning the play with a ship caught in a raging tempest was a stroke of entertainment genius on the part of our playwright. He was well known for his spectacular storms, which he would master in the Globe Theatre where audiences felt the blasts of thunder resonating through their bodies; pyrotechnics would dazzle and enthral spectators, who witnessed lightning in the Heavens or stage roof during performances of *Julius Caesar*, *Macbeth* and *King Lear*. The first recorded performance of *The Tempest* was November 1611 at Whitehall Palace, performed for King James I and his court. It was such a hit, it returned to court the following season 1612–13 as part of the entertainments celebrating the Princess Elizabeth's impending marriage to the Elector Palatine. The effects of the storm played at court would have been exhilarating and the themes of colonial expedition, magic, masque and marriage would have pleased the Jacobean nobles present.

It would have also found a home at the Blackfriars playhouse, Shakespeare's theatre north of the Thames. Smaller and a bit more intimate than the Globe, the Blackfriars was the company's candlelit, indoor playhouse and required a different aesthetic from the open-air, thatched Globe. While the plays in the repertory of the King's Men moved between playhouses and adjustments to acoustic, visual and even olfactory effects were made to suit the venue and the different social demographics of the audience, the plays, as they have come down to us, provide some evidence of their original performance. Storms were spectacular and visually affecting in the Globe. The use of a cannonball rolled upon the wooden floor of the Globe's attic or drummers making 'thunder in the Tiring-house', as seventeenth-century astrologer John Melton reveals, would have generated startling noise for an audience who had yet to encounter the internal combustion engine. Melton tells us too that 'the twelve-penny Hirelings make artificial Lightning in their Heavens'.[4] Firework effects packed with gunpowder helped create the flash and spark of lightning.

Shakespeare's audiences found such spectacle breath-taking, if not terrifying, experiencing it as nothing short of magic. But indoor theatres called for something subtler, less fiery, less smelly. So stage hands used aural techniques to create the meteorological events that were crucial to the dramatic story in plays like *The Tempest*. In addition to the drum of thunder, the sound of wind might be created by voices or instruments; the shouts of the boatswain and passengers would be fuelled with urgency and terror. The language of the play fills in the gaps where real fireworks might be too risky: the storm's 'fire and cracks' and 'sulphurous roaring' (1.2.203–4) leave 'flamed amazement' (1.2.198) upon the passengers. Combined with the visual capaciousness of Shakespeare's language, then, the theatre's use of illusion and aural special effects rendered the playwright and his company veritable magicians. Perhaps then it is not odd that Shakespeare's Prospero uses 'rough magic' to conjure the storm that opens the play:

> *A tempestuous noise of thunder and lightning heard; enter a* Shipmaster *and a* Boatswain.
> MASTER   Boatswain!
> BOATSWAIN   Here master. What cheer?
> MASTER   Good, speak to th' mariners. Fall
>   to't yarely or we run ourselves
>   aground. Bestir, bestir!
>
> (1.1.1–4)

Cosmic events showcased God's power. In God's fury, his subjects could be terrorised by earthquakes, meteors and *tempests*, defined by English lexicographer Randle Cotgrave in 1611 as 'storms', all 'bluster' and 'boisterous' natural events. They were portents of things to come, the weather read as a sign of divine judgment and authority. As sixteenth-century chronicler of London John Stow tells us in November of 1574, 'stormy and tempestuous winds' were 'received as tokens of God's wrath ready bent against the world for sin now abounding, and also of his great mercy, who doth but only show the rod wherewith we daily deserve to be beaten'.[5]

Some of the most bewitching and engrossing accounts of tempests at sea are found in the great sweep of travel literature that emerged in Europe between the fifteenth and seventeenth centuries, from the descriptions of the many storms suffered at sea by Columbus on his trading and settler expeditions to the vivid tale recounted by Strachey that opened this chapter. Storms and shipwrecks often accompanied the so-called 'discoveries' of remote territories. These same travel accounts tell of and illustrate vividly the encounters with indigenous people described as either welcoming and kind, or savage and murderous, with equal fervour and fantasy.

It is hardly surprising that since the decolonisation efforts of the mid-twentieth century, *The Tempest* is often viewed through a post-colonial lens, meaning that it is read historically within the context of European colonisation. That its chief character is a conjuror as well as a European settler (albeit temporarily) allows Shakespeare's play to mark England's increasing preoccupation with the world beyond its borders and its own colonial aspirations to dramatic effect. With its provocative exploration of European ideas of civility and barbarity through dramatic spectacle, the play stages the dangerous and opportunistic foray into 'brave new worlds', while interrogating the violent expression of white European expansionism.

'A PRINCE OF POWER'

What did it mean to 'prosper' in the sixteenth century? The word was linked to thriving but not purely in terms of material wealth;

it connoted luck, good fortune, felicity; it suggested happiness 'entire and unspotted', according to the linguist Thomas Thomas in 1587. Enshrined in the notion of prospering was also the idea of 'going forth' or proceeding. It meant making something better, improving it, 'waxing strong', blossoming, even. It was linked to power in that it meant having the 'world at will';[6] Shakespeare uses some form of the word 'prosper' over sixty times in his canon with these various meanings in mind. And then there's Prospero himself whose very name portends his success. The name of Shakespeare's magus matters, even in implying that the opening storm was not an accident of nature, but rather a timely conjuration.

The storm at sea threatens the lives of the passengers on a ship as they return from celebrating the wedding of the daughter of Alonso, the King of Naples to the African King of Tunisia. Once again, Shakespeare draws our attention to interracial marriage. Alonso's daughter Claribel is married off to the African King, a union that gestures to the vital importance of global alliances at this time. In such instances, racial suspicion is trumped by the necessities of trade relations, as dodgy nobleman Sebastian reminds his brother, the King, in Act 2, chiding him for lamenting the loss of his son at sea:

> Sir, you may thank yourself for this great loss,
> That would not bless our Europe with your daughter
> But rather loose her to an African...
>
> (2.1.124–6)

Sebastian crudely suggests that Alonso has prostituted his daughter to an African for the benefit of easy trade and that had it not been for that wedding, there'd have been no shipwreck

William Shakespeare. The Chandos portrait is very likely the only portrait painted in the playwright's lifetime, possibly by John Taylor. It hangs in the National Portrait Gallery, being the first portrait acquired when the Gallery was founded in 1856.

The memorial bust of Shakespeare in Holy Trinity Church, Stratford-upon-Avon. Already a controversial likeness, the bust was painted entirely white in the late eighteenth century and then repainted in the nineteenth century, many believing it did not do the elegance and mastery of William Shakespeare's legacy any justice.

Above: The 'Heavens' or the canopy roof above the reconstructed Globe stage.

Left: Douglas Hodge as Titus in the 2006 Globe Theatre production of *Titus Andronicus*. Titus enters in a Roman *triumphus* accompanied by his prisoners, the Goths and Aaron the Moor (not pictured).

The Moroccan Ambassador, Abd el-Ouahed ben Messaoud ben Mohammed Anoun, visited London and the court of Elizbeth I in 1600 as part of a royal delegation to create an alliance with the English crown. He may have been an inspiration for Shakespeare's creation of Othello.

Renaissance depictions of Cleopatra not only eroticised the Egyptian queen's death, but also tended to dismiss her racial heritage. In many paintings she is depicted as white, even if there are poems and plays (including Shakespeare's) that indicate either implicitly or explicitly that she was 'tawny' or black.

Mark Rylance's critically acclaimed portrayal of Cleopatra took place at the Globe Theatre in 1999. As part of the 'Original Practices' style of performance, all-male casting was preferred. Rylance did not perform Cleopatra's racial heritage, nor could he without donning black or brownface.

Joaquina Kalukango as Cleopatra (it is still a rare sight to see a black actress play the part of Shakespeare's Egyptian queen) and Jonathan Cake as Antony in a production that consciously cast with race in mind.

Above and left (detail): Anonymous painting of the King's Fountain (*Chafariz d'El-Rei*) in Lisbon shows Africans and Jews together and illustrates the kinds of identity-distinguishing accessories and garments minoritised communities were forced to wear. The Jewish figures are seen wearing red hats or turbans and yellow badges affixed to their sleeves.

Above: Carpaccio's *Miracle of the Relic of the True Cross at the Rialto Bridge* showcases the extraordinary reality of Venice's multicultural populace. In the centre of the frame, a Black gondolier can be seen rowing a passenger across the canal.

Right: Titian's painting of Laura dei Dianti, the wife of the Duke of Ferrara, shows an African child with her, holding a pair of gloves symbolising the status and wealth of the Duchess. The child wears a jewel in his ear, which echoes Shakespeare's imagery when Romeo describes Juliet as a 'rich jewel in an Ethiop's ear' (1.5.45).

Joe Dixon as Caliban in the Royal Shakespeare Company production of
The Tempest, 2016. His costume draws on the depiction of Caliban as
monstrous and 'savage'.

Kenny Leon's production of *Much Ado About Nothing* in the Delacorte Theater in Central Park staged in 2019 boasted an all-Black cast. He set the play in an affluent African American city in Georgia in 2020 and excised the anti-black humour from the play to 'place Black excellence front and centre'.

Adjoa Andoh on the poster used to promote her groundbreaking all–women of colour production of *Richard II* in the Globe's indoor theatre, the Sam Wanamaker Playhouse, in 2019. The deliberate placement of the St George's Cross behind Andoh was her way of claiming the flag, the country and its 'national' playwright.

and further loss. He continues, suggesting that this political marriage is detestable not just to the country but to the 'fair soul herself', the Princess Claribel, now Queen of Tunisia, who is 'Weighed between loathness and obedience' (130–1), implying she is balanced between her repulsion at being married to a black man and her filial duty to the King of Naples as well as her new husband. Sebastian, we learn is not to be trusted, since he convinces Antonio later in the play to help him plot against King Alonso and usurp his place, a plan foiled by Prospero's spirit-spy.

The story begins with the premise of interracial marriage between Claribel and the King of Tunisia, but we come to learn that Prospero has very different plans for *his* daughter. He and the now fifteen-year-old Miranda watch the storm from afar, our sensory immersion in it now perspectival, refracted through their gaze. Miranda's response to the suffering of the passengers at sea echoes two of Shakespeare's other late plays or 'romances' that involve shipwrecks and lost souls washed up on an unfamiliar shore. In *Pericles* (1609), the eponymous character's experience of migration and shipwreck finds him beached in Pentapolis. A fisherman laments the struggle at sea he has just seen: 'Alas, poor souls, it grieved my heart to hear what pitiful cries they made to us to help them…' (2.1.18). In *The Winter's Tale* (1611), a young shepherd also witnesses a shipwreck: 'O, the most piteous cry of the poor souls!' (3.3.90).

Compassion, Shakespeare seems to say, is the *only* appropriate response to maritime tragedy. The twentieth-century Caribbean novelist and essayist George Lamming considers a 'most appropriate parallel in contemporary history is the unforgettable transport of slaves from Africa to the Caribbean… On ship[s] the slaves were packed in the hold on galleries one above the other… [W]hen the cargo was rebellious or the weather bad, then they stayed below for weeks at a time'.[7] What would Shakespeare's call for compassion provoke us to make of the 'piteous cries of the poor souls' there? In Act 1, Miranda's response to the shipwreck follows suit, her empathy compounded by her utter powerlessness:

> If by your art, my dearest father, you have
> Put the wild waters in this roar, allay them.
> The sky, it seems, would pour down stinking pitch
> But that the sea, mounting to th'welkin's cheek,
> Dashes the fire out. O, I have suffered
> With those that I saw suffer – a brave vessel
> (Who had no doubt some noble creature in her)
> Dashed all to pieces. O, the cry did knock
> Against my very heart! Poor souls, they perished.
> Had I been any god of power, I would
> Have sunk the sea within the earth or ere
> It should the good ship so have swallowed and
> The fraughting souls within her.
>
> (1.2.1–13)

She feels acutely her own lack of capacity to help, while showing an awareness that her father can inflict as well as *end* suffering. 'Be collected,' he admonishes her. 'Tell your piteous heart / There's no harm done' (14,15–16).

Prospero proceeds to reveal to Miranda her origin story, explaining how, twelve years ago, he was a 'prince of power' but Antonio, his brother, also on the ship, betrayed him and stole his dukedom. Assisted by Alonso, Antonio sent Prospero and Miranda out to sea where they were finally shipwrecked upon the island he now commands. 'What foul play had we that we came from thence?' (60) Miranda asks, shocked at the revelation of betrayal and upon learning she is the daughter of a prince. 'By foul play, as thou sayst, were we heaved thence' (62), Prospero replies. The corruption that led to their exile is deemed 'foul', the opposite of 'fair' in Shakespeare's canon. 'Foul' denoted pollution, blackness and diabolism – this is not to suggest that Prospero means that black Africans were responsible for their loss, but he uses language that racialises political corruption because of the meanings the word 'foul' held in the period.

The play's image patterns corroborate Prospero's sense of good versus bad in this story. No further questions need be asked. Miranda is the repository of her father's narrative of their history and she represents us, the audience. As listeners to this one-sided exposition we end up believing the storyteller. He asserts his moral worth by deploying the language of exceptionalism coded by 'foul' and 'fair'; his Dukedom was 'fair Milan' (1.2.126), after all, full of beauty and virtue as well as justice. Additionally, when Miranda asks how they ended up on such an island, Prospero claims, 'By providence divine' (159). God brought them to this place. There's the crux. Shakespeare would have been well aware of the assertions of divine providence or Christian fate found in travel accounts documenting shipwrecks and new found territories as a means to justify their sustained presence, and the exploitation of natural resources and indigenous people.

The Duke-turned-magician has plans for all the passengers now washed ashore, including Gonzalo, an elder statesman who helped Prospero acquire his books of magic before departing Milan, and Sebastian, Alonso's scheming brother. We also meet the clowns Trinculo the court jester and Stephano the quaffing butler, there to serve as social foils to the indigenous Caliban. Last but not least in Prospero's view is the young prince Ferdinand, who in the mayhem of the tempest and shipwreck becomes separated from the other passengers and presumed lost to King Alonso. But as we learn, he is not lost, nor was it ever intended that he would be. Prospero's supernatural servant Ariel, while invisible, will lead Ferdinand to Prospero and Miranda and the two young people will fall in love. Then Prospero can proceed with his plans for revenge against his enemies. It is for these reasons he has conjured the storm to bring them onto the island. He then places a charm on Miranda so she falls asleep while he calls for Ariel, 'an airy spirit'. Ariel is the elusive conduit for Prospero's magic, the spirit who can 'fly', 'swim', 'dive into the fire' and 'ride on the curled clouds' all to perform his master's pleasure (1.2.190–1). Ariel reports that all the passengers on board are alive and scattered around the island in separate groups as instructed.

Despite his dazzling capacities and remarkable obedience, Ariel longs to be free. Prospero promises to liberate him from servitude after he has aided his plot against the European castaways, who Ariel charms, manipulates and spies upon throughout the play. Prospero's warmth towards his 'brave spirit' is tempered from time to time by terror. He reminds him that he saved him from confinement within a tree, set there by the previous matriarch of the island: 'Dost thou forget / From what a torment I did free thee?' (1.2.250–1). He triggers him by reminding him of the 'foul witch Sycorax, who with age and envy / Was grown into a hoop' (257–8), meaning the witch's old age had bent her body excessively.

But who is this 'foul witch'? What do we know about her? Why is she so terrifying? Misogyny, ageism and racism infuse

Prospero's language, reminding us of the associations made between witchcraft, race and gender in the language of the period's literature. Sycorax's 'black' magic is deliberately contrasted with Prospero's more learned occultic art, referred to in the Renaissance as 'white magic'. Sycorax is from Algiers, a city in North Africa; she is a 'damned witch' (263), full of 'mischiefs manifold' and 'sorceries terrible' (264), too terrible, in fact, for 'human hearing' (265); the 'blue-eyed hag' (269), with 'earthy and abhorred commands' (273) imprisoned Ariel but died before releasing him, leaving behind her only heir, '(A freckled whelp, hag-born) not honoured with / A human shape' (283–4). When Prospero awakens Miranda from the charm, he summons Caliban, this so-called 'hag-born' son of Sycorax.

The complex trio of Ariel, Caliban and Prospero has intrigued and perplexed people for centuries. Countless interpretations abound. Predominantly, Prospero is viewed as a sort of lord of a feudal manor or a coloniser, Ariel the preferred servant and Caliban the enslaved subject. There have been psychological readings too proposing Ariel and Caliban are not real, but rather manifestations of Prospero's psyche, or that all three are simply iterations of psychologist Carl Jung's id, ego and superego. But such readings tend to centralise the experience of the white European male settler and his counterpart reader, neutralising, if not normalising, Prospero's behaviour and its effects upon the prisoners and enslaved people of the island. Artists and poets have over the years analysed or adapted the play in ways that have enabled the colonised subject's experience to prevail instead, and it is important to engage with these interpretations to view the complete picture that Shakespeare himself has painted. George Lamming, for example, explicitly connects Shakespeare's play to what he calls

'England's experiment in colonisation', attesting to Caliban's 'spirit of freedom' despite his captivity and drawing our attention to his assertion that the island, in fact, belongs to him.[8] To view the play merely through a white 'universalist' prism is to miss its heart.

ENSLAVED SUBJECTS

Our empathy for Caliban is complicated by Miranda's reaction to his name and what we learn about their history: "'Tis a villain, sir, / I do not love to look on' (1.2.310–11). But Prospero reminds his daughter of Caliban's usefulness:

> ...he does make our fire,
> Fetch in our wood, and serves in offices
> That profit us.
>
> (312–14)

When Prospero summons him, he calls him 'slave' (313), 'earth' (314), 'tortoise' (317), 'poisonous slave' (320), and reminds him his 'witch' mother was impregnated by 'the devil himself' (320). We've seen this kind of prologuing of a character before in *Othello*, with Iago's use of language that dehumanises and racialises a figure before we meet him.

Slaves and slavery were not unfamiliar concepts in Shakespeare's England. The word 'slave' appears frequently throughout his works. It is not unreasonable to assume that first and foremost, it was understood as a person who labours for no money under the threat of brutal and systematic corporal punishment. By the 1600s Spain and Portugal had notoriously monopolised the trafficking of African people for the purposes of enslavement in the Caribbean and Americas. Elizabethans would have known of the slaving voyages of Francis Drake and John Hawkins, whose father William Hawkins, helped establish the triangular route. The term 'slave', therefore, was already linked to blackness by the time this play was written. In Shakespeare's canon, it is also a generic insult, indicating lowly status, linked also with servitude and used interchangeably with words like 'ass', 'rogue', 'villain' and 'servant'. Its subtler metaphorical uses allude to debasement, monstrousness and evil, such as in *Richard III* when Queen Margaret refers to the 'deformed' king as a 'slave of nature' (1.3.229). Thoughts could also be 'slaves', sent 'flying' to visit a lover, as in Valentine's letter expressing his love for Silvia in *Two Gentlemen of Verona* (3.1.141–5), highlighting the metaphor of servitude and slavery that underpinned rituals of courtship at the time.

Prospero's calling Caliban 'earth' draws attention to the possibility of his darker complexion – the colour of earth. It alludes to his perceived baser nature too, being a 'savage' as he is described in the *dramatis personae* of the text in the *First Folio*. Prospero's name-calling includes 'tortoise' because he's slow to arrive, but also, intriguingly, tortoises were linked in the period's allegories with the crass and lowly-ranked sense of touch in the Renaissance hierarchy of the senses because of their hard shells and reptilian textures – suggesting Caliban only thinks about satisfying primitive urges.

The exchanges between Caliban and Prospero are full of rage and curses. By juxtaposing these moments with the somewhat gentler interactions between Prospero and Ariel – who is a 'fine apparition' and 'my quaint Ariel' (1.2.317), Shakespeare is asking us to think critically about service and enslavement in the context of the natural world. As we try to grasp the differences between Ariel and Caliban, we need to consider their physical positioning in the play. Ariel is a spirit of the air, the space considered superior to the earth in Elizabethan cosmological thought; it is the realm of divinity and weather, impossible for humans to conquer. Caliban's work, such as his endless fetching of wood, is earth-focused, which makes us think about the destruction of the natural world even with its promise of fruitful abundance and mineral riches. It also forces us to concede that Caliban won't profit from that labour himself.

Prospero's mastery of air through Ariel and the earth through Caliban suggest an exceptionality, or a divine authority. His dominion over the island and its inhabitants appears justified in his god-like ability to command the elements, unlike the base crew and passengers of the ship that he wrecks onto the island, for example. As the Boatswain tells Gonzalo in the opening scene, 'You are a councillor; if you can command these elements to silence and work the peace of the present, we will not hand a rope more. Use your authority! If you cannot, give thanks you have lived so long' (1.1.19–22). Most European settlers assumed entitlement was theirs on the basis of their 'civility', knowledge, language and religion in the face of the 'savagery', incoherent language or 'gabble' (1.2.357) and supposed ungodliness of the people they encountered. Shakespeare is posing questions here that we are still grappling with today, such as what our relationship is to nature and whether it is one of mastery; what forces *do* we control? How have our attempts to *prosper* by subjugating the planet and many of its people, suppressing their culture and language, limited and endangered the existence of us all? In 1611, when *The Tempest* was being staged, these questions were already urgent.

WHOSE ISLAND IS IT?

Caliban's reactive curses speak to the charge that his mother was a witch, using language that is evocative of all that is rotten on the isle:

> As wicked dew as ere my mother brushed
> With raven's feather from unwholesome fen
> Drop on you both. A southwest blow on ye
> And blister you all o'er.
>
> (1.2.322–5)

At the time, 'wicked' meant 'foul', synonymous as we know with 'polluted', 'dirty', 'corrupt', 'deformed' and 'black'.[9] The native islander's hurt can be felt in his fiery evocation of his mother's tricks. We have heard throughout this book that dark complexions and idleness were attributes linked from the classical period through to the eighteenth century to sunny, warmer climes, while colder regions created hardy, vigorous white people. The 'southwest' wind would have been either a stormy gale or a hot wind. Caliban tries his best to curse the foreigners to his native land, drawing upon the natural conditions and objects of the island to wish upon them pain and blistering. But Prospero curses him harder, his occultic power having the greater material consequence for Caliban's body:

> For this, be sure, tonight thou shalt have cramps,
> Side-stitches, that shall pen thy breath up; urchins
> Shall forth at vast of night that they may work
> All exercise on thee; thou shalt be pinched

As thick as honeycomb, each pinch more stinging
Than bees that made 'em.

(1.2.326–31)

Pain is intrinsic to Prospero's 'rough magic' and his strategy. It was also an essential mechanism in servitude and its extreme, slavery. If we acknowledge that England was a culture of servitude at every echelon, whether to a master, parent, husband, lord, duke, monarch or God, then the relationships in the play begin to make more sense. Intrinsic to English ideas about service was physical punishment; beatings and whippings were commonplace. The painful promise Prospero makes prompts Caliban to assert his own identity with a tone that implies he has nothing further to lose as he unveils a counter history to the one Prospero narrated earlier:

> This island's mine by Sycorax, my mother,
> Which thou tak'st from me. When thou cam'st first
> Thou strok'st me and made much of me; wouldst give me
> Water with berries in't, and teach me how
> To name the bigger light and how the less
> That burn by day and night. And then I loved thee
> And showed thee all the qualities o'th'isle:
> The fresh springs, brine pits, barren place and fertile.
> Cursed be I that did so!

(332–40)

With this riposte, we are given both sides of the story. Caliban speaks directly to and about his new master. The travel narratives of the period are largely one-sided, framed through the white,

European perspective and skewed by its values. But here, Shakespeare changes the lens and we are given a different view. We see that there was affection between them once, that they educated each other, Caliban showing Prospero how to live off the island – what was 'barren' land and what was 'fertile' – and Prospero teaching him language. From Caliban's perspective, Sycorax is not a witch so much as she is a *mother*, a figure most people can relate to regardless of background and history.

But Caliban's tale moves from historical narrative to curse to accusation:

> ...All the charms
> Of Sycorax – toads, beetles, bats – light on you,
> For I am all the subjects that you have,
> Which first was mine own king; and here you sty me
> In this hard rock, whiles you do keep from me
> The rest o'th'island.
>
> (340–5)

He tells us the island was entirely his; he was its only subject and king. But now he is confined to a stone cave, unable to move beyond a certain perimeter. Consistently dehumanised and literally demonised, he is, according to Prospero's tale, the son of the devil.

But once we are able to read beyond the racialising rhetoric and open our minds to Caliban's named experiences, our feelings towards him become complicated by Prospero's revelation of the reason for this confinement:

> ...Thou most lying slave,
> Whom stripes may move, not kindness; I have used
> thee

(Filth as thou art) with humane care and lodged thee
In mine own cell, till thou didst seek to violate
The honour of my child.

(345–9)

The charge of attempted rape of the young, virtuous Miranda often closes off any possibility of redemption for Caliban. Prospero suggests the violation of his trust severed any hope that they could ever live harmoniously on the island. He uses this to illustrate that Caliban is unteachable. The 'lying slave' is more responsive to violent lashes – 'stripes' – than to kinship/family and compassion – 'kindness'. Even when he took him into his cell, Prospero always saw Caliban as 'filth', easily understood from his judgement in brackets – '(Filth as thou art)'. His prejudices were brutally confirmed in his view.

How do we read this through a decolonised perspective? Is it even possible? The importance of white women to the perpetuation of racial purity was ever present for Shakespeare. Tales of the assailable virtuous maid goes back centuries and are often related in terms that objectified her whiteness through the language of poetic praise, where terms like 'fair' are used to designate the most superior of white complexions. It's everywhere in Shakespeare too, whether he is reinforcing or mocking its overuse. His preoccupation with interracial marriage/relationships articulates, amongst other things, the premodern European anxiety about reproduction and racial purity. It is why his works contain so many fathers keen to arrange, manage and control their young daughters' futures with the aim of securing hereditary and genetic consistency. Given the failures of Lord Capulet in *Romeo and Juliet*, Egeus in *A Midsummer Night's Dream*, the dead father of Portia in *The Merchant of Venice* and Brabantio in *Othello*, Prospero is just one of many Shakespearean fathers determined to get it right. He won't let down white patriarchy like his predecessors or even King Alonso did; he exacts more studied control, using his 'art' of magic and his strategic skills as a 'prince of power'. Caliban admits wholeheartedly to the attempted rape if only to gall this anxiety of white, upper-class fathers, creating the fearful image of copies of himself populating the island:

> ...Would't had been done;
> Thou didst prevent me, I had peopled else
> This isle with Calibans.

> (350–2)

The oppression of white women feeds the religious and cultural emphasis upon their status as property and perpetuators of white racial purity. As a result, European women's bodies were excessively regulated throughout the premodern period and for centuries after. Early modern conduct manuals directed at young highborn women are full of admonitions managing their behaviour from the food they eat, the company they keep, the clothes they wear to how loudly they should laugh in public. Richard Dyer sees this as a phenomenon persisting in the modern era. In his view, 'inter-racial (non-white on white) rape is represented as bestiality storming the citadel of civilisation'.[10] Some of the most violent attacks on Black men and Black communities over the last two hundred years have cited accusations of rape or attempted rape of white women as justification for the violence and punishment exacted upon them.

Shakespeare does not allow us to empathise exclusively with either the coloniser or the colonised. Prospero's enslavement, torture and prejudgment of Caliban as 'filth' doesn't sit well with a modern audience, nor does Caliban's intent to rape Miranda. But Shakespeare was not one for making things easy for his audience.

'VILE RACE'

Throughout Caliban is called a 'freckled whelp' (spotted dog), a 'savage', a 'mooncalf' (possessing a deformity caused by a full moon), 'not honoured with human shape', 'hag-seed', 'monster', 'strange fish', 'misshapen knave', 'strange thing', 'disproportioned' and 'a devil born'. The fact that many depictions of him have struggled to see past this name-calling shows how easy it is to be manipulated by racialising rhetoric and coded language: to be upper-class, European and white is to be human; everything else is other, savage, threatening, or foolish.

On one part of the island, as another storm threatens, Caliban sees Alonso's court jester Trinculo and mistakes him for one of Prospero's spirits. He falls flat on the ground in the hopes of going unnoticed. But Trinculo sees the odd shape, or rather, smells him: 'What have we here, a man or a fish? Dead or alive? A fish: he smells like a fish, a very ancient and fish-like smell... A strange fish' (2.2.24–7). The reason so many staged Calibans are dressed as fish is because of these lines, but Trinculo is commenting more on the native islander's smell than his looks. He immediately fantasises about taking such an object to England where, apparently, 'any strange beast there makes a man. When they will not give a doit to relieve a lame beggar, they will lay out ten to see a dead Indian' (30–2). When indigenous people were brought to England, at times they were displayed publicly, as curiosities and exotic artifacts, and people willingly paid to gawk at them.[11]

To take shelter from the storm, Trinculo climbs under Caliban's cloak or 'gaberdine', lying head to foot across him. In productions this can make for a hilarious scene as the text suggests that Caliban's head would be partially visible with a pair of legs poking out of the gaberdine on both ends. When Stephano, the drink-loving butler, enters singing, he sees the oddly shaped figure on the ground: 'Have we devils here? Do you put tricks upon's with savages and men of Ind? Ha! I have not 'scaped drowning to be afeard now of your four legs' (2.2.56–9). When Caliban speaks up, Stephano remarks, 'This is some monster of the isle' and is flummoxed that he knows his language. But he does. And he speaks it eloquently.

The monstrosity rhetoric in the scene crescendos to absurd levels, echoing excessively the dehumanising language we first heard from Prospero. But the perspective of the butler and the clown are meant to be suspect – their foolishness is the main object to be gawked at here. The audience is in on the joke; we can see clearly that there are two people under the gaberdine, not a strange monster. In his lack of experience of Europeans other than Prospero and Miranda, Caliban mistakes them for gods, because they give him wine, the intoxicating effects of which drive him to offer them the riches of the island and his perpetual service. With Ariel listening in undetected, Caliban persuades them to help him murder Prospero with the promise that he will serve *them* as lords of the island. Caliban's attempt to conspire with the butler and the clown is eventually reported to Prospero by Ariel, so he never stands a chance.

Shakespeare was fond of dramatising the quirky encounters between people from different worlds. In *As You Like It*, for example, much humour is milked from Touchstone, the court jester, sparring with a rustic shepherd about the differences between their behaviours and customs as Shakespeare's way of interrogating snobbish courtly etiquette. Caliban's scenes with the two simple castaways provide a farcical parody of the colonial encounter, unpacking its tragic fallout through humour and folly.

In the final act, when Prospero tells all the castaways and islanders what has transpired, that because of his spirit spy he knows all the transactions that have occurred, he decides to forgive the castaways rather than avenge his own exile. Yet he points to Caliban to claim ownership of him: 'this thing of darkness, I / Acknowledge mine' (5.1.276). The term 'darkness' functions metaphorically and literally as part of the fabric of black and white imagery helping to keep us attentive to racial difference and its metaphorical importance. When considering the ethnicity of Caliban, we'd need to take note of Shakespeare's many references to Africa. Gonzalo says once washed up on the isle: 'Methinks our garments are now as fresh as when we put them on first in Africa, at the marriage of the King's fair daughter Claribel to the King of Tunis' (2.1.70–3). Caliban's mother, painted as black by the play's language – 'the foul witch Sycorax' (1.2.258) – was from Algiers (Algeria). Geographically, this fictional island, then, should be located between Europe and Africa, so Caliban is more likely to be of African descent. Shakespeare's lack of specificity is curious. After all, Aaron and Othello are repeatedly referred to as 'moors' so there could be no doubt about *their* ethnic backgrounds. Why? Shakespeare's vague relations of ethnicity in *The Tempest* makes us think allegorically and globally. Caliban's ambiguity helps us to see him as representative of indigeneity and enslavement more broadly; after all, no one single ethnicity suffers the oppression and tyranny of European colonisation.

Stories, images and descriptions of indigenous Americans circulating in Renaissance European travel narratives were easy to get hold of. Thomas Hariot's *Brief and True Report of the New Found Land of Virginia* describes people 'clothed with loose mantles made of Deere skins' or as 'attired in the most strange fashion'.[12] Milanese merchant Girolamo Benzoni relates in his account the moment Columbus and his fellow explorers encountered the 'gentle' Taíno (or Arawak) natives in Haiti (referred to then as 'Hispaniola' or 'Little Spain'). An engraving by Belgian artist Theodor de Bry harnesses visually

this encounter and highlights the principal binary that under-pinned colonisation: civility versus barbarity.

We can't help but notice the artistic privileging of the Europeans in their style of dress, strength of armour and weaponry, upright bodies and gestural poses, such as the power stance – arms akimbo. Contrast these features with the sparse clothing, bare feet, lack of weaponry, dynamic bodies and relaxed gestures of the Taíno greeting them with gifts; disturbingly in the background we see other Taíno people fleeing in terror from the Spanish ships.

In another example, the Englishman John White, who served as a mapmaker and illustrator on an expedition to found a colony on Roanoke Island in North Carolina – which apparently disappeared, becoming known as 'the lost colony' – produced a series of watercolours while there, detailing the native Algonquian (Algonkin) people of the Carolina coast, depicting their habits, customs and occupations. These remarkable illustrations are the earliest of their kind by an English artist that we know of.

The public depictions of indigenous Americans from this period to the present day are steeped in stereotype and bias. The problem with White's watercolours for us now, for example, as seemingly benevolent and skilful as they are, is that they were crafted through the white gaze at a time when it was deemed the only perspective that mattered.

STAGING THE 'SAVAGE DEFORMED SLAVE'

Perhaps Shakespeare was inspired by the tales and illustrations of the first Americans even if his geography says otherwise. But given the way Caliban is spoken of in the play, what would Shakespeare's original Whitehall or Blackfriars audience expect to see? At court sumptuous costumes and impressive spectacle were the norm, and from time to time the King's Men performed in the elaborate masques staged for the king. Court masques were allegorical pageants characterised by lavish spectacle, music and dance, with an 'anti-masque' that presented an interpretation of the grotesque as a foil to beauty. The primary purpose of these performances was to glorify the monarch; they were provocative, expensive affairs, and most popular during the reign of the Stuarts. In Shakespeare's play, Caliban is sparsely dressed when Prospero first encounters him, but by the time we meet him, he may be wearing rags of old clothes given to him by the ex-Duke, or dressed in a 'gaberdine', or cloak, and potentially adorned with objects associated with the sea such as shells or coral. Either way he needed visibly to contrast with Miranda and Prospero, who, we learn, had brought with them their expensive and exquisite clothing. It seems unavoidable that Caliban would have been painted in black or brown face to represent his African heritage or American indigeneity as well as gesture to his 'earthy' status.

He may have been represented as 'deformed' according to Renaissance definitions which meant disabled or merely 'ugly', a subjective value, I concede. Visible deformities in this period were viewed as marks of sin or moral depravity. Disabled or diseased bodies gestured to souls that were 'deceitful' or 'sloth-ful', 'malicious' and even 'evil'.[13] Some also questioned the full humanity of those 'rudely stamped', as Shakespeare's villainous king, Richard III, refers to himself (*Richard III*, 1.1.17). Caliban's 'deformity' would be represented through makeup, gesture or gait. It is unclear as to whether he was born with a deformity, as 'mooncalf' suggests, or grew misshapen from having performed hours upon hours of labour, being beaten and cursed with pain. Caliban has been pinched hard and feels

Prospero's phantom pinches upon his body frequently. According to the literary historian Patricia Akhimie, pinches can actually 'change the shape of men and Prospero's oddly specific punishments would transform bodies by degrading musculature and bone in much the same way old age would'.[14] But it is also very likely that he was not originally presented as deformed or disabled at all nor that he would have been staged as inhuman, or a grotesque monster with fish scales or animal-like features. There would be no dramatic tension otherwise, no signs of his history if he simply looked the way the racialising language makes him out to be. Shakespeare's text allows for a gap between what other characters say about him and what the audience actually sees.

Artistic renderings and theatre productions over the past four hundred years have portrayed Caliban through a mixed range of concepts and costume designs that speak to each generation's distinctive fantasies of primitivity, monstrosity or foreignness. During David Garrick's Stratford-upon-Avon Jubilee in 1769, actors paraded as different Shakespearean characters. Caliban was bestialised, as a Captain Edward Thompson, who attended the festival, describes:

> There was Caliban too, a most monstrous ape,
> No beast had before such a whimsical shape,
> Yet was nearly being hang'd for attempting a rape.[15]

An illustration copied by British engraver Peter Simon from Swiss artist Henry Fuseli's painting entitled *The Enchanted Island Before the Cell of Prospero*, depicts the magus and his daughter glowing white, gesturing gracefully with upright bodies, while on the opposite side crouches the hunched, more tawny, partially

human, satyr-like, devil-faced figure of Caliban. The contrast between civility and barbarity highlighted in de Bry's depiction of Columbus and the Taíno natives is captured more starkly here some two hundred years later.

Productions in theatres over the last two centuries have not strayed terribly far from these early interpretations. We have seen white actors in blackface or with dirt smeared on their faces; many actors have been costumed as fish- or swamp-like creatures with scales, or made up as half-man/half-beast, or as a devil; Black and Asian (East and South) actors have played the part, but in many productions, they have been the *only* ethnic minority to be cast, which simply objectifies their difference. Sometimes Caliban is depicted as crawling on all fours, at other times he is upright and human, but oppressed or enslaved.

Anti-colonial productions have tried to revise this depiction of Caliban and there have been illuminating adaptations and re-tellings, such as Aimé Césaire's powerful play, *Une Tempête* (1969) set on a Caribbean island with a clear postcolonial perspective: Prospero is a white master, Ariel a 'mulatto fairy' and Caliban an enslaved black man. Theatre critics have for decades derided postcolonial interpretations. In 1970, Jonathan Miller directed a production at the Mermaid Theatre in the UK which staged the first Black British Ariel and Caliban. Some reviewers thought the anticolonial stance of the production was laudable, while others such as Milton Shulman thought the production was attempting to 'squeeze' an 'imperialist allegory into a story that will obviously resist such an interpretation'.[16]

It is baffling that any reader of this play would think that it 'resists' a colonial interpretation, but I am not surprised at this reaction. For many, the Great White Bard is indestructible and if this play is his mythic 'farewell' to the stage, there has to be more beauty and aesthetic form than political challenge. But reading Shakespeare for the twenty-first century means not being afraid of 'more matter and less art' (*Hamlet*, 2.2.96).

Mainstream productions in our current moment still have a tendency to respond literally to the dehumanising tropes scattered all over the play. Time and again, theatre directors resurrect and normalise the premodern European point of view by staging Caliban as a monster. In the Stratford, Ontario Festival production in 2010, Black actor Dion Johnstone was costumed to represent the 'strange fish' imagery in the scenes with Stephano and Trinculo. Prospero was played by Shakespearean great Christopher Plummer. This casting perpetuates a benign reading of Prospero if the actor playing him is well established, beloved and, therefore, immediately sympathetic.

The 2016 Royal Shakespeare Company production marking four hundred years since Shakespeare's death deployed advanced digital technology to assert their Bard's relevance in the twenty-first century. A blog review notes that the RSC:

> collaborated with Andy Serkis's The Imaginarium Studio to have Ariel in a body suit with live action motion sensors, so that he can perform all the moves live, with his body projected on high on a gauze tube, twisting and turning in the air. The face is digital, produced after hours of work with Simon Russell Beale [who plays Prospero] to record Mark Quarterly's facial reactions. The technology owes a lot to Serkis's Gollum in the *Lord of The Rings/Hobbit* series.

Caliban was played by Joe Dixon in a fish-like costume with a large belly and spine meant to look misshapen. The same blogger, Peter Viney, muses, 'after complaining of productions where Caliban was reduced as a normal looking argument against colonialism, it was good to see the "monster" restored.'[17] Yet staging Ariel so spectacularly with CGI technology while keeping Caliban earth-bound simply reinforces the unhelpful binaries the play upholds.

During the 2021 Anti-racist Shakespeare Webinar on *The Tempest* hosted by the Globe, indigenous Shakespeare scholars Scott Manning Stevens and Madeline Sayet noted that when directors stage the play in literal terms, it often means people of colour end up 'playing the monster', or, I would add, white actors are overly monster-fied, neither of which help us to interrogate the systems of power the play's encounters rely upon. Stevens offers up an enticing challenge to theatre directors who want to decolonise the play more overtly: situate Caliban within the play's beauty; undercut the language of 'foulness' by staging its opposite. Cast a beautiful actor.[18] We would then be able to see through the play's rhetorical machinery of 'otherness' and its linguistic strategy to racialise and dehumanise the colonised.

WONDERS 'FAIR'

Miranda is proficient in the language of beauty. She recognises its object, though she has very little exposure to other people on the island; she is confident that Ferdinand is 'fair' – he is not just the ideal complexion and stature but virtuous too:

> There's nothing ill can dwell in such a temple.
> If the ill spirit have so fair a house
> Good things will strive to dwell with't.
> (1.2.459–61)

Ferdinand is Prospero's captive, forced to perform hours of labour like fetching wood to test his mettle. Later in Act 3 when Miranda and Ferdinand express their love for each other, they play upon the different connotations of slavery. She confesses her lack of experience or knowledge of other people, but swears she likes the look of him:

> ...I would not wish
> Any companion in the world but you,
> Nor can imagination form a shape,
> Besides yourself, to like of...
> (3.1.54–7)

Ferdinand replies that the moment he saw her, he too fell instantly in love – his heart, like his life, forever enslaved to her will:

> The very instant that I saw you did
> My heart fly to your service, there resides
> To make me slave to it, and for your sake
> Am I this patient log-man.
>
> (64–6)

In contrast with Caliban's enslaved condition, there are tangible rewards for Ferdinand's enforced labours of love. His enslavement is only a temporary condition imposed by Prospero and his conjurations. The young noble is an appropriate suitor, of the same status, of the same race and speaks the same language, superiorly, in fact, as he notes earlier: 'My language?' he says. 'Heavens! / I am the best of them that speak, / Were I but where 'tis spoken' (1.2.429–31). His breeding and the privileges associated, rather than his efforts, are what determine his successful marriage to the fair daughter of a duke.

When Prospero observes their confessions, he confirms as much, pleased all is going to plan: 'Fair encounter', he says to himself, 'Of two most rare affections! Heavens rain grace / On that which breeds between 'em' (3.1.74–6). The word 'breeds' indicates this union is sanctioned; it is a 'fair' match and a rare love. In *Titus Andronicus*, the word 'breeder' is also used in a racially charged context, but negatively, when Aaron and Tamora's mixed-race child is brought on stage: 'Here is the babe, as loathsome as a toad / Amongst the fair-faced breeders of our clime' (4.2.70–1). The notion of breeding in Shakespeare is tied to racial purity. In *The Tempest*, this moment is not one that calls for Prospero to conjure violent storms, but instead to summon the grace of heaven, or, Christian benevolence, to rain down on the *fair* couple ensuring that what they 'breed' is pure. When in Act 4 Prospero gives his permission to marry, Ferdinand reassures his future father-in-law that his intentions are virtuous: 'For quiet days, fair issue and long life' (4.1.24). Prospero approves: 'Fairly spoke' (32). 'Fair issue' recalls *Antony and Cleopatra*'s 'unlawful issue' and draws our attention to the foil that the theme of interracial marriage provides in Shakespeare's plays to the sanctioned unions of white nobility.

The Tempest has been celebrated for centuries for its aesthetic beauty. Its sublime poetic interludes, its wondrous charms and supernatural forces, its spectacle and themes of redemption, forgiveness and reconciliation have meant that it is seen as one of Shakespeare's most enchanting and evocative plays. As the play ends, the clash between beauty and monstrosity and between civility and barbarity becomes blurred. The mutability of humanity, its capacity to improve, is tested here amongst the different groupings of islanders and castaways that eventually come together in the final act. Sebastian's hope to rebel against King Alonso, colluding with Antonio, does not come to fruition; as the play closes, Prospero's adamant quest for revenge has evolved into redemption, inspired by the fair love of his daughter and a soon-to-be prince of power.

Prospero emerges in his European dress as the Duke of Milan to the amazement and awe of the courtiers, while Alonso, overwhelmed to see his son Ferdinand alive, bestows his blessings upon the nuptials. Prospero frees Ariel and acknowledges that what Caliban is is partly due to his own 'rough magic', a magic that has caused as much pain as reconciliation. So he drowns his famous books on the occult, renouncing his magic. But is he renouncing power? For centuries Prospero has been lauded, identified with, admired, played by the finest actors and even likened to Shakespeare himself, a view hailing from the eighteenth century, when lines from Prospero's infamous epilogue were engraved into the Bard's statue in Westminster Abbey:

> The Cloud capt Tow'rs,
> The Gorgeous Palaces,
> The Solemn Temples,
> The Great Globe itself,
> Yea all which it Inherit,
> Shall Dissolve;
> And like the baseless Fabrick of a Vision
> Leave not a wreck behind.

Prospero's combination of 'rough magic' and political strategy prove successful; he *prospers*. Yet, the island will be returned to Caliban. But what will the effect of Prospero's occupation and extraction of the island's natural resources be? Will he leave it better off than he found it? Has he, in fact, laid the groundwork for future European citizens to re-locate there? If the imperial history of Western Europe is anything to go by, we can easily guess the answer to that.

The example of Prospero and his occupation of this magical isle helps us as we try to engage honestly with our own history. What can this beautiful-ugly story of storms and magic, isolation and rediscovery, ownership and theft, torture and love, oppression and forgiveness do for us as we attempt to come to terms with the long-term and devastating effects of European colonialism? How can Shakespeare help us on that journey? Shakespeare cannot remedy the world but his work offers us a medium for exploring it and for harnessing hope from our own human-made catastrophes.

Seven

TRAGEDY AND
INTERRACIAL POETRY

After looking closely at six of Shakespeare's plays where race is dramatically invoked through the experiences of central minoritised characters, where do we go next? Shakespeare's fascination with the sociology and psychology of difference is not limited to the 'race plays'; it in fact also finds force in his tragedies and comedies that seem less obvious candidates for inclusion in a book about Shakespeare and race; but it is in these works that he explores different modes of racial formation with compelling poetic virtuosity.

In Chapter 2 we saw how the language Elizabethans and Jacobeans used to refer to racial difference as we understand it today is characterised by words and signifiers seemingly archaic or no longer in use – like 'Moor' and 'blackamoor'. But ideas about race can also be found in the distinctions made between classes or groups of people, in the multiple meanings and connotations of words like *kin/d* and *blood* and in references to night, servitude, monsters, animals and witchcraft; we see it in the classifying of the supernatural as *strange*, a word that explicitly meant *foreign*. Such words and ideas suggest a world where race is present, palpable and a preoccupation of not only Shakespeare in

213

his tragedies, but also of the culture and history he was embedded in. Grappling with tragedy and its relationship to race is vital to unlocking how we can intervene, as modern readers with our own unique perspectives, in the great and tumultuous world of Shakespeare's plays.

'RACECRAFT': MACBETH

Coined by Karen E. Fields and Barbara J. Fields, the term 'racecraft' refers to a system of beliefs about race created over a long period; it constructs a 'mental terrain' of ideas originating 'not in nature but in human action and imagination'. The term deliberately invokes witchcraft because it gestures towards the eagerness to embrace inane concepts as truth, to take as fact what is not real and to act 'upon the reality of an imagined thing'. Belief becomes accepted as 'truth about the world'.[1] Race is a fiction but there are inequities in society that make race feel real and racism even more so. Shakespeare's *Macbeth* is an appropriate site to explore how racecraft works through language in the early modern formation of racialised otherness. It is lore adopted as truth in this period, like the belief in witchcraft; both were purposely designed to trigger anxieties in the period about foreign threats of all kinds. Such belief permeates not only Shakespeare's play, but also the 'mental terrain' of his first audiences. *Macbeth* dramatises how unspeakable acts are brought about through the mere power of suggestion, or belief. We see how its sorcery and 'black' magic align with otherness while identifying fear as the most dangerous human emotion, and the one most often leveraged when political bodies aim to create societal division.

Set in Scotland in the 1100s, the 'Scottish play', as it is commonly referred to by actors, was written only a few years after

King James I ascended to the English throne. Some scholars conjecture that it was first played in the Great Hall at Hampton Court Palace to an audience that included James's wife, Queen Anna, and her brother, King Christian of Denmark. Imagine the gall of Shakespeare's acting troupe, to stage a play about the murder of a visiting king in front of a visiting king – that is, if this performance took place at all. Otherwise, it is certain that it was performed in the Globe around 1606 to crowds gunning for special effects, storms, political plots and witches. It is one of Shakespeare's most topical plays, with its inclusion of prophecy and witchcraft, themes popular at the time as well as being almost frenzied obsessions of the king himself.

James I was convinced that witches were out to get him. He was certain that they had raised a tempest at sea when he and his new bride had attempted to sail to Scotland after a sojourn in Denmark spent with astrologers, astronomers and people who studied the occult. When one of the ships of the royal fleet was lost in the storm, James frantically blamed it on witches – when he finally returned home, over one hundred women were arrested for their 'devilish' desires to murder the king and queen. Kangaroo trials and violent persecutions followed. The scandal was written up in a pamphlet called *News from Scotland* at the King's request, which served as an alarmist exposition of the bloody threat of witches. A few years later, James I published his own version – *Demonologie* – of witchcraft lore, which staged an intellectual debate that attempted to convince readers of the existence of witches, 'detestable slaves of the Devil'.[2]

Such pamphlets are examples of an entire genre sparked by the medieval publication of *Malleus Maleficarum* ('The Hammer of Witches'), written by Dominican clergyman Heinrich Kramer and published in 1486 in Germany; it was subsequently printed multiple times and in multiple languages, proving to be one of the most popular treatises on the subject of witches, how to hunt them down, torture them to extract confessions and prosecute them violently. The atrocious, bloody persecution of millions of European women as witches throughout this period has been documented, but what hasn't quite been established is one of its legacies: the way in which the act of 'othering' women in this way racialises them as oversexualised and innately satanic, traits associated firmly, time and again, with blackness. Nor has it been fully acknowledged how medieval and Renaissance witchcraft lore has contributed to Anglo-European/American racism. The belief in a looming threat that operates by stealth, trickery and deception and thus motivated by excessive fear characterises racism and the misogyny of witchcraft.

Macbeth was also shaped by the news of a planned act of religious terrorism. The Catholic plot to blow up the Houses of Parliament only the year before was buzzing in the printing presses and was an urgent topic at court.[3] Given the tragedy's preoccupation with treason, usurpation of the crown and the conspiratorial world of the supernatural, it is hard for historians to avoid aligning Shakespeare's play with this most famous regicidal conspiracy in English history – the so-called 'gunpowder plot'. A seventeenth-century treatise about the plot makes clear the collective response to it at the time, which was that a foreign, 'popish' figure, Guido (Guy) Fawkes, no doubt in league with the devil, had attempted to remove the king and destroy English Protestantism.[4]

An illustration and poem from a news pamphlet by John Vicars about 'Fawkes and his Father-Satan' demonstrate the contemporary English Protestant view of the ties between foreigners, witches, Catholics and the Devil. Satan is, of course, black and a vessel for all of the above (he is pictured conducting the 'Work of Darkness'), depicted as such in art and sermons such as *The Black Devil* (1615) delivered by preacher Thomas Adams. To add further excitement to this set of beliefs, witches were sexually linked to Satan: to become a witch in the first place, you had to have sex with the Prince of Darkness himself. As such, witches had extensive powers; primarily they could harm Christians and deliver prophecies as forms of temptation. In 1612, the scholar George Gifford tells us that witches 'worketh by the Devil or by some devilish or curious art, either hurting or healing, revealing things secret or foretelling things to come which the Devil hath devised to entangle and snare men's souls withal unto damnation'.[5]

Shakespeare would have been acutely aware of his audience's diabolical curiosities and the links they had to identity in their imaginations. In their view, the foiling of the gunpowder plot would have been due to God's preference for English Protestants. I hasten to add, as the chief writer for the King's Men, Shakespeare would also have been rather keen to trigger his monarch's most theatrically viable anxieties, while drawing on a language of racialisation and the occult.

The play follows a Scottish hero, Macbeth, who three witches prophecy will be advanced to Thane of Cawdor and then become King while his friend Banquo's descendants will inherit the Scottish throne. He sends his wife word of what has been prophesied and informs her that the king, trusting Macbeth after his victory, will come to stay at their castle in Dunsinane. After reading his letter, Lady Macbeth calls on spirits to 'unsex me here' and fill her with the cruelty necessary to spur her husband to ascend to power. When the couple reunite, she convinces him the only way he'll rise to power is through nefarious means; so they plot to murder the visiting King Duncan. After guilt-ridden and fearful meditations, Macbeth does the deed; Lady M (as she is affectionately known) rubs Duncan's blood on the faces of two of his drunken servants to frame them for the murder and because Macbeth loses courage; fearing for their own lives, Duncan's sons, Malcolm and Donalblain, run away, leaving the nobles to suspect even them. As the play progresses, Macbeth is King but becomes twisted by fear, declining further into evil while Lady Macbeth is tortured by guilt. Her famous sleepwalking scene has harrowed audiences for centuries as she attempts to wash the blood off her hands repeatedly each night, until she finally dies. The scene shows the extent to which her journey from unsexed cruelty to vulnerable trauma interrogates the hypermasculine system she sought power within.

Macbeth meets the witches again, who foretell events that Macbeth misinterprets or sees as impossible, such as Birnam Wood coming to Dunsinane (how can a forest move?) and that 'None of woman born shall harm Macbeth' (4.1.79–80). So Macbeth considers himself safe, though his heart sits in constant fear. He agonisingly presides over a murderous reign, killing his companion Banquo and attempting to have his son Fleance murdered too; this act haunts him, but he is literally haunted when Banquo's ghost appears during a banquet, shaking his 'gory locks' at Macbeth. When Macbeth fatefully orders the murders of his rival Macduff's family, his pact with the devil is sealed. Malcolm, Duncan's son, raises an army in England and with Macduff's help, defeats Macbeth's forces: 'black Macbeth / Will seem as pure as snow' compared to the damage Malcolm will do. The usurping king is finally killed by Macduff – who was from his mother's womb, it turns out, 'untimely ripped' (born by Caesarean). Throughout the play, the sights, sounds, smells of murder, the devil, witches and prophecy create the atmosphere of a play that, were he writing today, would place *Macbeth* squarely in the horror genre.

As with *The Tempest*, *Macbeth* gives Shakespeare an opportunity to illustrate in material terms the powerful intersection of theatricality and mythical sorcery. The only version we have is included within Shakespeare's *First Folio*. It opens spectacularly with the stage direction: '*Thunder and lightning. Enter three* WITCHES'. The incantations to follow give us a glimpse of what is to come but also centralise witchcraft as simultaneously terrifying and spurious:

> 1 WITCH
> When shall we three meet again?
> In thunder, lightning, or in rain?
> 2 WITCH
> When the hurly-burly's done,
> When the battle's lost and won.
> 3 WITCH
> That will be ere the set of sun.
> ...
> ALL
> Fair is foul, and foul is fair:
> Hover through the fog and filthy air.
>
> (1.1.1–5, 8–9)

The gunpowder-infused sparks permeated the air with thick smoke, making it dark, smelly and 'filthy' for certain: the sounds *and* smells recalling the 'Popish' plot to usurp the throne the year before. The smell of dung, an ingredient in gunpowder, would fill up the theatre, invoking scripture's promises of the filthy stench of hell, contextualising the witches there for the audience. Shakespeare's rich sensory awareness of the visceral effects of performance should not be taken for granted.

The witches deliver the prologue, preparing themselves to meet Macbeth on his return from battle. In their conclusion that 'Fair is foul, and foul is fair', they do not just simply remind us of the play's powerful attention to the tensions between familiar racialised binaries – white/black; light/dark – but also that these two categories are worryingly interchangeable. That one can easily become the other terrifies those who need stable categories to determine who is and isn't one of 'us'. What we deem 'fair' in this play will prove 'foul', as deception becomes the play's very operating system. The imagery, like it or not, points to race. It raises questions about the savage and diabolical versus the civilised and virtuous. We discover the play's linguistic investment in equivocation – or speaking in riddles to obscure the truth – which occurs consistently throughout in relation to political deception and identity; it reveals that racial formation like political stability is built on slippery vocabulary and precariously constructed ideas of what constitutes right and wrong.

When news broke of another white supremacist massacre, this time in Buffalo, New York, it reminded me how this kind of fear-fuelled violence is provoked by the rhetoric of those who espouse conspiracies; in this case, the 'great replacement theory' invented by French white nationalist Renaud Camus, who argued in 2011 that Europe's white population was in danger of extinction, to be replaced with Muslims, Jews, Black people or people of colour, Shakespeare's contemporaries were told to be afraid too that 'strange' diabolical figures – be they witches, demons, Muslims, Jews or Africans – would annihilate or replace them; modern white supremacist channels churn out a similar, codified rhetoric about Black people, Jews and immigrants. Little has changed in the methodology.

Exactly who or what the 'witches' are has been a point of debate amongst scholars for decades. In Shakespeare's source text, they are called 'nymphs'. But the play refers to them as witches and 'weyward' or 'weyard' (weird) sisters, which has been interpreted by some to be 'wyrd', meaning destiny. This holds up, given their prophetic powers. But 'weyward' has perhaps a more pertinent set of meanings when it comes to the othering of the three sisters – 'perverse', 'wilful', 'wrongheaded', 'erratic' and even 'fugitive'. Once we understand how the three sisters operate, witness their effect on the Macbeths and notice the ease with which they move between worlds, these meanings fit more seamlessly.

Macbeth and his companion Banquo encounter the 'weyward sisters' and immediately note their alien-like qualities:

MACBETH
So foul and fair a day I have not seen.
BANQUO
How far is't called to Forres? What are these,
So withered and so wiled in their attire,
That look not like th'inhabitants o'th'earth,
And yet are on't?

(1.3.38–41)

By now we are familiar with the semantic weight of words like 'fair' and 'foul', that they were signifiers that played a crucial role in the formation of race through all kinds of texts in sixteenth- and seventeenth-century England. Here Macbeth acknowledges prophetically that the day's value is ambiguous; it will bring the worst and the best to him. His unwelcome fate and his greatest, as yet untapped desires will be joined together in the prophecies he will hear. Black and white are intermingled, making the language interracial itself.

Banquo is unable to identify these 'withered' and wildly attired people that 'should be women, / And yet your beards forbid me to interpret / That you are so' (1.3.45–7). Most readers will assume this means they are old crones and the word 'hag' shows up in the play to help justify this. But it is not so straightforward. This exchange echoes some of the cross-cultural encounters seen in travel literature. In the geographer Richard Hakluyt's *Principal Navigations*, we find an account of the first English voyage to Africa in 1553, in which some of the people are described using the same tone as Banquo's of marvel and alienation: 'Among other things therefore touching the manners and nature of the people, this may seem strange, that their princes and noble men use to pounce and rase their skins'.[6] The othering of the witches is a racial strategy, and one way it is achieved is through the word 'strange', which turns up seventeen times. We might think of 'strange' as referring to that which is odd or unnatural in the modern sense, but in Shakespeare's time and earlier it explicitly meant 'alien', 'barbarous', 'exotic', 'uncouth', 'savage' or 'wild', as described by linguist John Palsgrave in 1530. The Tudor scholar Sir Thomas Elyot saw 'monstrous' as synonymous with 'strange', particularly in the context of portents or prophecies.[7] By the time Elizabeth was on the throne, the word referred to foreigners. In *Macbeth* the prophecy is 'strange intelligence' (1.3.75); 'garments' or clothes are 'strange' (147); Lennox hears 'strange screams of death' (2.3.56); an old man reports having seen 'Hours dreadful and things strange' (2.4.3); and when Macbeth sees Banquo's ghost he reckons he has a 'strange infirmity' (3.4.86), etc.

The witches greet Macbeth as Thane of Glamis, which he is; then Thane of Cawdor, which he is not yet; they tell him he 'shalt be king hereafter' (1.3.50). Banquo notes Macbeth's fearful demeanour and calls what they have just heard 'Things that do sound so fair' (52), so asks why he looks concerned. But the news is far from 'fair' really. Macbeth's mind is infected with the suggestion of his political rise, which simultaneously thrills and terrifies him; it is when he is met by nobles Ross and Angus with the title of Thane of Cawdor that the suggestion becomes fact and reinforced when King Duncan later praises him and proposes to visit his castle in Dunsinane. When Lady Macbeth is sent word by her husband of their guest, she retorts that 'The raven himself is hoarse / That croaks the fatal entrance of Duncan / Under my battlements' (1.5.38–40), invoking traditional harbingers of death. Literary readings of Lady M have often taken her to task as the head witch, as evil, more ambitious than her husband, coercive, manipulative and emasculating. In other words, most readings of her throughout the nineteenth and twentieth centuries were misogynistic.

When we first meet Lady Macbeth we can see how Shakespeare's heroine subscribes to the values of Machiavellian masculinity. The language in the play operates at times upon a colour continuum, and mingles the masculine with the racial. On such a continuum, 'fair' would be at one end – its whiteness with a lustre signifying purity and virtue, the highly prized shade of white observable across Shakespeare's works. At the other end lies 'foul', which links in the Renaissance imagination with blackness, repeatedly aligned with diabolism, witchcraft, barbarity and untamed sexuality. The variations that lie between these two extremes also matter when it comes to reading race in Shakespeare. We have seen how some characters become mobile on the colour continuum – early modern ideas of blackness are mapped on to Desdemona, for example – where white characters are dissociated from whiteness through the process of racialisation. In the Scottish play, 'fair is foul and foul is fair' suggests a hypermobility, or even a comingling, and interchangeable categories of racial distinction. This makes race and identity extremely unstable in a play where 'strangeness' dominates.

'SO FAIR AND FOUL A DAY'

In Act 1 scene 5, Lady Macbeth is centre stage reading a letter from her husband while worrying about the 'kind' of man he is:

> Glamis thou art, and Cawdor, and shalt be
> What thou art promised. Yet do I fear thy nature,
> It is too full o'th'milk of human kindness
> To catch the nearest way. Thou wouldst be great,
> Art not without ambition, but without
> The illness should attend it…
>
> (15–21)

She assumes that waiting for the crown to appear magically upon Macbeth's head is not an option, because her husband is 'too full o'th'milk of human kindness'; she equates Macbeth's particular whiteness – his 'kindness', signalled by the image of milk – with cowardice; the word 'kind' itself rooted in kinship, lineage and race. He is ambitious but he does not have the 'evil' or Machiavellian craftiness that must attend aspirations to great power, so she calls upon spirits to 'unsex' her and fill her with 'direst cruelty' (43) necessary to help her husband rise to power; she invokes 'thick night' (50), coded through images of darkness and diabolism: the 'dunnest smoke of hell' (51), 'blanket of the dark' (53) sky, and emphasising the role of deception and concealment in regicide.

The European assertion of white identity is cast in the image of fairness; but what is the link between whiteness and fear? Cowardice is unaligned to masculine ideals of honour and valour and therefore far removed from the ideal. Paleness in Shakespeare signals cowardice, is dissociated from the 'fair' whiteness of European exceptionalism: 'my hands are of your colour, but I shame / To wear a heart so white', says Lady Macbeth to her husband just after the regicide (2.2.65–6); Macbeth is kept 'pale' (3.2.51) by the bond he has made to murder his way to power; later on he admits his cheeks are 'blanched with fear' in contrast to his wife's 'ruby' cheek (3.4.114); more emboldened in Act 5, he tells his soldier to prick and 'over-red' his face to hide the 'linen cheeks' of *his* fear (5.3.16). This relationship between fear and paleness is elsewhere in Shakespeare – in *Hamlet* we hear how action is 'sicklied o'er with the pale cast of thought' (3.1.84).

The face is where we see these emotional and moral/spiritual changes. And like any regicidal Machiavellian pair worth their salt, from the start the Macbeths know they have to 'mock the time with *fairest* show: / False face must hide what the false heart doth know' (1.7.82–3). Faces and hearts become contrapuntal in this tragic narrative. At the time, the face was viewed widely as a map charting the inner workings of the mind; it should reveal one's character and signify the nature of their heart.

When Duncan hears of the execution of the first Thane of Cawdor, a traitor, he ruminates that there is 'no art / To find the mind's construction in the face' (1.4.11–12) to lament that he never would have guessed at such betrayal. The art that Duncan alludes to is physiognomy, the practice of reading the face to decipher morality, character and intentions. An art which Shakespeare debunks. Sadly, the Scottish king's lack of skill in the art of face-reading, evident also when he addresses Lady Macbeth as '*Fair* and noble hostess' (1.6.24), ends in his bloody murder.

Macbeth is the most mobile on this colour continuum as he increasingly is detached not just from 'fairness' but whiteness too. He gradually calls upon tropes of blackness to hide not only his intentions but to cover his pallid fear:

> ...ere the bat hath flown
> His cloistered flight, ere to black Hecate's summons
> The shard-born beetle, with his drowsy hums,
> Hath run night's yawning peal, there shall be done
> A deed of dreadful note.
>
> (3.2.41–5)

Like Lady Macbeth's 'Come you spirits, unsex me here', Macbeth too summons darker forces as he positions night as a sinister ally:

> ...Come, seeling night,
> Scarf up the tender eye of pitiful day
> And with thy bloody and invisible hand
> Cancel and tear to pieces that great bond
> Which keeps me pale. Light thickens,
> And the crow makes wing to th'rooky wood.

Good things of Day begin to droop and drowse,
While Night's black agents to their preys do rouse.
(47–54)

By Act 4, Macbeth is blackened by his deeds; according to
Malcolm, he is 'black Macbeth' (4.3.52). And his enemy Macduff
explicitly allies him with the devil:

Not in the legions
Of horrid hell can come a devil more damned
In evils to top Macbeth
(4.3.55–7)

The playwright knew the impact made on those quick to believe
in the diabolical practices of witches and the 'strange' ingredients
used to destroy Christian goodness; the language of sorcery aligns
with that of racecraft; it is coercive, provocative, colourful and
shocking:

Root of hemlock digged i'th'dark,
Liver of blaspheming Jew,
Gall of goat and slips of yew
Slivered in the moon's eclipse,
Nose of Turk and Tartar's lips,
Finger of birth-strangled babe
Ditch-delivered by a drab,
Make the gruel thick and slab.
(4.1.25–32)[8]

The cauldron serves as a receptacle for fearful misogynoir-rooted
imaginings about female sexuality and foreigners, a combination

that equates to 'black magic'. The 'liver of a blaspheming Jew' and nose of the Muslim 'Turk and Tartar's lips' invoke the violence against and the racially contaminating menace of 'infidels', who, like the witches, are spectres posing an existential threat to white Christianity. The complex portrayal of the witches in *Macbeth* shows us how language establishes difference. As England's encounters with non-European cultures created a need for differentiation, language developed that sought to demonise and diminish. We can use Shakespeare's play as a critical lens to our present moment to consider how conspiratorial language and dehumanising tropes continue to circulate, overtly as well as stealthily undergirding and perpetuating racial division.

But what do we make of Shakespeare's racialising methods when it comes to his most celebrated and seemingly harmless poetry? How do we read or listen to or perform the racial binaries in one of the greatest love stories ever written?

THE 'FAIR' ART OF LOVE: *ROMEO AND JULIET*

The Shakespeare scholar Kim F. Hall reminds us that 'Shakespeare and his contemporaries regularly use black as if it were a simple antonym for "beautiful"'.[9] Black and white were signs of what was considered ideal and what was not in Shakespeare's time, but they also had a deeper resonance grounded in the fledgling values attached to race and empire in this period. 'Oh dear, please don't ruin *Romeo and Juliet* by talking about race!' said a member of the public when the Globe hosted an anti-racist webinar on the play. You may be thinking this too. But worry not, because the play can't be ruined. It *can* be opened up, however, and questioned, unpacked, challenged even, but not much can be done to ruin a play that is perhaps the most beloved and the most globally popular in Shakespeare's canon. It is the gateway drug for school children. It was mine. I admitted when I introduced this book how my fifteen-year-old heart was stolen by the passion and intensity of this young, 'star-crossed' couple. But now that I'm older, more practised at reading Shakespeare, I want to consider what it means to think about race in relation to this play in the twenty-first century while keeping in view what it might have meant in its own time.

So many film versions, stage performances and adaptations exist, demonstrating the myriad ways this play can be read, how it can be transplanted into a vast variety of contexts, geographies and cultures. It is easy to see how the play's attention to conflict, kinship and blood might enable interpretations that consider race, ethnicity and colonialism. Two warring families – the Montagues and Capulets – are at the centre, but we never learn why they are feuding. We only know that each side is full of hate and fury for the other. The two families may be 'both alike in dignity' (or status), but in 'fair Verona' extreme devotion to kinship bonds dictates the rules. By staging the clandestine love of two young people who attempt to erase the identities that would keep them apart, Shakespeare throws light upon the tragic consequences of identity-based extremism. In 2023, we know something about that.

Shakespeare's interracial poetic strategy is heightened from the start in *Romeo and Juliet*. We meet two servants of the Capulet household who banter about servitude, the 'ancient' feud and raping virgins. It's a discomfiting conversation; perhaps that is why it is so often cut. They talk of carrying coals, being fouled by the filth of such a dirty job, and then talk of the incentive they have to 'thrust to the wall' the women of the Montague house-hold and take their 'maidenheads'. Samson says he will 'take the wall of any man or maid of Montague's' (1.1.11) meaning that part of a wall in a house/villa that is the cleanest, a proverbial assertion of his superiority and entitlement. But Gregory suggests that will make him a 'weak slave' (12). Aligning filth and coal with slavery and unrestrained sexual assault triggers the play's attention to racialised imagery and brings black stereotypes into the frame with the value judgments attached to colour-coded language.

We are fully aware that there is conflict and strife in the action of the play; we know that the two sides of the feud use violence, linguistic and bodily, to assert their identity and supremacy. But what occurs in the expressions of love and beauty sheds even more light upon the extent to which *Romeo and Juliet* participates in the racial formation in this era and how we, in a supposedly post-colonial moment, should talk about this play now. We should think about how students of colour in a classroom or actors of colour in a rehearsal room receive this language and can get to grips with the excessively valued and quite sublime poetry that just happens to, at times, diminish their own bodies.

In Act 1 scene 1, the young Montague displays the signs of a very typical Renaissance lover – the 'Petrarchan lover' named after fourteenth-century poet Francesco Petrarca, who is most famous for his sonnets written in praise of his idealised mistress Laura. It is a genre Shakespeare liked to poke fun at. Like any typical Petrarchan lover, when we first meet him Romeo is melancholy, sighing, brooding, despairing over his unrequited love, the ideal woman... Rosaline: 'She is too fair, too wise, wisely too fair, / To merit bliss by making me despair' (1.1.219–20). Rosaline is not deliberately trying to destroy him, though that's what it feels like. He puns on 'fair' to describe her white, shining beauty, but also her 'fair' mind; blessed with wisdom she has rejected love entirely. Romeo uses the hyperbolic poetry and imagery very fashionable in his day that idealised white women as virtuous ideals of beauty. Benvolio is more practical; he tells his kinsman to look at other women and enjoy their beauties. But Romeo says looking at other women would only amplify for him Rosaline's beauty:

> Show me a mistress that is passing fair,
> What doth her beauty serve but as a note
> Where I may read who passed that passing fair?
> Farewell, thou canst not teach me to forget.
>
> (1.1.232–5)

Shakespeare is renowned for the musicality of Romeo's romantic lamentations; the use of repetition – 'passing', 'passed', 'passing' and the puns 'fair', 'fair', 'farewell' – is also our playwright flexing his rhetorical muscles. Romeo draws on the language of ideal beauty to demonstrate the absolute impossibility that anyone could surpass or pass that 'fair' = beauty/whiteness. He suggests that Rosaline is not only the most beautiful woman in Verona, she is also the whitest.

THE FOIL OF BLACK

When we meet Juliet, she is with her nurse and her mother Lady Capulet tells her the 'valiant' gentleman Paris wants to marry her. Juliet is not enthusiastic. The Capulets are preparing for a ball and Romeo and his friends, Mercutio (cousin to

Prince Escalus, the Duke) and Benvolio with masques and torches prepare to attend. From this point (Act 1 scene 4) the language of the play conspires with the thematic focus on warring factions, on opposites and the unique effects if they mingle. Shakespeare's investment in the poetic potential of his go-to binaries should not be underestimated – brightness and darkness dominate: day and night; white and black; the sun and the moon. His poetic strategy, as I have said, feels inter-racial. For example, the word 'fair' alone is used over forty times in the first two acts alone, while after the play takes its tragic turn, darkness descends over the verse and we feel not just the emotional but also the visual tone alter as we are taken on this tragic journey through tropes of night and darkness. Light is everywhere in the early acts and when Romeo and his mates enter the ball, they have already poeticised about the flaming torches they carry. It's not just women who are fair, but Verona itself, moods, hearts and minds. Romeo is still melancholy in Act 1 scene 4 so he'll take the torches from his friends and watch from the sidelines – 'The game was ne'er so fair, and I am dun' (39); Shakespeare uses the word 'dun' to refer to brown, dusky, not-fair, but here it is also melancholy. Most of us know what happens when Romeo enters the Capulet ball. He lays eyes on Juliet and falls in love at first sight. She dazzles him as heavenly light seems to burst out from her entire being:

O, she doth teach the torches to burn bright

(1.5.43)

But then Shakespeare gives us an image, often ignored, un-noted, dismissed as trope, but it matters and I shall render it visible here:

232

It seems she hangs upon the cheek of night
As a rich jewel in an Ethiop's ear,
Beauty too rich for use, for earth too dear.
So shows a snowy dove trooping with crows
As yonder lady o'er her fellows shows.
The measure done, I'll watch her place of stand
And, touching hers, make blessed my rude hand.
Did my heart love till now? Forswear it, sight,
For I ne'er saw true beauty till this night.

(1.5.44–52)

Romeo has just contradicted his own assumption about Rosaline having seen someone even more beautiful. We know she is fairer because of the vivid pictures he creates to describe her unmatched beauty. Juliet is a 'rich jewel' that twinkles in an 'Ethiop's ear'. Her radiant beauty shimmers against the darkness of the night; the black skin of an Ethiopian provides the foil to showcase the combination of complexion and virtue. For years mainstream Shakespeare scholarship has ignored this image. And that might be understandable if it was an isolated one. But as we'll see in the next chapter, the image of an Ethiopian comes up again and again and not always in such seemingly pleasant moments. How blackness is used as a prop for whiteness is not confined strictly to poetry. In the art of the Renaissance there are numerous examples where a beautiful white woman is centred, the use of light and perspective making her skin glow while a black person, usually someone in service, is used not only to make the white subject appear more 'fair' but also to demonstrate imperial wealth and colonial ambition through 'exotic' acquisition.

The image of an African with a jewel delicately hanging from their ear is more commonplace in Renaissance European depictions than we might imagine. In Titian's painting of Laura dei Dianti, the wife of the Duke of Ferrara, the African child accompanying her holds a pair of gloves, which like the boy himself symbolises wealth, status and identity. You'll note a rich jewel hanging from his ear. While we know who the subject of the painting is, we know nothing of the identity of the child, whose story remains untold. Aristocratic households and courts across Europe collected Africans to be gazed at, as mere symbols of extravagance as well as domestic servants. Their darkened bodies sit like shadows against the rich, textural whitened bodies centred in these portraits showcasing the rising European power and hunger for colonial acquisition and the cultivation of entitlement amongst the upper classes. As the seventeenth century rolled on, more and more examples of such portraits emerged with black boys wearing a jewel earring providing the visual foil to white ladies, showcasing the deepening of England's involvement in the slave trade and imperialism.

Shakespeare's example, you may be thinking, is not about imperial acquisition; 'it's just a metaphor'. But metaphors are powerful signifiers of ideas, ideas rooted in social and cultural contexts; metaphors are portraits created through words. We have been reading this passage from *Romeo and Juliet* for centuries, revering it without necessarily realising how moved and intoxicated we are by the poetic descriptions that just happen to elevate whiteness above blackness. Discussing this passage with Alfred Enoch and Rebekah Murrell, two biracial actors who played Romeo and Juliet in the Globe's 2021 production, directed by Ola Ince, it was clear that these lines struck a nerve with them as they spoke about their love for Shakespeare and excitement about performing his words. In a 2020 documentary (*Behind Closed Doors*) created by Shakespeare's Globe to give audiences a glimpse into the kinds of conversations had in rehearsal rooms, we discussed the ways in which these lines impact upon performers who are not white: Enoch (who has starred in the hit TV series *How to Get Away with Murder* as well as the Harry Potter movies) is a devoted Shakespearean actor, and asked pointedly, 'As Black people, how do we make the language ours?' Both actors commented on the sense of internalised racism BME/BIPOC actors experience when they are told by Shakespeare's verse what beauty is – white – and what it isn't – black. The language seems rooted in burgeoning notions of Empire; the portraits above show just how tangible this association is. These tropes, which are part of the fabric of perception in the West, go some way towards colonising the minds of people of colour who also digest these images from an early age and then have to teach them, or learn about them, or deliver them on stage. Curious readers and lovers of Shakespeare who recognise the value in colour-conscious casting will understand that Shakespeare's moment and his work are not always inherently inclusive of non-white bodies. This means acknowledging that the poetry in some of our favourite plays can be beautiful to some and problematic for those who do not represent the traditional ideal.

As Romeo's apostrophe to Juliet's beauty continues, he doubles down on the white/black binary with Juliet contrasting directly with the women around her:

> So shows a snowy dove trooping with crows
> As yonder lady o'er her fellows shows.

Again, a poetically vivid image. We can picture a beautiful white dove triumphantly, almost militarily marching, its superiority and beauty enhanced by the blackness of the crows. Romeo's persistence in drawing on the imagery of brightness, lightness and whiteness culminates in their first encounter. It is one of my favourite moments in Shakespeare, full of passion, ecstasy, joy, wonder. Who hasn't felt the glory of falling in love? The sonnet (a fourteen-line poem usually in iambic pentameter – meaning each line has ten syllables where the first syllable is unstressed and the second is stressed) was hugely popular in Elizabethan England and was the chief vehicle for the passionate expressions of love and desire. The young couple speak in a shared sonnet. It starts with the line 'If I profane with my unworthiest hand' and ends fourteen lines later with 'Then move not, while my prayer's effect I take'. It's pretty smooth, actually. As they construct a poem spontaneously together, the young couple create a joint metaphor of saints and pilgrims which culminates in their first kiss:

> ROMEO
> Have not saints lips and holy palmers too?
> JULIET
> Ay, pilgrim, lips that they must use in prayer.
> ROMEO
> O then, dear saint, let lips do what hands do –
> They pray; grant thou, lest faith turn to despair.
>
> (1.5.100–4)

Juliet is the saint, worshipped by the somewhat baser pilgrim lover who has already been palm to palm with her only to propose that their lips do the same. Shakespeare takes the Petrarchan ideal of the pale, glistening female virtuous mistress to new heights.

'ANCIENT GRUDGE' AND RACIAL MUTINY

When Romeo and Juliet discover each other's identity, they both feel the premonition of darkness descend. This doesn't prevent them from sacrificing everything to be together. The famed 'balcony' scene gives Romeo another opportunity to elevate Juliet's beauty even higher. She goes from resembling a jewel in an 'Ethiop's ear', to a snowy dove 'trooping' amongst black crows, to a bright saint, then to the sun itself as she appears in her window:

> Arise, fair sun, and kill the envious moon,
> Who is already sick and pale with grief
> That thou her maid art far more fair than she.
>
> (2.2.3–5)

The backbone of the play, the 'ancient grudge', is tied to these racialised images of superiority and inferiority. Romeo, like all Petrarchan lovers, often places himself beneath his lady, and of course he is physically positioned below her to iconic effect in the balcony scene. In the metaphorical world of Shakespeare's play, this means he is darker, evident in his melancholic ramblings earlier in the play and in 'night's cloak to hide' his face from the Capulets; while Juliet is 'fair maid', sun and bright angel.

Earlier at the Capulet ball, Juliet's cousin Tybalt, known for being brilliant at fencing, spies Romeo and it fills him with fury. Old Capulet tells him to leave the issue alone so as not to disrupt his festivities, but Tybalt is not happy:

> This by his voice should be a Montague.
> Fetch me my rapier, boy. [*Exit Page.*]

What, dares the slave
Come hither, covered with an antic face,
To fleer and scorn at our solemnity?
Now by the stock and honour of my kin,
To strike him dead I hold it not a sin.

(1.5.53–8)

Tybalt's outrage at Romeo's unwelcome presence uses language which echoes fears at the time of the number of strangers infiltrating England.[10] Just by being there Romeo is dishonouring Tybalt's superior 'stock', his 'kin', his people. The Shakespeare scholar and novelist Margo Hendricks tells us that the word 'race' was important enough to be included in Renaissance dictionaries; for example, in Italian linguist John Florio's *World of Words* (1590), he 'offers the following entry for the Italian term for race: *Razza, Raza*, as *Raggia*, a kind of race, a brood, a blood, a stock, a name, a pedigree'.[11]

Despite the two families being 'alike in dignity', they are seen by each other as a different 'stock', as Tybalt says, a different race. I am not proposing this as certain or even probable, but it is a tantalising question: what if Romeo and Juliet are, in this way, another interracial couple on the Shakespearean stage?

We are privileged to follow Romeo into the Capulet orchard, his second invasion into their land, where he spies her at her window; now we overhear Juliet's desire for Romeo to *not* be of his stock or his name; in her iconic 'Romeo, O, Romeo' speech, she retorts that,

'Tis but thy name that is my enemy.
Thou art thyself, though not a Montague.
What's Montague? It is nor hand nor foot,

Nor arm nor face nor any other part
Belonging to a man. O be some other name!
What's in a name? That which we call a rose
By any other word would smell as sweet;

(2.2.38–44)

Juliet has been raised with the belief that Montagues are different and therefore enemies. Her sentiments somewhat resemble Shylock's 'Hath not a Jew eyes' speech in *The Merchant of Venice* in its attempt to point out what science has proven without a shadow of a doubt, that there is *no biological basis* for difference. Our names are not our bodies; in other words, the classifications and the labels we give each other to create distinctions that make us feel safe are rooted in myth, socially constructed and ultimately destructive. The essence of Romeo is that of a man and Juliet sees him and his beauty, thus she calls him 'fair Montague' (2.2.98).

When the lovers exchange vows of love and decide to marry, they part with bittersweet yearnings: 'Parting is such sweet sorrow / That I shall say goodnight till it be morrow' (184–5). But they have mingled their names and identities and Shakespeare's cosmic imagery conspires to create an interracial image of night becoming day, reflecting Romeo's melancholy being lifted by this newfound bright love, and for a moment both states coexist:

The grey-eyed morn smiles on the frowning night,
Chequering the eastern clouds with streaks of light,
And darkness, fleckled, like a drunkard reels
From forth day's pathway made by Titan's wheels.

(2.2.188–91)

This extraordinarily vivid depiction of night fading and dawn encroaching captures that sweet spot in time when it is at once day and night. The tone of the tragedy, joy of love, combined with death, loss and grief, are encapsulated by these racialised patterns of language.

With Romeo and Juliet's marriage aided by the well-intentioned Friar Laurence and the Nurse their happiness is tragically interrupted by another street brawl turned bloody. Tybalt and Mercutio's deaths as well as Romeo's banishment and Juliet's enforced marriage to Paris swerve the play sharply away from the giddy star-gazing poetry of love, longing and foreboding into the realm of despair that drives us towards the double suicide of two teenagers. When Ola Ince directed it at the Globe, she was determined not to romanticise the suicide. She examined the relationship between youth and depression, drawing upon the post-pandemic mental health crisis that has devoured young people across the world. Naturally, the production was criticised in a *Daily Mail* headline: 'Wokeo and Juliet'. Never mind; it is clear that if a theatre artist, particularly a Black woman, decides not to adhere to the conventional reading of the play, the 'safe' interpretation that simply makes us feel nostalgic about being young and in love, the Great White Bard's most avid bodyguards will always become enraged.

Contradiction, opposites, binaries, multivocality, mixed imagery and biraciality all characterise the language of the play. Its very pulse is contrapuntal and driven by a racialising linguistic energy. When Juliet hears that her cousin Tybalt is dead and that her husband has killed him, she does not know which news devastates her more. We then experience the emotional contradictions along with her; the poetics of white and black are woven together in Shakespeare's masterful use of paradox: 'O serpent heart hid with a flowering face!' (3.2.73), she says of Romeo the murderer of her kinsman; 'Did ever dragon keep so fair a cave?' (74). As we saw in *Macbeth*, the discrepancies between the face and the heart alert us to the popular motif of deception. Unlike Macbeth, Romeo is *not* a dragon, and Juliet knows it, but her fighting heart can't help but mingle the imagery both lovers have depended upon:

> Beautiful tyrant, fiend angelical,
> Dove-feathered raven, wolvish-ravening lamb,
> Despised substance of divinest show,
> Just opposite to what thou justly seem'st,
> A damned saint, an honourable villain.
>
> (75–9)

She recalls for us the black and white birds referenced earlier, but this time the bird is a hybrid of the dove and the raven, a biracial image that helps Juliet make sense of the duality of her affections, grief and betrayal mixed with love and desire:

> Was ever book containing such vile matter
> So fairly bound? O, that deceit should dwell
> In such a gorgeous palace.
>
> (3.2.83–5)

We know what happens at the end of this play, so I will conclude with Juliet's desires. The racialising language has a very different effect in this play than it does in *Macbeth*. There are moments that disturb us, like the Ethiop image, the comparison of unattractive women to 'crows', the promotion of whiteness and light above blackness and the dark. Teachers must discuss this openly with students to ensure diverse classrooms are able to question the poetry's meaning and not merely accept its splendour. Instead, it is helpful to ask *why* this is considered beautiful language; who says it is? What are we valuing in these images? Who is being diminished or erased by them? What is the legacy of this imagery today? Both Romeo and Juliet come to depend on such language to express the turmoil of love and grief; to aid their understanding of their emotions through paradox and contradiction as well as reversal. We may recall as Romeo kisses Juliet in the tomb when he thinks she is dead, he relies again on the same imagery: 'Ah, dear Juliet, / Why art thou yet so fair?' (5.3.101–2). While night was deemed terrifying in Shakespeare's time, the 'witching hour' as Hamlet called it, Juliet's summoning of night reverses these associations. Contrasting with Macbeth's invocation of night to hide his sins, recall in Act 3 Juliet's impatient urging of night's arrival so she can consummate her marriage:

> Come, civil night,
> Thou sober-suited matron all in black,
> And learn me how to lose a winning match,
> Played for a pair of stainless maidenhoods.
> Hood my unmanned blood, bating in my cheeks,
> With thy black mantle, till strange love grow bold,
> Think true love acted simple modesty.
> Come, night, come, Romeo, come, thou day in night,
> For thou wilt lie upon the wings of night
> Whiter than new snow upon a raven's back.
> Come, gentle night, come, loving black-browed night,
> Give me my Romeo, and when I shall die
> Take him and cut him out in little stars,
> And he will make the face of heaven so fine

That all the world will be in love with night
And pay no worship to the garish sun.

(3.2.10–25)

Here, night is desired, it is 'civil', 'sober-suited' and 'gentle'; it can cloak her as she loses her 'maidenhood' (her virginity) once and for all. Romeo will come with the night, his fairness or beauty will be like a 'day' in the night, recalling that image of the sweet spot of time – he will fly on night's wings as if he were snow on a raven's back. Again, we encounter an image in which blackness is praised precisely because its very presence asserts the indisputable primacy of whiteness. An image pattern with racial meanings we can no longer deny.

Eight

ANTI-BLACK COMEDY

...methinks she's too low for a high praise, **too brown for a fair praise**, and too little for a great praise...
(Benedick, *Much Ado About Nothing*, 1.1.163–5)

In 2019 the Public Theater in New York staged Shakespeare's popular comedy, *Much Ado About Nothing*, in the Delacorte Theater in Central Park. Tony Award-winning director Kenny Leon cast the play with an all-Black company, seeing the comedy as an appropriate site for exploring community and democratic values. Set in the aftermath of war, *Much Ado* stages what happens after the Prince of Aragon – Don Pedro – and his fellow soldiers return to Messina, Italy, to the home of Don Pedro's friend Leonato; romance, revelry, misunderstanding, deception and humorous word-play ensue. Leon's updated setting is just outside Atlanta, Georgia, in a town called Aragon in 2020. He felt Atlanta's substantial and affluent African American population would perfectly suit the play's concern with wealth and identity. After the civil rights movement, Georgia became an important site for protest and activism, which the production captures by way of the military theme. Opening with its lead actress singing Marvin Gaye's 'What's Going On?' was an explicit nod to this context. Stacy Abrams, the nearly elected Governor of Georgia who still contends the office was stolen through Black voter suppression, is proudly invoked on a banner hanging on the wall of the fairy-light-strewn festive set under the stars in Central Park. The director wanted to showcase the joy, pride and patriotism within the African American community despite America's turbulent history of racial oppression.

In this version of the play, the war is not traditional military combat against a foreign enemy but rather the war for equality, civil rights and the pursuit of racial justice; the soul of the nation is at stake rather than its territory. Because it was an all-Black cast, lines like those that opened this chapter were cut. In Shakespeare's text they are heard when the young soldier Claudio sees the daughter of Leonato, Hero, and asks Benedick (Grantham Coleman in the Public's production) what he thinks of her. Benedick's response is tepid if not cruel when he suggests she's not the prettiest woman he's ever seen. In a line that is meant to induce laughter, he comments that she is too short, too dark and too insignificant. 'Too brown for a fair praise' means she doesn't merit the kind of popular poetry that worships alabaster faces, or rose and lily cheeks. The actress playing Beatrice in Leon's production, Danielle Brooks (known for her role in the Netflix hit *Orange is the New Black*), remarked that it would have been offensive to make this joke in a production that promised to 'put black excellence front and centre'.[1] Brooks jubilantly noted that this was the first time she had 'seen a Beatrice be dark-skinned plus-sized with natural hair' and relished the opportunity to bring her own identity to the role. The racist joke about being too brown would have jarred violently in a production that was in part a 'celebration of black bodies'.[2]

Writing about the production, Bernadette Looney contends that while Shakespeare 'never claims that white-skinned

Englishmen are superior to others…he assumes that and builds metaphors around it'. The interventions of the director were essential so that the comedy could be served up to a diverse, twenty-first-century audience. Looney continues, 'Shakespeare can be made for everyone, with significant changes, but the original is not for all – never has been, never will be'.[3] Kenny Leon has a more positive take, seeing Shakespeare, along with August Wilson, as one of the greatest writers in the literary pantheon. For him the messages of the play say we need to 'live in a world that is embracing of love, that is embracing of laughter, of singing songs out loud'.[4] An all-Black cast is not an anti-white statement, as the director declares himself; it is the opposite, in fact, because it demonstrates that Shakespeare can be, with some mediation, for everyone.

RACIAL LAUGHTER

Shakespeare's comedies are as funny today as ever. There have been numerous times when I have stood in the Yard at the Globe and cried with laughter, as when watching the 'rude mechanicals' performing 'Pyramus and Thisbe' as if staging 'The Play That Went Wrong' in *A Midsummer Night's Dream*, or the time I howled at Mark Rylance's shocked whitened face when his Lady Olivia discovers Stephen Fry's yellow-stockinged Malvolio prancing across the stage during the 'Original Practices' performance of *Twelfth Night*. Laughter in the Globe Theatre is dangerously contagious; the spectators being visible to each other, the physicality of laughter and the sound of hilarity move through the crowd like electric currents zapping everyone in turn. The energy of a performance is born in the Yard where groundlings stand, seven hundred spectators shoulder to shoulder; so, whether it is laughter, amazement, fear or despair, the groundlings can dictate the emotional tenor of a performance, especially if the performers let it get away from them. Actors at the Globe often talk about how the electrifying energy of the groundlings affects their performances; the atmosphere helps nourish the intimate and playful relationship between them and the eager crowd. This dynamic between the actor, audience and the Globe's unique architecture is the defining feature of Elizabethan theatre. And it can be truly magical.

There is humour in most of Shakespeare's plays, tragedies *and* comedies. From the macabre humour in *Titus Andronicus* with its incessant punning on 'hands' during the amputation scene to the Nurse and Juliet's witty repartee in *Romeo and Juliet* to the drunken porter's quips and knock-knock jokes in *Macbeth*, Shakespeare often provides emotional relief for his audiences, who, at times, may be suffering or about to suffer the 'slings and arrows' of tragic pathos. Comedies are designed to be more consistently funny, though, and to end not on a tragic, but on an optimistic note. Shakespeare's 'problem' comedies such as *The Merchant of Venice* and *Measure for Measure* are a different story. Scholars labelled them 'problematic' because there's nothing funny *or* optimistic about the depiction of the Renaissance culture of antisemitism, nor about a play that handles themes like rape and consent in ways that disturb and taunt our modern and now post-MeToo sensibilities. And don't get me started on *The Taming of the Shrew*.

Perhaps it is wishful thinking, but I like to imagine that Shakespeare himself saw these ideas as problematic even then. Why else would he stage them other than to be provocative, political, and at times, critical, of his own moment? Some of the most challenging experiences I have felt as a spectator while watching a Shakespeare play have been while racist jokes or supposedly humorous stereotyping provoke gales of laughter from the audience. It makes me wonder how conscious audiences are of their responses during the opening scenes of *Othello* when Iago compares the Venetian Captain to a 'barbary horse' or a 'black ram tupping' a 'white ewe', for example. Why is this so funny? The way it is performed? The comedic structure of the scene? Or is it that racist humour is effective even to this day? It seems particularly funny when humans are compared to animals. That's a centuries-old favourite. It doesn't seem to matter in what type of venue *Othello* is performed; unless the opening scene is staged unconventionally, it almost always makes people guffaw, but it is unfortunately more noticeable in the Globe where audience emotions can fuel the engine of a performance. Being a person of colour while hearing and experiencing this kind of laughter (conscious or unconscious) is extremely unpleasant and makes Shakespeare seem like a writer who belongs only to white people after all. Not so magical then. Each time I witnessed such responses to the play in theatres in the US and Canada as well as in the UK, the spectators were predominantly white, and Iago really knows how to make them laugh.

Racist humour is a social tool that binds certain groups of people together and separates them from the 'other'. The sociologist Raúl Pérez tells us that:

> [H]umor holds significant affiliative power – something that is equally true in racist humor. This affiliative power enables humor to function as a mechanism that contributes to social alignment, building solidarity, and maintaining and reproducing a shared worldview. But while a key function of social humor is in drawing some

people closer together, an equally significant aspect is the capacity of humor to keep us apart.[5]

Humour and comedy establish bonds and produce solidarity, a powerful feeling of experiential sameness. When people laugh together, they become a community that, as Pérez notes, share a worldview. Let's remind ourselves that the Renaissance world-view was underpinned by the assertion of whiteness as marker of Anglo-European superiority as it relates to religion, power, culture and civility. During the Middle Ages and Renaissance period whiteness was becoming a symbolic lens through which purity, virtue and Christian goodness were viewed. Ever since, the supremacy of white identity has been leveraged and sustained through a variety of means, including humour.

Shakespeare's comedies contain a myriad of jokes, many of which mock or satirise women, 'Moors', Jews, Turks, the elderly, the young, the aristocracy, the working classes, farmers or rustics as well as kings and nobles. No one is spared. But as literary scholar Patricia Akhimie points out, 'Shakespeare's racist humor' needs to be looked at more closely.[6] When I set out to write this book, I had no intention of trying to separate Shakespeare from the racism that emerges from his texts. My goal was always to show how it rears its head, even in the scenes, lines, moments, characters, poetry that are the most unexpected or that seem innocuous if not delightful. I wanted to know why we still laugh at racial slurs and acts of exclusion. That the comedies demonstrate a racist edge is not in dispute. However, like any Shakespeare scholar who observes the tensions between fiction and the biographical details of an author in Elizabethan literary culture, I cannot with confidence claim Shakespeare's racist jokes point unequivocally to his own anti-black or antisemitic feelings. Then again, I am not interested in assessing whether the Bard was racist by our standards or not. He is dead. The plays are still here and very much alive. That's what we must grapple with if we are to continue enjoying, performing, reading and studying them.

We witnessed in *The Merchant of Venice* how harmful racist jokes can be not just to the emotional and social lives of the individual or group under attack. They also form part of the rhetoric that actually contributes to making the Jews in the play vulnerable to state authority and the law. *Merchant* contains so much racist rhetoric and offensive comedy that modern ears struggle to bear it even while the 'humour' continues to provoke laughter in some productions. But the humour that seemingly causes less offense in the unproblematic comedies like *Much Ado About Nothing* or *As You Like It* works on a subtler level. It is stealthy because it is part of the play's comedic preoccupation with courtly love, filial bonds, festivity and friendship. These themes are woven together with joyous poetry as well as biting sixteenth-century jest.

An example of such 'archaism' can be found in a number of plays. We saw in *Romeo and Juliet* Shakespeare's technique of using blackness as a poetic foil to enhance the beauty of Juliet with the reference to her as a jewel in an 'Ethiop's ear'. The comedies at various points take up this image but with a slightly different connotation and to more intentionally humorous effect, becoming overtly racist. In *A Midsummer Night's Dream* when Lysander is under the spell of the juice of love-in-idleness (the flower that makes someone fall in love with the first person/ thing they see), he is no longer interested in Hermia, the young lady he ran away with to the forest outside of Athens to escape the law that opposes their union. Oberon, king of fairies, orders

Robin Goodfellow – Puck – to place the magic juice on the eye of an Athenian, but he confuses Lysander with Demetrius, another young suitor who himself is being pursued desperately by Helena, Hermia's childhood friend. Oberon's pity over Helena's unrequited passion compels him to intervene, but Puck gets it so very wrong and now both young men are in love with the taller, fairer Helena, while Hermia is rejected, dismissed as 'low', 'little' and too dark. Trying to shake her off, Lysander cries out 'Away, you Ethiop' (3.2.256). I have seen this line in many productions provoke laughter. But why is it funny today?

The term shows up in an earlier Shakespearean comedy, *Two Gentleman of Verona*. Proteus (whose name means changeable) travels to Milan with his friend Valentine, and they both fall for Silvia. The only problem is that Proteus has a girlfriend at home, Julia, with whom he's exchanged vows. Proteus decides to pursue Silvia not least because she is of higher status, even if it means he has to betray his friend and neglect his vows to Julia:

> And Silvia – witness heaven that made her fair –
> Shows Julia but a swarthy Ethiop.
> I will forget that Julia is alive,
> Rememb'ring that my love to her is dead
>
> (2.6.25–8)

For extra effect, Shakespeare modifies 'Ethiope' with 'swarthy' to double down on the racist idea of Julia's looks being inferior to Silvia's 'fair'. Julia may as well be dead; she is, in his view, as he resolves to pursue this new love interest. The story doesn't end in his favour and he ends up contrite, begging the forgiveness of his friend and former lover, who, much to my dismay, takes him back.

Shakespeare's perhaps less well-known *Love's Labour's Lost* is a comedy about King Ferdinand of Navarre and his three friends, Berowne, Dumaine and Longueville, who decide to keep away from women for three years so they can spend that time cultivating their minds, their masculinity and their honour – a sort of sixteenth-century *voluntary* celibate men's group. When the Princess of France and her three ladies-in-waiting come to stay, they have to be housed a mile away from court, given the King's new rule, but eventually they are introduced and realise they all know each other. The King falls for the Princess, of course, and each lord falls for one of the ladies. Berowne and Rosaline become the centre of the play. She is not a conventional, fair beauty; she is darker. The play's poetry, therefore, is filled with racialising imagery as Shakespeare meditates, as he does so often in his romantic comedies, on the styles and methods of expressing love in his day. In Act 4 scene 3, the King and his companions discover they are all in love and writing sonnets to their ladies. The King asks Berowne if his 'lines' of poetry give away his love. Berowne answers:

> "Did they?" quoth you. Who sees the heavenly Rosaline
> That, like a rude and savage man of Ind
> At the first opening of the gorgeous East,
> Bows not his vassal head and, stricken blind,
> Kisses the base ground with obedient breast?
>
> (215–19)

For Berowne, young lovers are so inferior to the objects of their worship that they resemble 'savage' men of India; positioning himself as such shows how the play's language is invested in racial rhetoric as a way of describing, in overly poetic flourishes, how female beauty debases young men. Race and misogyny are intertwined in exchanges like this. Shakespeare is interrogating this Petrarchan idea of a woman being placed so high above the male lover. But why does he use racist imagery to do so?

When Berowne praises Rosaline as having a 'fair in her fair cheek', the King disputes with him, as part of their intellectual enterprise, and says 'thy love is black as ebony!'; but Berowne admits that 'fair' faces can be whitened with cosmetics, and therefore become artificial, whereas darker complexions are true and trustworthy, a sentiment about blackness we heard Aaron the Moor articulate in *Titus Andronicus*. Berowne uses the darker features of Rosaline to show how much more beautiful she is; she will in fact be the envy of all women, who will start dying their hair black 'to imitate her brow' (258). But then Dumaine and Longueville chime in:

DUMAINE
To look like her are chimney sweepers black.
LONGUEVILLE
And since her time are colliers counted bright.
KING
And Ethiops of their sweet complexion crack.
DUMAINE
Dark needs no candles now, for dark is light.
BEROWNE
Your mistresses dare never come in rain,
For fear their colors should be washed away.

(260–5)

Berowne's companions mock his attempts to poetically wash an Ethiopian white, which is in effect Berowne's tactic in his praise of Rosaline, who, like Hermia and unlike Juliet, is darker than the women around her. Note the unabashed pun of Berowne's name, signalling his role as advocate for darker complexions, which would align him with the narrator of Shakespeare's own double-edged 'dark lady' sonnets (Sonnets 127–152), which praise the darker features and more relaxed sexual inclinations of the lady. The gentlemen say Rosaline is as dark as soot, coal and an African, while Berowne mocks their ladies for wearing the fashionable white makeup that will wash off in the rain. The play is steeped in this kind of banter, quipping and metaphor, using blackness as a humorous weapon and 'Ethiop' as an insult to debate the value of conventional beauty versus a subjective alternative to the norm. The jokes also gesture to the relationship between blackness and female sexuality at the time. Misogynoir is detectable even in the most seemingly benign moments.

What do teachers, directors and actors do with such lines in a comedy? Do they continue to ignore the racism or dismiss it as being 'of its time'? It is unfortunate how often such lines are kept in scripts without having the conversations in the rehearsal room necessary to enable the actors to be in control of the interpretation, rather than allowing racist humour to run loose upon an audience. Racist slurs in classic texts hurt as much if not more because they get excused for being 'original', authentic and historically legitimated and this somehow means we have to keep them around like old relics or statues of slave traders. This desire to keep Shakespeare static normalises the racist language and its effects upon those of us who are Black, brown, Asian, Jewish or Indigenous. When racist slurs and jokes are ignored, the bodies of diverse performers are diminished.

MUCH ADO ABOUT MISOGYNOIR

Shakespeare's raucous comedy was written between 1598 and 1599 during the height of his writing career. It centres on the relationship between Benedick and Beatrice, niece to Leonato who hosts Don Pedro, Claudio and the perpetual bachelor Benedick after returning from war. Claudio falls for Hero, Leonato's young daughter, and asks Don Pedro to help him to court her. Beatrice has an acerbic wit and much of the play's comedy revolves around the word-play between Beatrice and Benedick whose tongues clash like swords as they attempt, like Katherine and Petruccio in *The Taming of the Shrew*, to win at the game of rhetoric, insult and clever put-down. It's an obvious formula for romantic comedies – the sparring couple eventually fall in love. But they finally unite because their friends trick them, in a wonderful eavesdropping sequence where, in one scene, the women – Hero, Margaret and Ursula – talk about how much Benedick says he loves Beatrice while the same device is enacted amongst the men; this time, Benedick is the one eavesdropping, delighting in what he hears: that Beatrice is in love with him! By this point, Claudio has successfully won the hand of Hero and their nuptials form the main event of the play. But there are other characters who have something to gain from it all going wrong.

Don John, the illegitimate or 'bastard' brother to Don Pedro, wants to disrupt the jollity simply because he is bitter. He plots with his accompanying soldiers, Borachio and Conrade, to convince Claudio that Hero has been unfaithful. As Borachio reports,

> … know that I have tonight wooed Margaret, the Lady
> Hero's gentlewoman, by the name of Hero; she leans

me out at her mistress' chamber window, bids me a
thousand times goodnight – I tell this tale vilely. I
should first tell thee how the prince, Claudio and my
master, planted and placed and possessed by my master
Don John, saw afar off in the orchard this amiable
encounter.

(3.3.138–42)

Convinced that Hero is disloyal, Don Pedro and Claudio plot to
humiliate her and her family at the altar. He denounces her
publicly as the ceremony begins, in terms that recall the
Renaissance ideal of virtue and its associations with natural glimmering, white beauty. Then he gives her back to her father, as if
she's property – 'take her back again' (4.1.28). Just as Othello does
in Shakespeare's tragedy written only a few years later, he then
rails against his bride's deceptive arts:

> She's but the sign and semblance of her honour.
> Behold how like a maid she blushes here!
> O, what authority and show of truth
> Can cunning sin cover itself withal!
>
> (31–4)

What are the 'signs' and 'semblances' of honour? Blushes on pale
cheeks? 'Behold how like a maid she blushes here!' Blushes are
visible upon a white woman's face if she is embarrassed or experiencing shame. The blush in the cheek was an appealing feature of
a young woman in Shakespeare's day; it indicated her purity and
pudeur. The beauty standard at the time dictated a preference for a
facial flickering between red and white, a rose and lily sparring for
dominance, as described in Petrarchan poetry: 'Her cheek, her

256

chin, her neck, her nose, / This was a lily, that was a rose'.[7] Claudio presumes however, that such blushing can be performed; that her virtuous complexion signalled above is faked – 'cunning sin' is good at covering up its presence in a woman's face – perhaps through makeup, that deceptive Jezebel-like weapon.

Claudio concludes that it is not modesty that makes Hero blush, but 'guiltiness,' assuming that 'She knows the heat of a luxurious bed' (4.1.39); that would bring colour to a woman's cheeks. The opposition between chaste white and dark sensual woman influences Claudio's accusations as he makes her sexual transgression a racial one: 'You seem to me as Dian in her orb' (56); Diana – the goddess of the hunt, also linked to the silvery moon and in poetry to Elizabeth I – represented chastity and virtue. But to Claudio's mind, Hero is 'more intemperate in [her] blood / Than Venus, or those pampered animals / That rage in savage sensuality' (57–60). The word 'savage' is a familiar stereotype in racial rhetoric, particularly when it comes to sexual behaviour. Claudio effectively calls Hero an animal and a savage unable to control her impulses.

The Elizabethan geographer and editor Richard Hakluyt's collection of travel writings contain an account of a voyage to Africa dated 1554, which describes the women of Libya as 'common: for they contract no matrimony neither have respect to chastity'.[8] This early Tudor account also tells of mythical creatures, cannibalism and monsters, so we cannot put much stock in it, but it illustrates the importance of chastity to European Christian ideals and how precarious virtue could be for women, who could easily be painted black through judgment, error, misunderstanding, accusation and humour.

Everyone at the wedding is in shock, not least Hero and Leonato, who is told by Don Pedro what he (thinks he) witnessed. Upon hearing the account again, Claudio berates Hero one more time: 'But fare thee well, most foul, most fair. Farewell / Thou pure impiety and impious purity' (4.1.102–4). This language is oxymoronic and steeped in pun. For Claudio, Hero is 'fair' and 'foul' because she appears to be innocent though beneath her deceptive looks she is corrupt. Leonato's reaction is disappointing. When he thinks it might be true that Hero has betrayed Claudio and shamed her family name, he says, 'Death is the fairest cover for her shame' (115); in other words, the only thing that can truly recover her modesty, her virtue, her 'fairness', is death. We soon see how misogynoir takes hold in Shakespearean comedy when Leonato continues with his metaphor of shame:

> …O, she is fallen
> Into a pit of ink that the wide sea
> Hath drops too few to wash her clean again,
> And salt too little which may season give
> To her foul-tainted flesh.
>
> (4.1.138–42)

It is hard to imagine that modern theatrical productions would want to hold on to such lines without serious consideration or intervention. Here the anti-black sentiment is not delivered in a comedic moment, but rather one potentially tragic. What is so troubling is the underlying notion that Black womanhood can be mapped upon Hero's supposed infidelity, which produces her 'foul-tainted' status. Disturbingly, this sentiment forms part of the fabric of thinking about race and gender in Western society today. Black feminist Mikki Kendall takes white feminism to task for writing about patriarchy and sexism in ways that have either elided, erased or perpetuated the debasement of Black women; it has meant,

> [describing] Black women in ways that play up their sexuality and remove their humanity. After all they are Other, so their skin is a foodstuff, the space between their thighs is mysterious, and they have never, ever been innocent. No need to mention virginity or purity; even when speaking of Black female infants, your focus must be on their sexuality...[9]

As difficult as it is to admit, Shakespeare's comedies take part in the process of racial formation that involves stereotyping Black or dark women as 'common' or sexually out of control and that has ramifications for Black women to this day.

When Beatrice can't account for Hero's whereabouts on the night in question because she didn't share her bed chamber as she normally does, Leonato sees this as proof to condemn his daughter. The Friar finally intervenes with his astute capacity to read faces and see the truth in Hero's 'thousand blushing apparitions' (159), which have made her pale with innocence and fear; all that can be seen is the 'angel whiteness' (160) that gives away her 'maiden truth' (164). This man of God can see through the slander to her fair qualities, her innocence and virtue. He comes up with a plan to save her honour – she will fake her death and the family outwardly mourn for her, so that the accusations and anger towards Hero transform to remorse. Beatrice and Benedick share an intimate moment when in tears she asks him to 'kill Claudio' (287) if he truly loves her. This line always makes audiences laugh: 'If you love me, commit murder for me' doesn't strike us as the dialogue of a happy couple. Yet if Beatrice's suggestion is irrational, her anger is not. Benedick will seek out the truth and challenge his friend's behaviour in person.

The bumbling constable, Dogberry, with the 'Watch' – a sort of Elizabethan voluntary night patrol assembled to keep order in cities and towns – are keen to report to Don Pedro and Leonato that they overheard Borachio boasting about the plot to set up Hero. But what does that mean for Hero's fake death? Claudio is truly repentant for what he did and he is told he must go to her tomb and hang an epitaph or poem on her monument then sing to her 'bones'; after this, he must marry Hero's identical cousin (who is actually Hero) as recompense for his error. When Claudio arrives to marry Hero's 'cousin', Leonato asks him if he is still determined to 'marry with my brother's daughter?' (5.4.37), to which he responds: 'I'll hold my mind were she an Ethiope' (38). It is hard not to wonder if every time the word 'Ethiop/e' is used in Shakespearean comedy, original audiences would have been expected to laugh. They probably found racial slurs quite funny, the way many people continue to do so today when they see exaggerated portrayals of any ethnic or racial stereotype. I suspect it was comedy gold for Shakespeare, which is why the word appears only once in a tragedy – *Romeo and Juliet*. Claudio's meaning here is that he is committed to the marriage no matter what the bride looks like – if she's black, he'll marry her anyway. He's a man of his word, after all... The irony is that he chose to reject Hero because of her association with racialised femininity – her metaphorical blackness – but manages to inadvertently racialise her again to demonstrate his commitment to her memory.

Hero is veiled until they get to the altar and it is finally revealed to him that she is alive. Somehow, she is able to forgive him. In the final moments of Act 5 Benedick and Beatrice realise they were duped in the eavesdropping scenes but can't deny their love for each other, Benedick declaring proudly that he intends to marry Beatrice; 'man is a giddy thing' (5.4.105), so changeable and uncertain, he concludes. The play then ends with much celebration, quite unproblematically, and so not really classed by literary critics as troublesome for years. But it's time we see, as insightful theatre directors like Kenny Leon does, that Shakespeare's comedies can be thrilling and delightful especially when we account for all identities that may engage with them on our own terms. That a black woman can joyfully perform in a play whose original language maligns black femininity testifies to the flexibility of these texts and their robust welcoming of each generation that claims them as their own.

RACE AND CLASS: *AS YOU LIKE IT*

I still recall my first encounter with *As You Like It* as an undergraduate student; my professor pointed out the many hilarious sexual puns and the play's incredibly modern concerns with feminism and gender-fluidity, but I recall bristling at lines that resonated with me in a way they didn't with most of the students in the class. And we never discussed them. We spoke a lot about class difference against the backdrop of Shakespeare's stratified society. That's pretty standard. But no discussion of race; analysis of the play was racially neutral. After all, it is not a play *about* race. However, the relationship between class and race is clearer to me now than it was back in 1991. I believe Shakespeare was alive to these intersections too; we see it actually staged in *The Tempest* in the comedic episode that brings Caliban together with Trinculo and Stephano.

Although economic prosperity became available to more than just the landed gentry in the sixteenth and seventeenth centuries, social differentiation and class structure were nonetheless embedded in Shakespeare's England. After all, this was when sumptuary laws dictated the clothing, including fabrics and colours, that could be worn based on social status, and a time when sermons were preached and pamphlets were written insisting that crossdressing made people monstrous and unidentifiable. The anti-cross-dressing treatise *Haec-Vir, or The Womanish Man* (1620) addresses many arguments, including the racialised charge that wearing the clothing of the opposite sex makes you barbarous.[10] The lack of a European humanist education and upper-class breeding united those in the lower echelons of society with the 'savages' or strangers encountered in new worlds and on England's own shores. But so did their dissociation from the perfect, white complexion that reflected not just class but national exceptionality. Class, gender *and* ethnicity were required to be visible identities at this time so that one could discern an enemy, a friend, a potential lover, a stranger, a foreigner, a cony-catcher (con-artist) or a fool.

As You Like It is one of Shakespeare's 'festive' comedies, classified as such by twentieth-century critic C.L. Barber. The plays in this category are usually set during the holidays taking place across the English festive calendar – whether it's May Day, Midsummer, or Twelfth Night – and they revel in the transgression of social boundaries. Here, the natural world threatens urban decorum. Evoking the classical celebration of pastoral settings, nature is a space for freedom, reflection, revelry, love and poetry, but it is also steeped in the festive tradition in England that included role reversal, misrule, games, disguise and confusion. By contrast, the urban or court world is where government, patriarchal authority and the rule of law feel tangibly oppressive. When these two worlds clash, social encounters become cross-cultural meetings of a more global kind, where exile, alienation and difference are heightened.

As the play opens, we meet Orlando, the discontented younger son of the deceased Sir Rowland de Boyes; he complains to Adam, an old servant, that he is sick of being mistreated by his cruel elder brother Oliver. Orlando introduces the important theme of breeding as he compares his sad condition to his brother's horses. He is not allowed access to the court nor to the rituals necessary for him to fashion himself a gentleman, yet Oliver's 'horses are bred better, for besides that they are fair with their feeding, they are taught their manage and to that end riders dearly hired; but I, his brother, gain nothing under him' (1.1.10–14). The horses clearly have a much better deal. He finally confronts his brother: 'I know you are my eldest brother, and in the gentle condition of blood you should so know me. The courtesy of nations allows you my better in that you are the first-born, but the same tradition takes not away my blood, were there twenty brothers betwixt us' (1.1.42–5). He alludes here to the law of primogeniture, which stipulated direct inheritance through the first-born son. What stands out is the importance of blood and his own sense of his proximity to racial purity because of his noble blood – he may be the youngest son, but his blood indicates his exceptional breeding.

At court, the usurper, Duke Frederick, has exiled his brother Duke Senior to the forest of Arden with his companions, where they live in community, feasting and singing, evoking the medieval nostalgia of Robin Hood and his band of merry men. His companions include the melancholy Jacques whose famous 'seven ages of man' speech articulates the cynical note in this otherwise festive play. Frederick's daughter Celia is close to her cousin,

Rosalind, who, despite her father Duke Senior's banishment remains at court because these ladies' 'loves / Are dearer than the natural bond of sisters' (1.2.264–5). When we meet them, they are bantering about how Lady Fortune (the personification of luck itself) has inadequately distributed natural gifts to women. Celia notes that, 'for those that she [Fortune] makes fair she scarce makes honest, and those that she makes honest she makes ill-favouredly' (1.2.37–9). 'Honest' means true/chaste. She places in opposition fair and 'ill-favoured' (foul/ugly), an opposition that occurs throughout. I don't need to point out the familiar binary being alluded to here. But Shakespeare sets up these two courtly ladies as the fairest in the land and they are called as much several times in the comedy 'fair princess' (1.2.92 – to Celia; 159 – to Rosalind) – a standard greeting in Elizabethan England, but only to women who are on the highest end of the colour continuum.

At a wrestling match involving Charles, Duke Frederick's champion, Rosalind and Celia meet Orlando, his challenger, and Rosalind falls in love with him speedily; after he wins against Charles, Rosalind gives him her necklace and he is left speechless, having fallen for her too. Then, discovering there is a plot against him by his brother, Orlando flees to the forest of Arden. The turn of events goes a bit sour for Rosalind too, who is, for no apparent reason other than her uncle's insecurity, banished to the forest. Celia's bond with her is so powerful she clandestinely accompanies her. They disguise themselves to ensure their safety: Rosalind will dress up as a boy and call herself Ganymede – a reference to the Greek god Zeus's gender-fluid cup-bearer and homoerotic object of desire; Shakespeare was clearly playing with gender fluidity in ways that seem progressive for his time, but this should hardly surprise us given the commercial theatre companies consisted of only men and adolescent boys. These were boys who played the parts of women and, as we see the actor playing Rosalind doing, they did so virtuosically, moving easily between male and female attributes with the help of gender prosthetics like costume, makeup and wigs. Celia chooses to disguise herself as a lower-class woman she'll call 'Aliena':

> I'll put myself in poor and mean attire,
> And with a kind of umber smirch my face –
> The like do you; so shall we pass along
> And never stir assailants.
>   ROS. Were it not better,
> Because that I am more than common tall,
> That I did suite me all points like a man?
>
>   (1.3.108–13)

Celia weaves low status together with a dark complexion in a sweeping example of anti-black comedic language. Umber is a pigment that would show as a dark, yellowish-brown colour or, if it is burnt, a dark brown. Celia's disguise would remind original audiences of England's repeatedly legislated vagrant culture, in particular of 'wildmen' or gypsies, who were heavily racialised and demonised as the Roma people still are. We might recall early modern satirist Thomas Dekker's complaint that if someone saw them, they'd swear 'they had all the yellow jaundice or that they were Tawny Moors' bastards, for no red-ochre man carries a face of more filthy complexion'.[11] In *King Lear*, Shakespeare makes this reference again: Edgar disguises himself as Tom o'Bedlam since he has been banished by his father, the Duke of Gloucester, who mistakenly believes he is corrupt. He decides, like Celia, 'To take the basest and most poorest shape... My face I'll grime with filth' (2.2.178, 180). Celia's adopted name, 'Aliena', explicitly captures the relationship between class and difference – if you do not belong to a society, you are an alien, a stranger. Touchstone, the court jester or fool, accompanies the disguised ladies into the forest, keeping them cheered with his witticisms and folly.

Orlando and his man servant Adam come across Duke Senior and his companions, who invite them to partake in their feast. Before you know it, Petrarchan poetry has invaded the forest of Arden as Ganymede and Aliena find verses addressed to Rosalind hung on trees. This is a glorious device, particularly in a theatre like the Globe where badly rhyming love poems can be hung on the pillars and all the posts around the auditorium. Ganymede/Rosalind is moved by this but deeply unimpressed by the verse and the empty similes they present. She is the mouthpiece for Shakespeare's own distaste for Petrarchan flourish that adheres more to convention than true feeling. She decides that she'll tutor Orlando how to woo a lady – as Ganymede, of course. Orlando, clueless that the person tutoring him is the woman he loves, agrees and Shakespeare gives a lady an opportunity to influence the poetry that shapes their eventual union.

While in the forest, the aristocrats encounter rustic clowns, in the form of shepherds. One of them, Silvius, is lovesick for Phoebe, who spurns him. Rosalind sympathises with Silvius, but when she berates Phoebe for rejecting him, Phoebe falls in love with her, thinking she's a young pretty-faced man, while Silvius is still pursuing Phoebe – it's a triangle encapsulating Shakespeare's playful insertion of homoerotically-charged desire and gender fluidity. Phoebe's confession shows how the distinction between the classes can be evident in facial complexions: 'The best thing in him / Is his complexion' (3.5.116–7). Noting that Ganymede's face has the ideal conflation of red and white, she remarks:

There was a pretty redness in his lip,
A little riper and more lusty red
Than that mixed in his cheek. 'Twas just the difference
Betwixt the constant red and mingled damask.

(120–3)

But Rosalind/Ganymede's take on Phoebe is far less generous. Rosalind is hard on Phoebe, using anti-black comedy to make her point:

I see no more in you than in the ordinary
Of Nature's sale-work.
…
'Tis not your inky brows, your black silk hair,
Your bugle eyeballs, nor your cheek of cream,
That can entame my spirits to your worship.

(3.5.43–4; 47–9)

Rosalind tells another woman she is not so special as to be able to have whomever she desires, which always provokes laughter in a modern audience. Reading these lines as an undergraduate, I remember wondering with furrowed 'inky brow', what's wrong with black eyebrows and black hair?

While Rosalind describes Phoebe's hair as 'silk', which may sound like a compliment, she goes on to chide her 'bugle eyes'. Meanwhile, when she says Phoebe's cheeks are like 'cream', this is not praise. In the Elizabethan period, cream was thicker, described in dictionaries of the time as 'coagulate'; Rosalind is implying that Phoebe attempts to *appear* whiter by wearing thick and poorly applied white makeup. Tudor makeup was mostly lead-based at court, while more organic ingredients were in use in the rural countryside; cream itself may have even formed part of a concoction to make the face whiter. Either way, it was popular to make fun of overly painted ladies in this way. The seventeenth-century anti-cosmetic writer Thomas Tuke refers to these women being 'whited' 'over with painting laid one upon another, in such sort: that a man might easily cut off a curd of cheesecake from either of their cheeks'.[12] Phoebe is being slighted here: no matter how hard she tries, she'll never be as fair as an upper-class lady like Rosalind.

But it not just Phoebe's face that is racialised, it is her hand too – and not just her anatomical hand, but also her handwriting. In Act 4 scene 3, Silvius delivers a letter to Rosalind from Phoebe without knowing its contents. Rosalind assesses: 'She says I am not fair…and that she could not love me' (15–16), convinced a man wrote it. Silvius swears he didn't know what was in it. Rosalind conflates Phoebe's actual hand with what she has written:

> I saw her hand – she has a leathern hand,
> A freestone-coloured hand – I verily did think
> That her old gloves were on, but 'twas her hands.
> She has a housewife's hand – but that's no matter.
>
> (4.3.24–7)

In Shakespeare's time, hands were indicative of class, identity, character, virtue and intelligence. Phoebe's hands are so brown and leathery they look like old gloves. How can someone with that kind of hand have the wit to write a letter? 'Leathern' implies brown and rough, while 'freestone-coloured' suggests a gritty texture and dark sandy colour. Why are Phoebe's hands brown and rough? Because she is a labourer who uses them, working out in the elements and under the sun. According to premodern racial climate theory, which many of Shakespeare's contemporaries subscribed to, darker complexions were explicable due to generations of exposure, what Morocco referred to as the 'the shadowed livery of the burnished sun' (*The Merchant of Venice*, 2.1.2).

Rosalind drives the point home further, equating Phoebe's identity and personality with the words she has written:

> Why, 'tis a boisterous and a cruel style,
> A style for challengers. Why, she defies me,
> Like Turk to Christian. Women's gentle brain
> Could not drop forth such giant-rude invention,
> Such Ethiop words, blacker in their effect
> Than in their countenance.
>
> (4.3.31–6)

Phoebe is racialised based on her social status here, and mocked for her presumption in writing such a letter. Rosalind effectively charges Phoebe with being *uppity* – a more modern term with anti-black connotations in its accusation of haughtiness. It appeared in the 1952 edition of the Oxford Dictionary with the N-word – together the two words were defined as 'above oneself, self-important'.[13] For a woman, and a low-status woman at that, to pen a letter attempting to woo (who she thinks is) a man is the height of 'giant-rude' presumption. What's worse, she writes like a 'Turk to' a 'Christian' – in other words, with cruelty, alluding also to the folk or 'Mummers plays' performed by amateur actors in premodern England in which masking, blackface and characters like a Turkish knight would combat with either St. George or Robin Hood. Essentially, Phoebe is an amateur at best.

Unfortunately, the word 'Ethiop' is used yet again, this time to describe Phoebe's words, hence her intelligence. Using racializing language, Rosalind attributes the lack of eloquence and effectiveness in this letter to the social status of its writer. It's not a great look for Rosalind in a twenty-first-century production – this kind of racist metaphor is outdated. But it is surprising how many productions present these lines as race-neutral, even today.

Shakespeare likes to end his festive comedies with double or triple marriages. Even jesters need love; Touchstone wants to marry a country girl who, as Touchstone says himself, is a 'poor virgin', an 'ill-favoured thing' (5.4.57); her virginity is like a 'pearl in your foul oyster' (61). The racist language points here to another woman's lowly status in the societal structure of this play. Once Duke Frederick discovers Orlando has fled into the woods, he sends Oliver after him – but Oliver is attacked by a lion and saved by his brother Orlando, and they ultimately reconcile. Meanwhile, Rosalind devises a plan in which all the 'appropriate' pairs are matched by the end. Still disguised as Ganymede, Rosalind artfully manipulates and convinces Phoebe to marry Silvius if for any reason she can't marry Ganymede. Aliena/Celia falls for the newly reformed Oliver and they shall also get married. On the day of the nuptials, the god Hymen (of marriage) descends from the Heavens to bless the couples, while Duke Frederick has left the court to become a bit of a hermit and reflect on his wrongdoing; Duke Senior is restored. Rosalind and Orlando will marry, blessed by the heavens. It is clear that even with all of the co-mingling in the forest, everyone ultimately has their place on the social scale and by the end of the play, this varied cast of characters return to the status quo, having only enticed us in that Shakespearean green-world way with the possibilities inherent in an alternate universe.

REVERSING ANTI-BLACK COMEDY

The comedies required jokes – lots of them – to make audiences laugh and willingly pay money to return to the playhouses again and again. Some of the jokes and witty exchanges we see in them echo those found in early Henrician and late Elizabethan joke manuals. In the 1500s jest books – books containing funny or witty anecdotes, quips and insults – were extremely popular, starting with *An Hundred Merry Jests* (1526), from which Beatrice in *Much Ado* supposedly acquires her wit. Shakespeare would have had access to such popular volumes, which spoke to the age's thirst for tales of humiliation, beatings, stereotyping and misogyny as well as stories of cross-cultural encounters and interracial courtship. But not all of the stories tell of racist humour. One anecdote in a jest book by Catholic poet Anthony Copley, in fact, has a twist:

> A Blackamoor king, coveting a French woman, [who]… told him his complexion was so ugly she could not love him: thou art deceived said he, it is the baseness of thy mind which is so filthy a glass that my beauty cannot be seen in thee.[14]

It is more of a witticism than a joke. The blackamoor king expresses, like Aaron and the Prince of Morocco, a deep knowledge of his own value as he calls out the French woman's prejudice, expressed here as her dirty mind resembling a mirror. It is not his face that is ugly; it is her perspective. Perhaps this is Shakespeare's message when he uses phrases like 'too brown for a fair praise' or 'Away, Ethiop' – that the minds of those who shout or quip using these pejoratives are actually what is defiled by hate, prejudice, xenophobia or white supremacy. We could take that message away from Shakespeare's anti-black comedy, or we could sit in the discomfort of never really knowing if that is indeed the message he intended. The fact is these are living, breathing, fluid plays and we use them to communicate with each other today – whether it's in a classroom, a theatre or an armchair by a fire. Normalising or pretending we don't see Shakespeare's racist humour just won't do anymore.

Epilogue

WHO'S ENTITLED
TO THE BARD?

When it was announced that Denzel Washington would be playing Macbeth in a new film version in 2021, the news was met
with expected enthusiasm. Given Washington's reputation, talent
and platform, it is hardly surprising that this adaptation of
Shakespeare's play would attract much publicity and anticipation.
Unfortunately, it also brought forth hate in certain spaces of the
internet known for cradling white supremacist sentiment about
all aspects of culture, including film, television and even
Shakespeare. On 24hourcampfire.com, a site for those primarily
interested in hunting, a member with the handle 'Valsdad' posted
on 5 December 2021, 'They've made a MacBeth where he's a
Black guy!' Responses to this simple statement read like a guide
to 'how to be a racist and proud'. 'elkcountry' intimated that he
had had enough: 'saw a commercial the other day that had a black
Santa! There is nothing the left won't touch to force feed the
racism card down your throat!' 'JoeBob' had a slightly different
take, however: 'I [usually] like to complain about putting blacks
in historical roles that were white people, but I really like Denzel.
And anyway, Macbeth is almost mythical, so I don't think it
matters too much'. What JoeBob gets right is that Shakespeare's

play is hardly concerned with realism – it features witches, ghosts and all manner of supernatural intervention. Reading on would make your stomach turn. 'Pharmseller' asks wryly, 'Does Macduff still kill him, or is that racist?' and DigitalDan asks 'When do they use whitey to pick cotton?' It degenerates further when a meme of a Black girl is posted with the line: 'When Disney makes a movie about Greta Thunberg'. As the thread continues, racist stereotypes worsen and the site seems nothing more than a safe haven for hate speech. All because a talented Black actor was cast in a Shakespeare play.

Ironically, in an interview with NBC news to promote the film, Denzel Washington insisted that 'we ought to be at a place where diversity shouldn't even be mentioned, like it's something special.'[1] If only. Directed by Joel Coen and co-starring Francis McDormand and Kathryn Hunter, the film side-stepped the question of race and attempted a colour-blind depiction, presumably assured that Washington's blackness would be less detectable than his celebrity. But Denzel Washington missed the irony of his comments. To what extent is it possible to separate his race from the play's own insistence that race matters in more ways than one? In the racist reaction online, we can see that Shakespeare is viewed by many, still, as the property of white culture; only white actors are entitled or legitimately able to play the starring roles. But isn't it naïve to assume race can be masked, or that Washington's race wouldn't count when Shakespeare has always been a contested figure in the racial divide? Shakespeare cannot be bracketed from race, as the entitled hunters who fiercely protect the Great White Bard so grossly remind us.

Bardolatrous critic Harold Bloom argued that 'we keep returning to Shakespeare because we need him; no one else gives us so much of the world most of us take to be fact'; he continues: 'Shakespeare is not only himself the Western canon, he has become the universal canon'. He argues in fact that we are all 'reinvented by Shakespeare'.[2] It's a lovely thought. But it's also skewed by a colossal sense of Anglo-European self-importance. The Shakespeare that we think we know was invented in the eighteenth century by a nation bent on defining itself as an empire, a conqueror of the world and all the atrocities that brought with it. It is not *that* Shakespeare that we need, nor should we want it. As the writer and academic Emer O'Toole put it in an opinion piece for the *Guardian*, Shakespeare's construction as universal is dangerous because 'if we can root Shakespeare's dominance in his universality, rather than in history, we can bask in the cosy knowledge that our culture is just a tad superior after all.'[3]

This universal ideal motivates the rallying cries against casting actors of colour. The racist conversations on websites such as 24hourcampfire.com site in response to the casting of an Oscar-winning actor as Macbeth illustrate an extreme, perhaps minority view, but nevertheless they reveal how over-invested we have been in expressing Bardolatry in this way and how this attitude is dangerously on the rise. Clearly, for some, casting Black actors in these so-called universal and iconic parts is historically problematic – and that's at best! At worst it is seen as a defilement of the Bard's sacred intentions. As Ayanna Thompson has stated, 'while we may want Shakespeare to be for everyone, all too often Shakespeare has been used as a gatekeeper; that is as a barrier to exclude and subjugate people of colour'.[4]

In 2022, both the Royal Shakespeare Company and Shakespeare's Globe were targeted and heavily criticised for advertising new productions of Shakespeare plays with Black actors pictured on their publicity posters. Fury at what is termed 'woke' attempts to fill a 'diversity quota' suggested the actors and creatives in those productions, who had to persevere through rehearsals and full runs of the shows in order to rise above the racist fray, did not belong there in the first place.

Many of Shakespeare's characters are indeed based on historical figures, but Shakespeare himself was never invested in natural realism. A young white male was the first person to ever play his black and quixotic Cleopatra. The fiery-tongued Queen Margaret in *Richard III* was played by a boy actor. Shakespeare's theatre company was subject to all the conventions of the day where boys played the parts of women, where instead of seeing horses during a performance of *Henry V*, the audience would be accustomed to imagining them there instead. But original performance practices are still not even the reason why *anybody* can play Shakespeare in theatres around the world. The plays lend themselves to diversity because of their creation within the context of racial formation. Black characters, and those from a range of ethnic minorities, are the subject of some of the plays *because* Shakespeare's England was populated by people from many racial and geographical backgrounds. It's hardly a stark intervention for a Black man to play Hamlet, or a Black woman to play Henry V or Richard II. Moreover, Black actors have been making Shakespeare on both sides of the pond for two hundred plus years, from the African Company (which produced Ira Aldridge), the first Black theatre troupe established in New York City in 1821 by James Hewlett and William Alexander Brown, to the all-Black London-based Talawa Theatre Company set up by Yvonne Brewster in 1986 and still going strong. Many choose to deny or diminish such histories. Yet, as scholars Patricia Cahill and Kim F. Hall articulate perfectly, Black people 'have fought for the right to perform Shakespeare', seeing in the playwright 'a source of joy, inspiration, and innovation even as they resist his use as an agent of dominion',[5] a view Kenny Leon, the Public Theater's director of *Much Ado About Nothing*, would agree with wholeheartedly.

As I pointed out in Chapter 1, Shakespeare was constructed as an emblem of English exceptionalism, as a native genius.

It is time to let that go.

This is harder for some than it is for others, regardless of his global appeal. Some of Shakespeare's plays, particularly the English history cycle that chronicles the Wars of the Roses, would appear to encourage or license such rhetoric. On Shakespeare's birthday in 2022, the conservative British government minister in charge of culture, Oliver Dowden, tweeted an image of the St George's flag with a seemingly patriotic excerpt from Shakespeare's *Richard II* spoken by the King's uncle, the aging John of Gaunt: 'This blessed plot, this earth, this realm, this England. Happy St George's Day'. The Shakespearean actor Samuel West tweeted fiercely in response: 'Oh Oliver. Know your Shakespeare' and pointed out that the rest of that infamous speech protests the harm England has inflicted upon itself: England 'is now leased out...now bound in with shame' (2.1.59, 63),

> With inky blots and rotten parchment bonds.
> That England, that was wont to conquer others
> Hath made a shameful conquest of itself.
>
> (64 –6)

West's riposte reminds us to read Shakespeare more diligently, more interrogatively, rather than cherry-picking the famous or comforting bits for the sake of flag waving.

Earlier in the speech, Gaunt points out that the kings of England are indeed 'Feared by their breed and famous by their birth' (52) – English royalty is exceptional because of its ancestral legitimacy and prowess. Gaunt laments the loss of England's superiority and advocates 'making England great again'. But *Richard II* is not a straightforward history play, nor is it strictly jingoistic. It presents an ambiguous picture of a spoiled king having been on the throne since he was ten years old; he banishes his cousin, takes his lands and titles but then is challenged by a rebellion. When he is finally defeated, he is forced to give up the throne. Shockingly, Shakespeare stages a deposition scene, which was considered unwise to include in performances as Elizabeth I was beginning to age; a scene in which the King hands his crown to the usurper – his cousin, Henry Bolingbroke, who goes on to become Henry IV in Shakespeare's history cycle – would not have gone down well in a country with a government fond of capital punishment. Surprisingly the play does not overly advocate for English patriotism even if John of Gaunt speaks about a time when England was at its best. Instead, collectively, Shakespeare's history plays illustrate how each generation looks back yearningly at the past as a golden age that never really existed.

Perhaps the most striking thing about the play is how often it has been used as a tool for political resistance. In 1601, six years after it was written and first staged, Robert Devereux, the 2nd Earl of Essex, led an unsuccessful rebellion to attempt to overthrow Elizabeth I's government. On 7 February, the Lord Chamberlain's Men were asked by the Earl's followers to stage a performance of the play with the deposition scene intact. The acting troupe were paid very handsomely to take this dangerous risk, as Essex believed he would have had the good and great of London on his side. Was he wrong! The rebellion failed and Essex and his followers were duly executed. Elizabeth I, aware of the political ramifications of being likened to a king like Richard II, apparently retorted, 'I am Richard II, know ye not that?' I'd say Shakespeare's company got off lightly.

In 2003, as Tony Blair's government marched into Iraq despite the British public's fury and opposition, Mark Rylance staged a season of work called 'Regime Change', the centrepiece of which was an Original Practices production of *Richard II*, broadcast by the BBC – despite the Renaissance clothing and music, it was a production that spoke angrily and urgently to the moment while also showcasing the Globe's power as a political space. In more recent times, the speech Oliver Dowden quoted on the Bard's birthday was particularly pertinent in the chaos of Brexit. As a political statement about English identity, the play was staged in the Globe's indoor, candlelit Sam Wanamaker Playhouse by a cast and creatives made up entirely of women of colour, conceived and directed by Adjoa Andoh, who played the title role, and co-directed by Lynette Linton.

The poster was deliberately provocative and epitomised Andoh's motivation for the production. In reclaiming the St George's flag, an archetypal symbol of English white nationalism, Andoh intervened in its meaning:

> when we talk about who belongs where, as we discover more with science and history it becomes nonsense that only racists and fascists have a claim to this flag. In a way, staging *Richard II* with all women of colour is about saying let's double down on this ownership and have the people who are at the bottom of the heap of Empire, whose ancestors' lives fuelled the growth of empire and who continue to contribute to this country, let's have them tell the story of this nation.[6]

The production was widely acclaimed by critics and scholars alike, hailed as no less than a game-changing event in the history of Shakespearean theatre, the *Guardian* declaring: 'If one definition of a first-rate Shakespeare production is that it makes one view the play afresh, this pioneering show preeminently passes the test'.[7] Acting greats such as Doña Croll, who, as we know from Chapter 3, was the first Black woman to play Cleopatra in a full British stage production, formed part of this all-woman-of-colour troupe. Croll stepped into the role of Gaunt no less, her performance of the lines lamenting the decline of 'This blessed plot' as classically distinguished as it was charged with defiance and contemporary urgency. Andoh's vision of reclaiming England firmly put to bed the lie that when Shakespeare's plays are in the hands of non-white artists they are on loan. This was not a case of colourblind casting – the practice that historically enabled actors of colour to perform in Shakespearean roles since the nineteenth century. Rather Andoh's production invited actors of colour to convey their identities, their bodies, their histories and lineages in their characters.

Most powerfully, the production shed light upon Shakespeare's presence within the history of race, slavery and empire and made clear that white Britain (or America for that matter) is *not* synonymous with Shakespeare. No one group can claim entitlement over these works or has special access to the gloriously diverse, discomforting and capacious store of words that is Shakespeare. Andoh's proud declaration will resonate with many: 'my connections to this country are deep. I was born in this country, I was raised in this country, I have a right to claim that flag.'[8]

And we *all* have the right to claim the Bard.

ACKNOWLEDGEMENTS

While I was writing this book, my 29-year-old nephew, Julian A. Karim, was murdered. He was and always will be so very dear to my heart. There were times when I thought I couldn't finish writing, because…why? How could I write about Shakespeare in the midst of such profound loss and grief? But I realised that Shakespeare has much to say about loss and his tragedies suggest that humans are built for grief. So, I did finish the book, but it is also because Julian would have wanted me to.

If it hadn't been for the love and support of my family, I certainly would not have made it through such a challenging time. In particular, I have felt so honoured by the support of my husband, Angus Lamming. On many a night, he gently lifted my chin and practically placed my fingers on the keyboard, brought me countless cups of coffee and read every word avidly and lovingly and then told me what he thought about it constructively and compassionately. There are no words to describe the gratitude and love I feel for him. I am grateful for my incredible daughter Sabreena Karim-Cooper, a writer herself, whose passion for drama and love for me inspires all that I do. The endless encouragement of my step-daughter Kate Lamming, while she was writing her own undergraduate dissertation, was also a huge boon. I'm so grateful for my parents, Fazal and

Fawzia Karim, themselves descendants of colonisation who, through their extraordinary example, have shown me how to overcome oppression and difficulty. The strength to continue writing was inspired by the titanic courage displayed by Julian's family – Julian's parents, Reshad and Rosanna Karim, Julian's siblings, Kesandra and Alex, and Julian's children, 'Bubba' and 'Skilly'. The loss they suffered is unimaginable and yet they are each finding a path through the most unspeakable pain. I will forever be in awe of them.

My agent Charlie Brotherstone has been tremendous from the moment we fashioned the proposal to the final submission. I am so grateful for his belief in me and this book, and for his endless generosity and kind support. My editor, Cecilia Stein, has been incredible. I am so grateful to her, to Rida Vaquas and all the team at Oneworld for their enthusiasm for *The Great White Bard*. I am also hugely grateful to my amazing US editor Patrick Nolan and the team at Viking Books for their immense moral and editorial support.

Thanks are due to colleagues and PhD students at Shakespeare's Globe and King's College London. Special thanks go to Hanh Bui for reading chapters and delicately providing feedback. I am also grateful to the scholars, artists and friends who believed in *The Great White Bard* from the start: Emma Smith and Ayanna Thompson for reading chapters and giving me honest and enthusiastic feedback; heartfelt thanks to Adjoa Andoh, Bill Barclay, Lolita Chakrabarti, Neil Constable, Claudia Conway, Lucy Cuthbertson, Nandini Das, Jennifer Edwards, Alfred Enoch, Kyle Grady, Margo Hendricks, Peter Holland, Jonathan Hope, Adrian Lester, Brendan O'Hea, James Shapiro, Chris Stafford, Michelle Terry, Will Tosh, Claire van Kampen and Michael Witmore for their friendship and encouragement.

ACKNOWLEDGEMENTS

The 'ShakeRace' and RaceB4Race collectives are my second family and I owe them all a debt of gratitude – not just for producing so much incredible work but for their generous solidarity and support. Having a space for scholars of colour to talk about legitimate, deeply rigorous scholarship has been a godsend and this book could not exist without this community. In particular, I want to acknowledge Kim F. Hall, Margo Hendricks, Ian Smith and Ayanna Thompson whose work inspired this book and who continue to ignite the advanced study of Shakespeare.

LIST OF TEXT ILLUSTRATIONS

1. The *alto relievo* in the front of the Shakespeare Gallery, Pall Mall, sculpted by Thomas Banks, c. 1789.
2. Engraving of Shakespeare on the title page of the *First Folio* by Flemish-born painter Martin Droeshout, 1623.
3. An engraving of Shakespeare illustrating Alexander Pope's 1725 edition of Shakespeare's works, based on the funerary bust in Stratford-upon-Avon.
4. William Shakespeare statue in the Poets' Corner, Westminster Abbey by Peter Scheemakers, 1740.
5. A composite sketch depicting a scene from *Titus Andronicus* drawn by Henry Peacham, c. 1594.
6. Pauline Black in *Cleopatra and Antony*, Actors Touring Company, photographed by David Corio, 1989.
7. *A Bed Chamber, Desdemona in bed asleep* (*Othello* Act 5, Scene 2), painted by Josiah Boydell, engraved by George Noble, 1800.
8. 'Moro di conditione' (A Wealthy Moor) by Cesare Vecellio from *De gli habiti antichi et moderni di diversi parti del mondo*, 1590.

BIBLIOGRAPHY AND
FURTHER READING

The Great White Bard is the culmination of my twenty-five years as a Shakespeare scholar, writing and publishing on Shakespeare's plays, the culture, theatrical history and social history of the early modern period. It is also the result of a deep enquiry into premodern critical race studies and postcolonial literary studies, two areas of research that are decades old. The scholarship in this area is incredibly rich, rigorous and thankfully ever expanding. Exciting new studies emerging from scholars working in this field range from new histories of slavery, colonialism and the artistic and literary response to Europe's expanding empire to exciting deep dives into Shakespeare and race and its intersections with ecological, indigenous, disability and gender studies. In other words, *The Great White Bard* is a book with deep roots in a scholarly field with many practitioners. I am indebted to those whose work has been foundational to my own and I am honoured *not* to take credit for every thought in this book.

PRIMARY SOURCES

Adams, Thomas, *The Black Devil or the Apostate Together with the Wolf Worrying the Lambs* (London: 1615).

—*The White Devil, or The Hypocrite Uncased* (London: 1612).

Africanus, Leo, *A Geographical History of Africa, written in Arabic and Italian by John Leo a Moor*, trans. John Pory (London: 1600).

Alison, Archibald, 'Of the Sublimity and Beauty of the Material World', in *Essays on the Nature and Principles of Taste* (Edinburgh, 1790).

Anonymous, *Haec-Vir, or The Womanish Man: Being an Answer to a Late Book Entitled Hic-Mulier* (London: 1620).

Applebaum, Stanley (ed.), *Il Pecorone* in *Medieval Tales and Stories: 108 Prose Narratives of the Middle Ages* (New York: Dover Publications, 2012).

Ashley, Robert, *A Comparison of the English and Spanish Nation* (London: 1589), cited in Noémie Ndiaye, 'Aaron's Roots: Spaniards, Englishmen, and Blackamoors in *Titus Andronicus*', *Early Theatre*, 19.2 (2016), pp. 59–80.

Best, George, *A True Discourse of the late voyages of discoverie, for the finding of a passage to Cathaya by the Northwest...* (London: 1578), cited in Ania Loomba and Jonathan Burton (eds), *Race in Early Modern England* (2007).

Buoni, Thomas, *Problemes of Beautie and humane affections*, trans. S.L. Gent (London: 1606).

Carlyle, Thomas, 'Lecture III. The Hero As Poet. Dante; Shakespeare', in *On Heroes, Hero-Worship, and The Heroic in History: Six Lectures, Reported with Emendations and Additions* (London: James Fraser, 1841).

Cobb, Keith Hamilton, *American Moor* (London: Bloomsbury, 2020).

Contarini, Cardinal Gaspar, *The Commonwealth and Government of Venice*, trans. Lewes Lewkenor (London: 1599).

Copley, Antony, *Wits, Fits, and Fancies* (London: 1614).

Coryat, Thomas, *Coryat's Crudities* (London: 1611).

Cotta, John, *The Trial of Witch-Craft* (London: 1616).

Dante, *The Divine Comedy*, ed. David H. Higgins and C.H. Sisson (Oxford: Oxford University Press, 1998).

Dekker, Thomas, *Lantern and Candlelight, or the Bell-mans second nights walk* (London:1608).

della Rocca, Bartolommeo, *The Rebirth of Chiromancy and Physiognomy* (1504), trans. Thomas Hill, *The Whole Art of Phisiognomie* (London: 1556).

Dryden, John, *Of Dramatick Poesie, An Essay* (London: 1668).

Duff, William, 'An Essay on Original Genius', cited in Robert Babcock, *The Genesis of Shakespeare Idolatry, 1766–1799* (Chapel Hill: University of North Carolina Press, 1931).

Edwards, Bryan, *The History, Civil and Commercial, of the British Colonies in the West Indies*, 5th edn. (London: 1819), i.3, cited in Morgan, *Slavery and the British Empire*.

Elyot, Thomas, *The Dictionary of Sir Thomas Elyot* (London: 1538).

Emerson, Ralph Waldo, 'Notes on Shakespeare', *The Atlantic* (September 1904): https://www.theatlantic.com/magazine/archive/1904/09/shakespeare/539499/

England, George (ed.), *The Creation, The Townley Plays* (London: 1897).

Ficino, Marsilio, *Commentary on Plato's Symposium*, in Albert Hofstadler and Richard Kuhns (eds), *Philosophies in Art and Beauty: Selected Readings in Aesthetics from Plato to Heidegger* (Chicago: University of Chicago Press, 1964).

Firenzuola, Agnolo, *On the Beauty of Women* (1541), trans. Konrad Eisenbichler and Jacqueline Murray (Philadelphia: University of Pennsylvania Press, 1992).

Furnivall, F.J., *The Leopold Shakespeare: The Poet's Works in Chronological Order from the Text of Professor Delius* (London: 1877).

Gifford, George, *The Witches of Northampton-shire Agnes Browne, Joane Vaughan, Arthur Bill, Hellen Jenkenson, Mary Barber. Witches. Who were all executed at Northampton the 22 of July last* (London: 1612).

Gouge, William, *Of domestical duties* (1622), in *Renaissance Woman: Constructions of Femininity in England*, ed. Kate Aughterson (London and New York: Routledge, 1995).

Greene, Robert (or Chettle, Henry), *Greenes Groats-Worth of Wit Bought with a Million of Repentance* (London: 1592).

Hakluyt, Richard, *The Principall Navigations, Voyages and Discoveries of the English Nation* (London: 1589).

Hariot, Thomas, *A Brief and True Report of the New Found Land of Virginia* (London: 1590), illustrated by Theodore de Bry (Charlottesville: University of Virginia Press, 2007).

Hazlitt, William, *Characters of Shakespeare's Plays*, 4th edn, ed. John Templeman (1838).

Hemmingsen, Niels, *A Postle, or Exposition of the Gospels* (London: 1569).

Hentzner, Paul, *Paul Hentzner's Travels in England During the Reign of Queen Elizabeth, Tran. By Horace, Later Earl of Oxford, to Which is Now Added Sir Robert Naunton's Fragmenta Regalia; Or, Observations on Queen Elizabeth's Times and Favourites with Portraits and Views* (London: 1797): https://www.elfinspell. com/HentznerModern.html

Herodotus, *Famous History of Egypt*, trans. Barnaby Rich (London: 1584).

Hilliard, Nicholas, *A Treatise Concerning the Arte of Limning* (1601), ed. R.K.R. Thornton and T.G.S Cain (Mid Northumberland Arts Group, 1981).

Horace, *Satires, Epistles, Ars Poetic* 1.IV. 85, cited in Anthony Gerard Barthelemy, *Black Face Maligned Race: The Representation of Blacks in English Drama from Shakespeare to Southerne* (Baton Rouge: Louisiana State University Press, 1987).

Hume, David, 'Of National Characters', in *Essays: Moral, Political, and Literary*, ed. Eugene F. Miller, Thomas Hill Green and Thomas Hodge Grose (Indianapolis: Liberty Gund, 1987).

James I, *Demonologie, in Form of a Dialogue* (Edinburgh: 1597).

Jefferson, Thomas, Letter to Robert Skipwith, 3 August 1771, in *The Works of Thomas Jefferson*, vol. 2: 1771–1779, Federal Edition (New York and London: G. P. Putnam's Sons, 1904–5).

Johnson, Samuel, *The Plays of William Shakespeare...to which are added Notes by Sam. Johnson*, vol. 6 (London: 1765).

Lomazzo, Paulo Giovanni, *A Tracte Containing the Artes of Curious Painting, Carving and Building*, trans. Richard Haydocke (London: 1598).

Melton, John, *Astrologaster, or the Figure-Caster* (London: 1620).

Münster, Sebastian, *Cosmographia* (1575), cited in David C. McPherson, *Shakespeare, Jonson, and the Myth of Venice* (Newark: University of Delaware Press, 1990).

Plutarch, *De Iside et Osiride* ('On Isis and Osiris'), cited in Benjamin Isaac, *The Invention of Racism in Classical Antiquity* (Princeton and Oxford: Princeton University Press, 2004).

—*The Lives of the Noble Grecians and Romans Compared*, trans. Thomas North (London: 1579).

Pope, Alexander, *The Works of Shakespeare in Six Volumes* (London: 1725).

Puttenham, George *The Arte of English Poesy* (1578), cited in Robert Hornback, *Racism and Early Blackface Comic Traditions* (New York: Palgrave, 2018).

—*Partheniades* (London: 1579).

Rhymer, Thomas, *A Short View of Tragedy* (1693), cited in Brian Vickers, *William Shakespeare: The Critical Heritage*, vol. 2: 1693–1733 (London and New York: Routledge, 1974).

St Augustine of Hippo, *The Expositions on The Psalms* (Jazzybee Verlag, 2012).

Shakespeare, William, *Antony and Cleopatra*, ed. Ania Loomba, Norton Critical Editions (New York and London: W.W. Norton & Company, 2011).

—*Antony and Cleopatra*, ed. John Wilders, The Arden Shakespeare (London: Bloomsbury, 1995).

—*As You Like It*, ed. Juliet Dusinberre, The Arden Shakespeare (London: Bloomsbury, 2006).

—*Cymbeline*, ed. Jean E. Howard, in *The Norton Shakespeare*, ed. Gordon McMullan, Suzanne Gossett, Stephen Greenblatt et al. (New York and London: W. W. Norton & Company, 2016).

—*Hamlet*, ed. Ann Thompson and Neil Taylor, The Arden Shakespeare (London: Bloomsbury, 2006).

—*King Henry V*, ed. T. W. Craik, The Arden Shakespeare (London: Bloomsbury, 1995).

—*King Lear*, ed. R. A. Foakes, The Arden Shakespeare (London: Bloomsbury, 1997).

—*King Richard II*, ed. Charles R. Forker, The Arden Shakespeare (London: Bloomsbury, 2002/2014).

—*Love's Labour's Lost*, ed. Walter Cohen, in *The Norton Shakespeare*, ed. McMullan, Gossett, Greenblatt et al. (New York and London: W.W. Norton & Company, 2016).

—*Macbeth*, ed. Sandra Clark and Pamela Mason, The Arden Shakespeare (London: Bloomsbury, 2015).

—*The Merchant of Venice*, ed. Katharine Eisaman Maus, in *The Norton Shakespeare*, ed. McMullan, Gossett, Greenblatt, et al. (New York and London: W.W. Norton & Company, 2016).

—*A Midsummer Night's Dream*, ed. Sukanta Chaudhuri, The Arden Shakespeare (London: Bloomsbury, 2017).

—*Much Ado About Nothing*, ed. Claire McEachern, The Arden Shakespeare (London: Bloomsbury, 2006).

—*Othello: The Moor of Venice*, The Arden Shakespeare, ed. E.A.J. Honigmann, with a new introduction by Ayanna Thompson (London: Bloomsbury, 2016).

—*Othello: The Moor of Venice*, The New Cambridge Shakespeare, ed. Norman Sanders, 3rd ed., with revised introduction by Christina Luckyj (Cambridge: Cambridge University Press, 2018).

—*Othello: The Moor of Venice*, The Oxford Shakespeare, ed. Michael Neill (Oxford: Oxford University Press, 2008).

—*The Rape of Lucrece* in *Shakespeare's Poems*, ed. Katherine Duncan-Jones and H.R. Woudhuysen, The Arden Shakespeare (London: Bloomsbury, 2007).

—*Romeo and Juliet*, ed. René Weis, The Arden Shakespeare (London: Bloomsbury, 2012).

—*The Tempest*, ed. Virginia Mason Vaughan and Alden T. Vaughan, The Arden Shakespeare (London: Bloomsbury, revised edition, 2011).

—*Titus Andronicus*, ed. Jonathan Bate, revised edition, The Arden Shakespeare (London: Bloomsbury, 2018).

—*The Two Gentlemen of Verona*, ed. Jean E. Howard, in *The Norton Shakespeare*, ed. McMullan, Gossett, Greenblatt, et al. (New York and London: W.W. Norton & Company, 2016).

Spenser, Edmund, *Epithalamion*, in *Amoretti and Epithalamion* (London: 1595).

Stevens, George, *The Plays of William Shakespeare in Fifteen Volumes* (London: 1793), cited in Emma Smith, *Shakespeare's First Folio: Four Centuries of an Iconic Book* (Oxford: Oxford University Press, 2016).

Strachey, William, *A true repertory of the wreck, and redemption of Sir Thomas Gates Knight; upon, and from the Islands of Bermudas: his coming to Virginia, and the estate of that Colony then, and after, under government of the Lord LA Warre, July 15 1610*, from Samuel Purchas, *Purchas His Pilgrimes* (London: 1625), vol. 4.

Thomas, William, *Principal Rules of the Italian Grammar* (London: 1550).

Tuke, Thomas, *A Treatise Against Painting* (London: 1616).

Varchi, Bernadetto, *The Blazon of Jealousy* (London: 1615).

Vecellio, Cesare, *De gli habiti antichi et moderni di diversi parti del mondo* (Venice, 1590).

Vicars, John, *November the 5 1605: The Quintessence of Cruelty, or Masterpiece of Treachery* (London: 1641).

Vives, Juan Luis, *The instruction of a Christian woman*, in *Renaissance Woman: Constructions of Femininity*, ed. Kate Aughterson (London and New York: Routledge, 1995).

Winckelmann, Johann, *History of the Art of Antiquity*, ed. Alex Potts, trans. Harry Francis Mallgrave (Los Angeles: The Getty Research Institute Publications Program, 2006).

Winstanley, William, *Lives of the Most Famous English Poets* (London: 1687), cited in Peter Holland, 'David Garrick: Saints, temples and jubilees', in *Celebrating Shakespeare: Commemoration and Cultural Memory*, ed. Clara Calvo and Coppélia Khan (Cambridge: Cambridge University Press, 2015).

SECONDARY SOURCES

Akhimie, Patricia, '"Qualities of Breeding": Race, Class and Conduct', in *The Merchant of Venice: The State of Play*, ed. M. Lindsay Kaplan (London: Bloomsbury, 2020).

—'Racist Humor and Shakespearean Comedy', in *The Cambridge Companion to Shakespeare and Race*, ed. Ayanna Thompson (Cambridge: Cambridge University Press, 2021).

—*Shakespeare and the Cultivation of Difference: Race and Conduct in the Early Modern World* (London and New York: Routledge, 2018).

Arshad, Yasmin, *Imagining Cleopatra: Performing Gender and Power in Early Modern England*, The Arden Shakespeare (London: Bloomsbury, 2019).

Babcock, Robert Witbeck, *The Genesis of Shakespeare Idolatry, 1766–1799: A Study in English Criticism of the Late Eighteenth Century* (Chapel Hill: University of North Carolina Press, 1931).

Bailey, Moya, 'More on the origin of Misogynoir', *Moyazb*, 27 April 2014: https://moyazb.tumblr.com/post/84048113369/more-on-the-origin-of-misogynoir

Baldwin, James, *Collected Essays*, ed. Toni Morrison (New York: The Library of America, 1998).

Barber, C.L., *Shakespeare's Festive Comedy: A Study of Dramatic Form and Its Relation to Social Custom* (New Jersey: Princeton University Press, 1959).

Bartels, Emily C., *Speaking of the Moor: From Alcazar to Othello* (Philadelphia: University of Pennsylvania Press, 2008).

Bate, Jonathan, *The Genius of Shakespeare* (Oxford: Oxford University Press, 1998).

Bloom, Harold, *Shakespeare and the Invention of the Human* (London: Penguin, 1999).

Brazaitis, Sarah J., 'White Women-Protectors of the Status Quo; Positioned to Disrupt It', in *Group Dynamics, Organizational Irrationality and Social Complexity: Group Relations Reader*, ed. Solomon Cytrynbaum and Debra A. Noumair, vol. 3 (A.K. Rice Institute, 2004).

Brewster, Yvonne, cited in Carol Rutter, *Enter the Body: Women and Representation on Shakespeare's Stage* (Abingdon: Taylor & Francis, 2002).

Britton, Dennis, *Becoming Christian: Race, Reformation, and Early Modern English Romance* (New York: Fordham University Press, 2014).

—'Flesh and Blood: Race and Religion in *The Merchant of Venice*', in *The Cambridge Companion to Shakespeare and Race*, ed. Ayanna Thompson (Cambridge: Cambridge University Press, 2021).

Brotton, Jerry, 'The First Muslims in England', BBC News, 20 March 2016: https://www.bbc.co.uk/news/magazine-35843991

—*This Orient Isle: Elizabethan England and the Islamic World* (London: Allen Lane, 2016).

Brown, David Sterling and Sandra Young, '(Un)Just Acts: Shakespeare and Social Justice in Contemporary Performance', *Shakespeare Bulletin* 39.4 (2021), pp. 529–535. Also: https://www.davidsterlingbrown.com/research.

Burton, Jonathan and Ania Loomba (eds), *Race in Early Modern England: A Documentary Companion* (New York: Palgrave Macmillan, 2007).

Cahill, Patricia A. and Kim F. Hall, 'Forum: Shakespeare and Black America', *Journal of American Studies*, 54.1 (February 2020), pp. 1–11.

Carbado, Devon and Mitu Galati, *Acting White: The Good Black/ Bad Black Problem*: https://law.vanderbilt.edu/files/archive/ActingWhiteintro.pdf

Centerwall, Brandon S., 'Who Wrote William Basse's "Elegy On Shakespeare"?': Rediscovering A Poem Lost from the Donne Canon', *Shakespeare Survey*, vol. 59 (2006).

Chakravarty, Urvashi, *Fictions of Consent: Slavery, Servitude and Free Service in Early Modern England* (Philadelphia: University of Pennsylvania Press, 2022).

Chapman, Matthieu, *Anti-Black Racism in Early Modern English Drama* (New York: Routledge, 2017).

Cobb, Keith Hamilton, 'The Irony of the American Moor', *Shakespeare and Beyond*, 14 July 2020: https://shakespeareand-beyond.folger.edu/2020/07/14/american-moor-irony-keith-hamilton-cobb/

Crenshaw, Kimberlé, Luke Charles Harris, Daniel Martinez HoSang and George Lipsitz (eds), *Seeing Race Again: Countering Colorblindness across the Disciplines* (Los Angeles: University of California Press, 2019).

Dadabhoy, Ambereen, 'The Moor of America: Approaching the Crisis of Race and Religion in the Renaissance and the Twenty-First Century', in *Teaching Medieval and Early Modern Cross-Cultural Encounters*, ed. Karina F. Attar and Lynn Shutters (New York: Palgrave 2014).

—'Two-Faced: The Problem of Othello's Visage' in *Othello: The State of Play* (London: Bloomsbury, 2014), pp. 121–47.

Das, Nandini, 'The Stranger at the door: belonging in Shakespeare's Ephesus', *Shakespeare Survey*, vol. 73 (2020), pp. 10–20.

Das, Nandini, Joao Vecente Melo, Haig Smith, and Lauren Working, *Keywords of Identity, Race, and Human Mobility in Early Modern England* (Amsterdam: Amsterdam University Press, 2021).

Dimmock, Matthew, *New Turkes: Dramatizing Islam and the Ottomans in Early Modern England* (Aldershot: Ashgate, 2005).

Dobson, Michael, *The Making of the National Poet: Shakespeare, Adaptation and Authorship, 1660–1769* (Oxford: Oxford University Press, 1994).

Dyer, Richard, *White* (London and New York: Routledge, 1997).

Earle, T.F. and K.J.P. Lowe (eds), *Black Africans in Renaissance Europe* (Cambridge: Cambridge University Press, 2005).

Erickson, Peter, '"God for Harry, England, and Saint George": British National Identity and the Emergence of White Self-Fashioning', in *Early Modern Visual Culture: Representation, Race, and Empire in Renaissance England*, ed. Peter Erickson and Clark Hulse (Philadelphia: University of Pennsylvania Press, 2000), pp. 315–45.

—and Kim F. Hall, '"A New Scholarly Song": Rereading Early Modern Race', *Shakespeare Quarterly*, 67.1 (August 2016), pp. 1–13.

Escolme, Bridget, *Shakespeare and Costume in Practice* (London: Palgrave Macmillan, 2020).

Espinosa, Ruben, *Shakespeare on the Shades of Racism* (London and New York: Routledge, 2021).

—and David Ruiter (eds), *Shakespeare and Immigration* (London and New York: Routledge, 2014).

Fernie, Ewan, *Shakespeare For Freedom* (Cambridge: Cambridge University Press, 2017).

Fields, Karen E. and Barbara J. Fields, *Racecraft: The Soul of Inequality in American Life* (London and New York: Verso, 2014).

Fisher, Michael H., *Counterflows to Colonialism: Indian Travellers and Settlers in Britain 1600–1857* (Ranikhert: Permanent Black, 2004).

Frederickson, George M., *Racism: A Short History* (Princeton: Princeton University Press, 2002).

Furness, Henry Howard Furness (ed.), *A New Variorum Edition of Shakespeare: The Merchant of Venice* (London: J.B. Lippincott Company, 1888).

Gikandi, Simon, *Slavery and the Culture of Taste* (Princeton: Princeton University Press, 2014).

Grady, Kyle, "'Envy Pale of Hew": Whiteness and Division in "Fair Verona"', in *White People in Shakespeare: Essays on Race, Culture and the Elite*, ed. Arthur L. Little, Jr. (London: Bloomsbury, 2023).

Grier, Miles, 'Inkface: The Slave Stigma in England's Early Imperial Imagination', in *Scripturalizing the Human: The Written as the Political*, ed. Vincent L. Wimbush (New York: Routledge, 2015), pp. 193–220.

Greenblatt, Stephen, 'Shakespeare's Cure for Xenophobia: What *The Merchant of Venice* taught me about ethnic hatred and the literary imagination', *The New Yorker*, 3 July 2017: https://www. newyorker.com/magazine/2017/07/10/shakespeares-cure-for-xenophobia

—'Shylock in Red?: James Shapiro, reply by Stephen Greenblatt', *The New York Review*, 14 October 2010: https://www.nybooks. com/articles/2010/10/14/shylock-red/

Grinnell, Richard 'Witchcraft, Race and the Rhetoric of Barbarism in *Othello* and *1 Henry IV*', *The Upstart Crow*, 24 (2004), pp. 72–80.

Habib, Imtiaz, *Black Lives in the English Archives 1500–1677* (London and New York: Routledge, 2008).

Hall, Kim F., 'Guess Who's Coming to Dinner? Colonisation and Miscegenation in *The Merchant of Venice*', *Renaissance Drama* 23 (1992), pp. 87–111.

—*Things of Darkness: Economies of Race and Gender in Early Modern England* (Ithaca: Cornell University Press, 1995).

Hall, Stuart, *Selected Writings on Race and Difference*, ed. Paul Gilroy and Ruth Wilson Gilmore (Durham and London: Duke University Press, 2021).

Haynes, Alan, *The Gunpowder Plot* (Stroud: The History Press, 1994, 2005).

Hendricks, Margo, "'Obscured by dreams": Race, Empire, and Shakespeare's *A Midsummer Night's Dream*', *Shakespeare Quarterly* 47.1 (Spring 1996), pp. 37–60.

—'Race: A Renaissance Category', in *A New Companion to English Renaissance Literature and Culture*, ed. Michael Hattaway, vols. 1 & 2 (Oxford: Wiley/Blackwell, 2010), pp. 535–44.

—'Surveying "race" in Shakespeare', in *Shakespeare and Race*, ed. Catherine M.S. Alexander and Stanley Wells (Oxford: Oxford University Press, 2000).

—'Visions of Color: Spectacle, Spectators, and the Performance of Race', in *A Companion to Shakespeare and Performance*, eds Barbara Hodgdon and W.B. Worthen (Oxford: Wiley/ Blackwell, 2005), pp. 511–26.

Heng, Geraldine, *The Invention of Race in the European Middle Ages* (Cambridge: Cambridge University Press, 2018).

Holland, Peter, 'David Garrick: saints, temples and jubilees', in *Celebrating Shakespeare: Commemoration and Cultural Memory*, ed. Clara Calvo and Coppelia Kahn (Cambridge: Cambridge University Press, 2015), pp. 15–37.

hooks, bell, *Black Looks: Race and Representation* (Boston: South End Press, 1992).

Hornback, Robert, *Racism and Early Blackface Comic Traditions: From the Old World to the New* (London: Palgrave Macmillan, 2018).

Hughey, Matthew, 'Backstage Discourse and Reproduction of White Masculinities', *The Sociological Quarterly*, 52 (2011), pp. 132–153.

Jones, Gwilym, *Shakespeare's Storms* (Manchester: Manchester University Press, 2015).

Jowitt, Claire, *The Culture of Piracy, 1580–1630: English Literature and Seaborne Crime (Transculturalisms, 1400–1700)* (London and New York: Routledge, 2010).

—'Francis Drake's forgotten role in the English slave trade', *History Extra*, 16 June 2020: https://www.historyextra.com/period/tudor/francis-drake-slave-trade-english-history-elizabeth-i-why-forgotten-legacy-john-hawkins/

Kane, Brendan and Malcolm Smuts, 'The Politics of Race in England, Scotland and Ireland', in *The Oxford Handbook of The Age of Shakespeare*, ed. Malcolm Smuts (Oxford: Oxford University Press, 2016).

Karim-Cooper, Farah, *Cosmetics in Shakespearean and Renaissance Drama*, revised edition (Edinburgh: Edinburgh University Press, 2019, originally published 2006).

—'Emotions, Gesture, and Race in the Early Modern Playhouse', in *Playing and Playgoing in Early Modern England: Actor, Audience and Performance*, ed. Simon Smith and Emma Whipday (Cambridge: Cambridge University Press, 2022), pp. 57–76.

—*The Hand on the Shakespearean Stage: Gesture, Touch and the Spectacle of Dismemberment* (London: Bloomsbury, 2016).

—(ed) *Titus Andronicus: The State of Play* (London: Bloomsbury, 2019).

Kaufmann, Miranda, *Black Tudors: The Untold Story* (London: Oneworld Publications, 2017).

—'Caspar van Senden, Sir Thomas Shreley and the 'Blackamoor Project', *Historical Research*, 18.212 (May 2008), pp. 366–371: http://www.mirandakaufmann.com/caspanvansenden.html

—'"Making the Beast with two Backs": Interracial relationships in Early Modern England', *Literature Compass*, 12.1 (2015), pp. 22–37.

Kendall, Mikki, *Hood Feminism: Notes from the Women White Feminists Forgot* (London: Bloomsbury, 2021).

Kerrigan, John, *Revenge Tragedy: Aeschylus to Armageddon* (Oxford: Clarendon Press, 1996).

Kirk, Genevieve, '"And his Works in a Glass Case": The Bard in the Garden and the Legacy of the Shakespeare Ladies Club', *Shakespeare Survey*, 74, ed. Emma Smith (28 August 2021) (Cambridge: Cambridge University Press).

Kolin, Philip C., '*Titus Andronicus* and the Critical Legacy', in *Titus Andronicus: Critical Essays*, ed. Philip C. Kolin (London and New York: Routledge, 1995).

Lamming, George, *The Pleasures of Exile* (Ann Arbor: The University of Michigan Press, 1992).

LaPorte, Charles, *The Victorian Cult of Shakespeare: Bardology in the Nineteenth Century* (Cambridge: Cambridge University Press, 2021).

Little Jr., Arthur L., 'Is It Possible to Read Shakespeare Through Critical Whiteness Studies?', in *The Cambridge Companion to Shakespeare and Race*, ed. Ayanna Thompson (Cambridge: Cambridge University Press, 2021), pp. 268–80.

—'Re-Historicizing Race, White Melancholia, and the Shakespearean Property', *Shakespeare Quarterly*, 67.1 (Spring 2016), pp. 84–103.

—*Shakespeare Jungle Fever: National-Imperial Re-Visions of Race, Rape, and Sacrifice* (Redwood City: Stanford University Press, 2002).

Loomba, Ania, *Shakespeare, Race, & Colonialism*, Oxford Shakespeare Topics (Oxford: Oxford University Press, 2002).

Looney, Bernadette, "Making Shakespeare Not Racist" in 'Black Lives Matter in the Public Theater's *Much Ado About Nothing*: Five Perspectives on Race and Shakespeare in 2020', Literary Hub, 14 August 2020: https://lithub.com/black-lives-matter-in-the-public-theaters-much-ado-about-nothing/

MacDonald, Joyce Green, *Women and Race in Early Modern Texts* (Cambridge: Cambridge University Press, 2002).

Maguire, Laurie and Emma Smith, *30 Great Myths about Shakespeare* (Oxford: Wiley/Blackwell, 2013).

Mare, Margaret and W.H. Quarrell, ed., *Lichtenberg's Visits to England, as Described in his Letter and Diaries* (Oxford: Clarendon Press, 1938).

Markey, Lisa and Noémie Ndiaye (eds), *Seeing Race Before Race: Visual Culture and the Racial Matrix in the Pre-modern World* (Tempe: Arizona Center for Medieval and Renaissance Studies Press, 2023).

McCarthy, Harry, *Boy Actors in Early Modern England: Skill and Stagecraft in the Theatre* (Cambridge: Cambridge University Press, 2022).

Morgan, Kenneth, *Slavery and the British Empire: From Africa to America* (Oxford: Oxford University Press, 2007).

Morrison, Toni, *Mouth Full of Blood: Essays, Speeches, Meditations* (London: Vintage/Penguin Random House, 2019).

Munro, Lucy, *Children of the Queen's Revels: A Jacobean Theatre Repertory* (Cambridge: Cambridge University Press, 2005).

Ndiaye, Noémie, 'Aaron's Roots: Spaniards, Englishmen, and Blackamoors in *Titus Andronicus*', *Early Theatre* 19.2 (2016), pp. 59–80.

—*Scripts of Blackness*: *Early Modern Performance Culture and the Making of Race* (Philadelphia: University of Pennsylvania Press, 2022).

Nubia, Oneyka, *Blackamoores: Africans in Tudor England, Their Presence, Status and Origins* (London: Narrative Eye and The Circle with a Dot, 2013).

—*England's Other Countrymen: Black Tudor Society* (London: Zed Books, 2019).

Omi, Michael and Howard Winant, *Racial Formation in the United States* (New York: Routledge, 1995, 2015).

Otele, Olivette, *Africans in Europe* (New York: Basic Books, 2020).

Painter, Nell Irvin, *The History of White People* (New York and London: W.W. Norton & Company, 2010).

Parvin, Shahnaz, 'Darkness and Women: An Appraisal of Colourism in Shakespeare's "Sonnets" and Tagore's "Krishnakaly"', *International Journal of Multidisciplinary Informative Research and Review* 1.3 (30 November 2020), pp. 133–142.

Pérez, Raúl, *The Souls of White Jokes: How Racist Humor Fuels White Supremacy* (Redwood City: Stanford University Press, 2022).

Rambaram-Olm, Mary and Erik Wade, *Race in Early Medieval England* (Cambridge: Cambridge University Press, forthcoming).

—and Matthew Gabriele, 'The Middle Ages Have Been Misused by the Far Right. Here's Why It's So Important to Get Medieval History Right', *TIME* (Nov 2019).

Renniger, C. and J. Williams, 'Black-White color connotations and race awareness in preschool children', *Perceptual and Motor Skills* (1966), pp. 771–785, 783, cited in Douglas Longshore, 'Color Connotations and Racial Attitudes', *Journal of Black Studies*, 10/2 (Dec. 1979), pp. 183–197.

Ritchie, Fiona, *Women and Shakespeare in the Eighteenth Century* (Cambridge: Cambridge University Press, 2014).

Rogers, Jami, *British Black and Asian Shakespeareans: Integrating Shakespeare, 1966–2018*, The Arden Shakespeare (London: Bloomsbury, 2022).

Nicola Rollock, 'The Heart of Whiteness: Racial gesture politics, equity and higher education', in Jason Arday and Heidi Safia Mirza (eds), *Dismantling Race in Higher Education: Racism, Whiteness and Decolonising the Academy* (New York: Palgrave Macmillan, 2018), pp. 313–330.

Royster, Francesca T., *Becoming Cleopatra: The Shifting Image of An Icon* (New York: Palgrave Macmillan, 2003, 2016 edition).

Said, Edward, *Orientalism* (London: Penguin Books, 1978, 2019 edition).

Schiff, Stacy, *Cleopatra: A Life* (New York: Random House, 2010).

Shahani, Gitanjali G., *Tasting Difference: Food, Race, and Cultural Encounters in Early Modern Literature* (Ithaca and London: Cornell University Press, 2020).

Shapiro, James, *Shakespeare and the Jews* (New York: Columbia University Press, 1997).

Shaw, Justin, '"Rub Him About the Temples": Othello, Disability, and the Failures of Care', *Early Theatre*, 22.2 (2019), pp. 171–84.

Singh, Jyotsna (ed.), *A Companion to the Global Renaissance: Literature and Culture in the Era of Expansion, 1500–1700* (Oxford: Wiley/Blackwell, 2021).

—*Shakespeare and Postcolonial Theory* (London: Bloomsbury, 2020).

Smith, Ian, 'Barbarian Errors: Performing Race in Early Modern England', *Shakespeare Quarterly*, 49.2 (Summer 1998), pp. 168–186.

—*Black Shakespeare: Reading and Misreading Race* (Cambridge: Cambridge University Press, 2022).

—'Othello's Black Handkerchief', *Shakespeare Quarterly*, 64.1 (Spring 2013), pp. 1–25.

—*Race and Rhetoric in the Renaissance: Barbarian Errors* (London: Palgrave, 2009).

Steggle, Matthew, 'Othello, the Moor of London: Shakespeare's Black Britons' in *Othello: A Critical Reader*, ed. Robert C. Evans (London: Bloomsbury, 2015), pp. 103–24.

Stern, Tiffany, *Rehearsal from Shakespeare to Sheridan* (Oxford: Oxford University Press, 2007).

Thompson, Ayanna, *Blackface* (London: Bloomsbury, 2020).

—ed. *The Cambridge Companion to Shakespeare and Race* (Cambridge: Cambridge University Press, 2021).

—'Introduction', *Othello* (London: Bloomsbury, 2016).

—'Introduction', *Red Velvet*, by Lolita Chakrabarti (London: Methuen Drama, 2014).

—*Passing Strange: Shakespeare, Race and Contemporary America* (Oxford and New York: Oxford University Press, 2011).

Vaughan, Virginia Mason, 'Race Mattered: Othello in Late Eighteenth-Century England', *Shakespeare Survey*, 51 (2003), pp. 57–66.

—and Alden T. Vaughan, *Shakespeare's Caliban: A Cultural History* (Cambridge: Cambridge University Pres, 1991).

Waller, Gary, *Edmund Spenser: A Literary Life* (Basingstoke: Macmillan, 1994).

Whittaker, Cord J., *Black Metaphors: How Modern Racism Emerged from Medieval Race-Thinking* (Philadelphia: University of Pennsylvania Press, 2019).

Wickham, Glynne, Herbert Berry and William Ingram (eds), *English Professional Theatre 1530–1600* (Cambridge: Cambridge University Press, 2000).

Wilson, John Dover, *The Essential Shakespeare: A Biographical Adventure* (Cambridge: Cambridge University Press, 1932).

Wootton, David (ed.), *John Locke: Political Writings* (Indianapolis/Cambridge: Hackett Publishing Company, Inc., 2003).

DATABASES

The Centre for the Study of the Legacies of British Slavery, UCL.

Cooper, Thomas, *Thesaurus Linguae Romanae et Britannicae* (London: 1578), LEME

Cotgrave, Randle, *A Dictionary of the French and English Tongues* (London 1611), LEME

Lexicons of Early Modern English: https://leme.library.utoronto.ca/lexicon/entry/1400/54687

Lexicons of Early Modern English: https://leme.library.utoronto. ca/search/quick

PODCASTS, YOUTUBE AND RADIO

Brooks, Danielle, 'Danielle Brooks on Bringing Herself to Beatrice': https://www.youtube.com/watch?v=H9KpiQ0RwHI

'Kenny Leon, Danielle Brooks & Grantham Coleman on The Public's "Much Ado About Nothing"', 28 May 2019: https://www.youtube.com/watch?v=ApgPOYfi9OM

Stevens, Scott Manning and Madeline Sayet, 'Anti-Racist Shakespeare: *The Tempest*', Shakespeare's Globe: https://www.youtube.com/watch?v=Rh8XKqgaSOc

Thompson, Ayanna, Ep. 6 'Shakespeare and Race', *Such Stuff Podcast*, Shakespeare's Globe (2020): https://www.shakespearesglobe.com/discover/blogs-and-features/2020/05/26/such-stuff-s5-e6/

NEWSPAPER ARTICLES AND BLOGS

Billington, Michael, 'Richard II review – Women of colour's blazing show reflects our current chaos', *Guardian*, 7 March 2019: https://www.theguardian.com/stage/2019/mar/07/richard-ii-review-lynette-linton-adjoa-andoh-sam-wanamaker-playhouse

Cavendish, Dominic, 'The Woke Brigade are close to "cancelling" Shakespeare', *The Daily Telegraph*, 9 February 2020: https://www.telegraph.co.uk/theatre/what-to-see/woke-brigade-close-cancelling-shakespeare/

Clark, Nick, 'Globe Theatre takes out 100 audience members with its gory *Titus Andronicus*', 22 July 2014: https://www.

independent.co.uk/arts-entertainment/theatre-dance/news/globe-theatre-takes-out-100-audience-members-with-its-gory-titus-andronicus-9621763.html

Conde, Arturo, 'Denzel Washington wants viewers to look past Macbeth's race', NBC News, 14 January 2022: https://www.nbcnews.com/news/nbcblk/denzel-washington-wants-viewers-look-macbeths-race-rcna12143?cid=sm_npd_nn_tw_ma

Dickson, Andrew, 'Harriet Walter on *Antony and Cleopatra:* "You have to play it fast or it falls apart"', *Guardian*, 4 January 2016: https://www.theguardian.com/stage/2016/jan/04/harriet-walter-on-antony-and-cleopatra-shakespeare-400-anniversary-interview

Fram, Alan, 'New conservative group would save "Anglo-Saxon" traditions', AP, 17 April 2021: https://apnews.com/article/politics-marjorie-taylor-greene-immigration-eefdf-9c180f69008d60ed92b9ef2ce03

Furness, Hannah, 'Globe audience faints at "grotesquely violent" Titus Andronicus', *The Daily Telegraph*, 30 April 2014: https://www.telegraph.co.uk/culture/theatre/william-shakespeare/10798599/Globe-audience-faints-at-grotesquely-violent-Titus-Andronicus.html

Golby, Joel, 'A bat signal has gone out to Britain's proud patriots: Save Our Statues', *Guardian*, 10 June 2020: https://www.theguardian.com/commentisfree/2020/jun/10/britain-statues-edward-colston-bristol-slaver?CMP=gu_com

Grant, Justin, 'Racial Offense Taken When "Uppity" Rolls Off Certain Tongues', ABC NEWS, 17 September 2008: https://abcnews.go.com/US/story?id=5823018&page=1

Hughes, Ian, 'Shakespeare Still Shocks', *Stratford Observer*, October2017:https://stratfordobserver.co.uk/news/shakespeare-still-shocks-research-reveals-2976/

Johnson, Boris, 'For their sake, immigrants must speak the language of Shakespeare', *The Telegraph*, 8 March 2015: https://www.telegraph.co.uk/news/uknews/immigration/11457877/For-their-sake-immigrants-must-speak-the-language-of-Shakespeare.html

@LiteraryMouse Twitter post, 9 January 2021: https://twitter.com/LiteraryMouse/status/1347903604196306953

Lodge, Guy, 'Streaming: *The Tragedy of Macbeth* and the best Shakespeare on film', *Guardian*, 15 January 2022: https://www.theguardian.com/film/2022/jan/15/streaming-the-tragedy-of-macbeth-and-the-best-shakespeare-on-film

Merrick, Rob, 'Schools minister rejects lessons about colonialism and slave trade in case they "lower standards"', *Independent*, 25 February 2021: https://www.independent.co.uk/news/uk/politics/school-compulsory-lessons-colony-slave-trade-b1807571.html

Morrison, Greg, 'Making Sense of history: Adjoa Andoh on Richard II', Shakespeare's Globe Blog, 12 September 2019: https://www.shakespearesglobe.com/discover/blogs-and-features/2019/09/12/making-sense-of-history/

Najib, Farah, '*The Merchant of Venice* at the Sam Wanamaker Theatre review: a fresh look at a problematic play', *Evening Standard*, 3 March 2022:

https://www.standard.co.uk/culture/theatre/the-merchant-of-venice-at-the-sam-wanamaker-theatre-review-shylock-anti-semitism-b985742.html

O'Toole, Emer, 'Shakespeare universal? No, it's cultural imperialism', *Guardian*, 21 May 2012: https://www.theguardian.com/commentisfree/2012/may/21/shakespeare-universal-cultural-imperialism

Strauss, Valerie, 'Teacher: Why I don't want to assign Shakespeare anymore (even though he's in the Common Core)', *Washington*

Post, 13 June 2015: https://www.washingtonpost.com/news/ answer-sheet/wp/2015/06/13/teacher-why-i-dont-want-to-assign- shakespeare-anymore-even-though-hes-in-the-common-core/

Vilas-Boas, Eric, 'An All-Black Production of *Much Ado About Nothing* Comes to Central Park', *Hyperallergic*, 28 May 2019: https://hyperallergic.com/502422/all-black-much-ado- about-nothing-shakespeare-in-the-park/

Viney, Peter, *The Tempest* RSC 2016: https://peterviney.com/ stage/the-tempest-rsc-2016/

NOTES

PROLOGUE

1. Rollock, 'The Heart of Whiteness', pp. 313–30, 313.
2. Strauss, 'Teacher: Why I don't want to assign Shakespeare anymore'.
3. Cavendish, 'The Woke Brigade are close to "cancelling" Shakespeare'.
4. Omi and Winant, *Racial Formation in the United States.*
5. Renniger and Williams, 'Black-White color connotations and race awareness in preschool children', p. 783.

1. THE MAKING OF THE GREAT WHITE BARD

1. Jowitt, 'Francis Drake's forgotten role in the English slave trade'.
2. Merrick, 'Schools minister rejects lessons about colonialism...'
3. Greene, *Greenes Groats-Worth of Wit.*
4. Winstanley, *Lives of the Most Famous English Poets*, p. 130.
5. Sawyer, 'Prologues and Epilogues', p. 135.
6. Dryden, *Of Dramatick Poesie*, p. 48.
7. Pope, *The Works of Shakespeare.*
8. Duff, 'An Essay on Original Genius', p. 287.
9. Bate, *The Genius of Shakespeare*, p. 163.
10. Alison, 'Of the Sublimity and Beauty of the Material World', p. 114.
11. *John Locke: Political Writings.*
12. Gikandi, *Slavery and the Culture of Taste*, p. 3.
13. The Centre for the Study of the Legacies of British Slavery, UCL, identifies the 3rd Duke of Chandos as joint owner of the Hope Estate between 1777 and 1789: https://www.ucl.ac.uk/lbs/person/view/2146640767

14. Dover Wilson, *The Essential Shakespeare*, p. 10.
15. Smith, *Shakespeare's First Folio*, p. 31.
16. Hume, 'Of National Characters', p. 208.
17. Winckelmann, *History of the Art of Antiquity*, p. 195.
18. Ritchie, *Women and Shakespeare in the Eighteenth Century*, p. 46.
19. Centerwall, 'Who Wrote William Basse's "Elegy On Shakespeare"?'.
20. Babcock, *The Genesis of Shakespeare Idolatry, 1766–1799*, p. 430.
21. Pope, *The Works of Shakespeare*, p. vii.
22. Kirk, 'And his Works in a Glass Case', pp. 298–316.
23. I am grateful for Michael Dobson's groundbreaking work on this subject in *The Making of the National Poet: Shakespeare, Adaptation and Authorship, 1660–1769*.
24. Babcock, *The Genesis of Shakespeare Idolatry*, p. 122.
25. Fernie, *Shakespeare For Freedom*, p. 114.
26. *Lichtenberg's Visits to England*, p. 15.
27. Fernie.
28. Holland, 'David Garrick: Saints, temples and jubilees', p. 30. [Italics my own.]
29. Cook, *Memoirs of Charles Macklin, Comedian*, p. 113.
30. Hedgecock, *David Garrick and his French Friends*, p. 34.
31. Kaufmann, 'Making the Beast with Two Backs', p. 23.
32. Thompson, Introduction, *Othello*.
33. Morgan, *Slavery and the British Empire*.
34. Draper, 'The City of London and slavery', pp. 432–66.
35. Morgan, *Slavery and the British*, p. 30.
36. Gikandi, pp. 24–35.
37. Johnson, 'For their sake, immigrants must speak the language of Shakespeare'.
38. Carlyle, 'Lecture III. The Hero As Poet. Dante; Shakespeare'.
39. Rambaram-Olm and Gabriele, 'The Middle Ages Have Been Misused by the Far Right'.
40. Jefferson, *The Works of Thomas Jefferson*, vol. 2.
41. Painter, *The History of White People*, p. 164.
42. Emerson, 'Notes on Shakespeare'.
43. Emerson, *English Traits*, cited in Painter, *The History of White People*, p. 170.
44. Fram, 'New conservative group would save "Anglo-Saxon" traditions'.
45. Twitter Post, @LiteraryMouse, 9 January 2021.
46. Statement from Michael Witmore, Director of the Folger Shakespeare Library, 7 January 2021.

47. Golby, 'A bat signal has gone out to Britain's proud patriots: Save Our Statues'.

2. BARBAROUS SPECTACLE

1. Clark, 'Globe Theatre takes out 100 audience members with its gory *Titus Andronicus*'.
2. Furness, 'Globe audience faints at "grotesquely violent" Titus Andronicus'.
3. Hughes, 'Shakespeare Still Shocks'.
4. Johnson, *The Plays of William Shakespeare*, vol. VI, p. 364.
5. Hazlitt, *Characters of Shakespeare's Plays*, p. 332.
6. Eliot, 'Seneca in Elizabethan Translation', p. 82, cited in Kolin, *Titus Andronicus*, pp. 4–5.
7. Hemmingsen, *A Postle, or Exposition of the Gospels*, sig. xxiy.
8. Horace, *Satires, Epistles, Ars Poetic* 1.IV. 85.
9. Smith, 'Barbarian Errors', p. 168.
10. Das et al., *Keywords of Identity, Race, and Human Mobility*, p. 219.
11. Otele, *Africans in Europe*.
12. Thomas, *Principal Rules of the Italian Grammar*.
13. Das et al., *Keywords of Identity*, p. 41.
14. Ibid., p. 40.
15. Stow, *The Survey of London*, cited in Brotton, 'The First Muslims in England'.
16. Brotton, *This Orient Isle*.
17. England, ed., *The Creation*, l. 132.
18. Africanus, *The History and Description of Africa*, pp. 42, 41.
19. Ashley, *A Comparison of the English and Spanish Nation*, p. 62.
20. *Paul Hentzner's Travels in England*.
21. St Augustine of Hippo, *The Expositions on The Psalms*.
22. Dante, *The Divine Comedy*.
23. hooks, *Black Looks: Race and Representation*, pp. 10, 20.
24. Thompson, Ep. 6 'Shakespeare and Race', *Such Stuff Podcast*.

3. MYTHOLOGISING THE TAWNY QUEEN

1. Maguire and Smith, *30 Great Myths about Shakespeare*, p. 164.

2. Coryat, *Coryat's Crudities*, p. 247.
3. Bailey, 'More on the origin of Misogynoir'.
4. Royster, *Becoming Cleopatra*, p. 9.
5. Smith, *Race and Rhetoric in the Renaissance*, p. 2.
6. Plutarch, *The Lives of the Noble Grecians and Romans Compared*, pp. 981, 995.
7. Plutarch, *De Iside et Osiride*, p. 371.
8. Africanus, *A Geographical Historie of Africa*, p. 162.
9. *Oxford English Dictionary*.
10. Shakespeare and race theorist Kim F. Hall wrote in 1995 that 'despite contemporary disagreement about the very existence of "races" and therefore the viability of "race" as a term in cultural or literary studies, I hold onto the idea of a language of race in the early modern period' (*Things of Darkness*, p. 6).
11. Orientalism – this term established by the theorist Edward Said (*Orientalism*, 1978) refers specifically to Western concepts of the East or the 'orient'; it suggests that the West predominantly created the idea of the Orient in order to dominate it. Such representations of the 'exotic' are often presented through a Western lens, making the East passive and assailable and the West the primary creators of culture.
12. Gouge, *Of domestical duties*, p. 90.
13. *Oxford English Dictionary*.
14. Hughey, 'Backstage Discourse and Reproduction of White Masculinities', p. 147.
15. Best, *A True Discourse of the late voyages of discoverie*, p. 108.
16. Kaufmann, 'Making the Beast with Two Backs', p. 26.
17. Ibid., p. 29.
18. In 'Guess Who's Coming to Dinner? Colonisation and Miscegenation in *The Merchant of Venice*', Kim F. Hall points out that 'this pregnant, unheard, unnamed, and unseen (at least by critics) black woman is a silent symbol for the economic and racial politics' of the play (p. 94).
19. Furnivall, *The Leopold Shakespeare*, p. lxxxii.
20. Schiff, *Cleopatra: A Life*, p. 89.
21. Hall, *Things of Darkness*, p. 153.
22. Herodotus, *Famous History of Egypt*, ff. 75, 96.
23. Dekker, *Lantern and Candlelight*, p. 132.
24. Talawa, 'Antony & Cleopatra: A Theatre First'.
25. Rutter, *Enter the Body*, p. 86.

26. 'Harriet Walter on *Antony and Cleopatra*'.
27. For more on this portrait see Arshad, *Imagining Cleopatra*.

4. MODEL MINORITY

1. Hamilton Cobb, 'The Irony of the American Moor'.
2. Thompson, Introduction, *Othello*, p. 63.
3. Ibid., p. 65.
4. Cotta, *The Trial of Witch-Craft*, p. 29.
5. Cooper, *Thesaurus Linguae Romanae et Britannicae*.
6. McPherson, *Shakespeare, Jonson, and the Myth of Venice*, p. 30.
7. Contarini, *The Commonwealth and Government of Venice*, p. 18.
8. Carbado and Galati, *Acting White: The Good Black/Bad Black Problem*, p. 5.
9. Vickers, *William Shakespeare: The Critical Heritage*, vol. 2, p. 51.
10. Smith, 'Othello's Black Handkerchief', pp. 1–25.
11. Hornback, *Racism and Early Blackface Comic Traditions*, p. 190.
12. Shaw, 'Rub Him About the Temples', pp. 171–84.
13. Parvin, 'Darkness and Women', p. 133.
14. Luckyj, 'Introduction', the New Cambridge *Othello*, p. 2.
15. *Othello: The Moor of Venice*, ed. Neill, pp. 10, 9.
16. Africanus, *A Geographical History of Africa*, p. 154.
17. Varchi, *The Blazon of Jealousy*, p. 21.
18. Lomazzo, *A Tracte Containing the Artes of Curious Painting, Carving and Building*, pp. 112, 114.
19. Erickson, 'God for Harry, England, and Saint George', p. 315.
20. Dyer, *White*, p. 29.
21. Ficino, *Commentary on Plato's Symposium*, p. 213.
22. Firenzuola, *On the Beauty of Women*, p. 15.
23. Buoni, *Problemes of Beautie and humane affections*.
24. Heng, *The Invention of Race in the European Middle Ages*; Hall, *Things of Darkness*.
25. Dyer, *White*.
26. Hilliard, *A Treatise Concerning the Arte of Limning*, p. 91.
27. Edmund Spenser's *View of the Present State of Ireland* (1596) is seen as a heavily racially charged anti-Irish, pro-English colonial treatise. According to Gary Waller, race 'was starting to acquire some of its

modern impact in Spenser's time, and his career and writings make distinctive contributions to those later developments' (*Edmund Spenser: A Literary Life*, p. 18).

28. Vives, *The instruction of a Christian woman*, p. 70.
29. Harriot, *A Brief and True Report*, p. 16.

5. STAGING HATE

1. Thompson, *Blackface*, p. 68.
2. Cited in *English Professional Theatre 1530–1600*, p. 182.
3. Lodge, 'Streaming: The Tragedy of Macbeth and the best Shakespeare on film'.
4. Habib, *Black Lives in the English Archives 1500–1677*; Nubia, *England's Other Countrymen*; Kaufmann, *Black Tudors: The Untold Story*.
5. Cited in Greenblatt, 'Shylock in Red'.
6. Vecellio, *De gli habiti antichi et moderni di diversi parti del mondo*.
7. Cited in Greenblatt, 'Shakespeare's Cure for Xenophobia'.
8. Sauter, 'Thirty Years of Reception Studies', p. 257.
9. Najib, 'The Merchant of Venice at the Sam Wanamaker Theatre'.
10. Fredrickson, *Racism: A Short History*, p. 19.
11. Histories of antisemitism are too many to list, but Geraldine Heng's *The Invention of Race in the Middle Ages* and James Shapiro's *Shakespeare and the Jews* provide extensive histories.
12. Applebaum, ed., *Il Pecorone* in *Medieval Tales and Stories*.
13. Brazaitis, 'White Women – Protectors of the Status Quo; Positioned to Disrupt It', p. 114.
14. The warrants were unsuccessful, but the language in them clearly states the presence of blackamoors in England was a concern. Kaufmann, 'Caspar van Senden, Sir Thomas Shreley and the "Blackamoor Project"', pp. 366–371.

6. SHAKESPEARE'S WHITE SETTLER

1. Strachey, *A true repertory*, in Purchas, *Purchas His Pilgrimes*, vol. 4, pp. 1734–6.
2. Ibid.
3. Hakluyt, *The Principall Navigations*, epistle dedicatory to Sir Francis Walsingham.
4. Melton, The *Astrologaster*, fol. 31.

5. Stow, *Survey of London*, cited in Jones, *Storms in Shakespeare*, note 42.
6. Cotgrave, *A Dictionary of the French and English Tongues*.
7. Lamming, *The Pleasures of Exile*, p. 97.
8. Ibid., pp. 13, 101, 113.
9. Thomas, *Principal Rules of the Italian Grammar*.
10. Dyer, *White*, p. 27.
11. Mason Vaughan and Vaughan, *The Tempest*, p. 230.
12. Hariot, *A Brief and True Report of the New Found Land of Virginia*, p. 34.
13. Rocca, *The Rebirth of Chiromancy and Physiognomy*.
14. Akhimie, *Shakespeare and the Cultivation of Difference*, p. 172.
15. Vaughan and Vaughan, *Shakespeare's Caliban: A Cultural History*, p. 100.
16. Escolme, *Shakespeare and Costume in Practice*, p. 150.
17. Viney, *The Tempest* RSC 2016.
18. Manning Stevens and Sayet, 'Anti-Racist Shakespeare: *The Tempest*'.

7. TRAGEDY AND INTERRACIAL POETRY

1. Fields and Fields, *Racecraft*, pp. 17–18.
2. King James I, *Demonologie*, Preface.
3. Haynes, *The Gunpowder Plot*.
4. Vicars, *November the 5 1605*.
5. Gifford, *The Witches of Northampton-shire*.
6. Hakluyt, *Principal Navigations*, p. 96.
7. Elyot, *The Dictionary of Sir Thomas Elyot*.
8. Scholars accept that the Jacobean playwright Thomas Middleton very likely had a hand in writing some of the scenes involving the witches.
9. Hall, *Things of Darkness*, p. 70.
10. Elizabethan letters and a Proclamation that seemed to be expelling 'blackmoors' from England, for example, contain rhetoric that makes clear the fear of infiltration: 'there are of late divers Blackmoores brought into the Realm, of which kind of persons there are already here too many, considering how God hath blessed this land with great increase of people of our own nations as any country in the world, whereof many for want of service and means to set them on work, fall to idleness and to great extremity; Her majesty's pleasure therefore is, that those kind of people should be sent forth of the

land' (Letter to Lord Mayors, July 11, 1596, in *Blackamoores: Africans in Tudor England, Their Presence, Status and Origins*, p. 4).
11. Hendricks, 'Surveying "race" in Shakespeare', p. 17.

8. ANTI-BLACK COMEDY

1. Vilas-Boas, 'An All-Black Production of *Much Ado About Nothing* Comes to Central Park'.
2. 'Danielle Brooks on Bringing Herself to Beatrice'.
3. Looney, 'Making Shakespeare Not Racist'.
4. 'Kenny Leon, Danielle Brooks & Grantham Coleman on The Public's "Much Ado About Nothing"'.
5. Pérez, *The Souls of White Jokes*, https://www.google.co.uk/books/edition/The_Souls_of_White_Jokes/Z2BsEAAAQBAJ?hl=en&gbpv=1&kptab=getbook.
6. Akhimie, 'Racist Humor and Shakespearean Comedy', p. 56.
7. Puttenham, *Partheniades*.
8. Hakluyt, *The Principal Navigations*, p. 90.
9. Kendall, *Hood Feminism*, p. 86.
10. Anonymous, *Haec-Vir*.
11. Dekker, *Lanthorne and candle-light*, H1r-v.
12. Tuke, *A Treatise Against Painting*, B3v.
13. Grant, 'Racial Offense Taken When "Uppity" Rolls Off Certain Tongues'.
14. Copley, *Wits, Fits, and Fancies*, p. 13.

EPILOGUE

1. Conte, 'Denzel Washington wants viewers to look past Macbeth's race'.
2. Bloom, *Shakespeare and the Invention of the Human*, p. 17.
3. O'Toole, 'Shakespeare universal? No, it's cultural imperialism'.
4. Thompson, Introduction, *Red Velvet* by Chakrabarti.
5. Cahill and Hall, 'Forum: Shakespeare and Black America', p. 4.
6. Morrison, 'Making Sense of history: Adjoa Andoh on Richard II'.
7. Billington, 'Richard II review – women of colour's blazing show reflects our current chaos'.
8. Morrison, 'Making Sense of History'.

INDEX

References to images are in italics; references to notes are indicated by n.